Trends in Special Medicare Payments and Service Utilization for Rural Areas in the 1990s

Donna O. Farley ◆ Lisa R. Shugarman
Pat Taylor ◆ Moira Inkelas ◆ J. Scott Ashwood
Feng Zeng ◆ Katherine M. Harris

T0308564

RAND Health

RAND

Prepared for the Centers for Medicare and Medicaid Services

The research described in this report was sponsored by the Centers for Medicare and Medicaid Services (formerly the Health Care Financing Administration). The research was conducted within RAND Health.

Library of Congress Cataloging-in-Publication Data

MR-1595 : trends in special medicare payments and service utilization for rural areas in the
    1990s / Donna O. Farley ... [et al.].
        p. cm.
    Includes bibliographical references.
    ISBN 0-8330-3213-5
    1. Rural hospitals—Prospective payment. 2. Medicare. 3. Medicare—Cost control. 4.
Rural health services. I. Title: Trends in special medicare payments and service utilization
for rural areas in the 1990s. II. Farley, Donna.

RA412.3 .M7 2002
368.4'26'00973091734—dc21

                                                                                2002026557

A profile of RAND Health, abstracts of its publications, and ordering information can be found on the RAND Health home page at www.rand.org/health.

RAND is a nonprofit institution that helps improve policy and decisionmaking through research and analysis. RAND® is a registered trademark. RAND's publications do not necessarily reflect the opinions or policies of its research sponsors.

Published 2002 by RAND
1700 Main Street, P.O. Box 2138, Santa Monica, CA 90407-2138
1200 South Hayes Street, Arlington, VA 22202-5050
201 North Craig Street, Suite 202, Pittsburgh, PA 15213-1516-1516
RAND URL: http://www.rand.org/
To order RAND documents or to obtain additional information, contact Distribution
Services: Telephone: (310) 451-7002; Fax: (310) 451-6915; Email: order@rand.org

PREFACE

The Centers for Medicare and Medicaid Services (CMS, formerly the Health Care Financing Administration) contracted with RAND to analyze Medicare special payments to rural providers and implications for access and costs of care for rural Medicare beneficiaries, with a focus on underserved areas. The payment provisions examined included (1) special payments for sole community hospitals, Medicare-dependent hospitals, rural referral centers, networks of Essential Access Community Hospitals and Rural Primary Care Hospitals (EACH/RPCH), and Medical Assistance Facilities; (2) reimbursements to rural health clinics and federally qualified health centers; (3) bonus payments to physicians in rural Health Professional Shortage Areas (HPSAs); and (4) capitation payments in rural counties. In addition, the effect of special payments for designated rural hospitals on Medicare Part A costs per capita was estimated.

This report presents the findings of our analysis of payment trends for providers qualifying under these Medicare special payment provisions.

The research results will be of interest to policymakers, researchers, and other parties involved with rural health policy or Medicare payment policy. The trend information and findings generated by the research can be used to formulate future Medicare payment policy as well as to guide subsequent research on relevant issues. The research was performed under Task 11 of Centers for Medicare and Medicaid Services Contract Number HCFA-500-96-0056, Project Officer William Buczko.

CONTENTS

TABLES

SUMMARY

The Centers for Medicare and Medicaid Services (CMS, formerly the Health Care Financing Administration) contracted with RAND to analyze special payments that Medicare has been making to rural providers and the implications for access and costs of care for rural Medicare beneficiaries. CMS is interested in developing information for use in formulating future Medicare policy for rural health care services and payments. Although the special payment provisions are diverse, they all are intended to support the rural health care infrastructure to help ensure access to care for Medicare beneficiaries residing in rural areas. These provisions were introduced at various times during the past decade or earlier.

The purpose of this research was to provide a comprehensive overview of Medicare special payments to rural providers over the last decade, including documentation of the supply of providers, trends in payments made by Medicare, resulting Medicare costs per beneficiary, and implications for access to care for Medicare beneficiaries living in rural areas. One focus of the study was on services in geographic areas designated as underserved areas by the Health Resources and Services Administration (HRSA), using either Health Professional Shortage Area (HPSA) or Medically Underserved Area (MUA) designations. The special payment provisions examined were:

- Special payments for sole community hospitals, rural referral centers, and Medicare-dependent hospitals;

- Reimbursements to Rural Health Clinics (RHCs) and Federally Qualified Health Centers (FQHCs);

- Bonus payments to physicians in rural HPSAs; and

- Medicare Adjusted Average per Capita Cost (AAPCC) capitation payments for rural counties, especially underserved areas.

Using results of the trend analyses, we estimated the relative contribution of special payments for rural hospitals to the Medicare per capita costs in rural counties, which are the basis for Medicare capitation rates. The results of this analysis also are presented in this report. Similar analyses were not performed for RHC/FQHC services or for physician bonus payments because the trend analyses showed that both of these payment provisions had quite small effects on Medicare costs per beneficiary.

BACKGROUND

The access of the rural elderly to health care services has been a continuing source of concern for policymakers. Elderly people live in rural areas in disproportionate numbers, and a larger proportion of them suffer from activity-limiting chronic diseases (Rogers et al., 1993; Schlenker and Shaughnessy, 1996). Elderly people in rural areas also travel longer and wait longer for outpatient care and use fewer preventive services than their non-rural counterparts (Taylor et al., 1993; Van Nostrand et al., 1993). Rural communities face difficulties protecting provider supplies, including recruitment and retention of physicians and the viability of rural hospitals. Rural hospitals tend to be small and offer a more limited range of services than their counterparts in more densely populated regions, and their numbers continue to decline. Rural hospitals with fewer than 100 beds are less likely to offer a range of acute care services. Instead, outpatient and long-term care services have become more important shares of total rural hospital services during the 1990s (Moscovice et al., 1999).

Congress created several new categories of rural hospitals with more favorable payment provisions to improve their financial performance. Sole community hospitals were designated early in the 1980s to ensure access for Medicare beneficiaries residing in non-metropolitan counties. Rural referral centers (RRCs) are larger rural hospitals with a range of services that offer specialty referral resources for other rural hospitals. Small rural Medicare-dependent hospitals were designated from April 1990 through September 1994, and the Balanced Budget Act (BBA) reactivated them in 1997. Two demonstrations also were in operation during the 1990s to test alternative models for limited-service rural hospitals that refer to larger, full-service facilities, including the Montana Medical Assistance Facility demonstration and the Essential Access Community Hospital program. These hospitals transitioned to Critical Access Hospitals after passage of the BBA.

Rural Health Clinics were created by the Rural Health Clinics Act (P.L. 95-210) of 1977 to extend Medicare and Medicaid coverage and cost-based reimbursement to support health care services for beneficiaries in underserved rural areas, including non-physician practitioner services. Separate designations were created for independent and provider-based RHCs. The Omnibus Budget Reconciliation Act (OBRA) of 1989 created the FQHC program to establish cost-based reimbursement for services provided to Medicaid beneficiaries by an existing network of federally funded community health centers, migrant health centers, and similar facilities. OBRA 1990 extended FQHC reimbursement to cover services provided to Medicare beneficiaries. Both urban and rural health centers are eligible for designation as FQHCs, and the scope of services the clinics are required to provide is broader than those required for RHCs.

To encourage physicians with established practices to relocate to rural areas, a payment incentive program was identified as a method to help offset the opportunity costs associated with relocation and starting a new practice (PPRC, 1992). Congress enacted a bonus payment program in 1989 that provided additional payments to physicians, above the amount paid by Medicare under the Physician Fee Schedule, for providing health care services in HPSAs. The original program gave 5 percent bonus payments to physicians providing care in rural HPSAs. In 1991, the bonus payment was increased to 10 percent and eligibility was expanded to include reimbursement for services provided by physicians in urban HPSAs.

Medicare spending for rural fee-for-service beneficiaries is the basis for the county-level AAPCCs that serve as the basis for capitation payments to Medicare health maintenance organizations. In general, the AAPCC rates for counties outside Metropolitan Statistical Areas (MSAs) are lower than those for more urbanized counties, reflecting lower rural utilization and payment rates. AAPCC rates for these counties also tend to fluctuate from year to year because they are based on spending for smaller populations. Given these payment issues and rural provider supply problems, few HMOs have contracted to serve Medicare beneficiaries in rural areas (PPRC, 1995), and several that entered these areas have subsequently withdrawn.

Eligibility for many of the rural programs and payments being addressed by this project requires service providers to operate in underserved areas, which are designated based on Congressional provisions for Medically Underserved Areas/Populations (MUA/P) and HPSAs. These areas are designated by HRSA through its regulatory process. HRSA reviews HPSA designations every three years, adding or deleting area designations as appropriate. In 1997, roughly 64 percent of counties outside MSAs contained at least one region officially designated as an HPSA and roughly 10 percent of non-MSA counties had no active primary care physician (NC-RHRPAC, 1998). In response to the Health Centers Consolidation Act of 1996, HRSA is revising the criteria and procedures for designating MUA/Ps and HPSAs, with plans to publish the new provisions in the near future. (See Section 1 for designation criteria.)

The 1997 BBA, as well as follow-up legislation in subsequent years, contained a number of provisions with important implications for the financing and delivery of Medicare-funded services in rural areas. Some provisions addressed fee-for-service payments for rural hospitals, skilled nursing facilities (SNFs), and home health agencies, which can be anticipated to have complex effects for rural providers. Some changes also were made in payment provisions for Rural Health Clinics and Federally Qualified Health Centers. Other provisions established a new methodology for capitation payments for the new Medicare+Choice organizations, including provisions to encourage plans to serve rural areas. The 1997 AAPCC rates were the baseline rates for this new payment formula.

METHODS AND DATA

With a few exceptions, the analyses performed in this research were descriptive analyses of trends in the supplies of providers qualified for Medicare special rural payment provisions, utilization of services, and Medicare spending for these services. The data, key variables derived, and analytic methods are described in detail in Section 2. The method we used to define rural locations was based on whether or not a county is part of an MSA, as defined by the Census Bureau. All counties outside an MSA were considered to be rural for purposes of this analysis. We note that this is an imperfect definition of rurality because each county contains a mix of urbanized and more truly rural locations and county boundaries obscure a wide range of local characteristics. Counties outside MSAs have fewer and smaller urbanized locations than MSA counties, but they are not uniformly rural in nature. Therefore, we use the term "non-metropolitan" counties, rather than "rural."

For all analyses, we compared measures across five categories of non-metropolitan counties that group counties according to their extent of rurality. We used the Urban Influence Codes (UICs) to establish these categories, collapsing the codes for non-metropolitan counties from seven to five categories (see Section 2 and Appendix B). In addition, non-metropolitan counties were classified as frontier counties if they were in the western part of the country and had population densities of fewer than 6 persons per square mile.

The various analyses of trends in special payments for rural providers and AAPCC payments involved linking data for 1992 through 1998 from several sources. Public use data sources included the annual Medicare Provider of Service (POS) files, annual Provider Specific Files, annual Medicare Impact files for hospital inpatient payment factors, an extract of the Area Resource File (ARF extract), summary files containing county-level counts of Medicare beneficiaries and Medicare health plan enrollees, and county-level files of AAPCC capitation rates for 1990 through 1997. We also used Medicare data for 1992 through 1998 for the 100 percent denominator files, MEDPAR claims for short-term inpatient hospital services for the 100 percent sample of Medicare beneficiaries, Medicare institutional outpatient claims from RHCs and FQHCs for the 5 percent sample of Medicare beneficiaries, and Medicare Part B claims for physicians' services for the 5 percent sample of beneficiaries.

Social Security Administration (SSA) state and county codes were used to link provider-level data or Medicare claims to county-level measures (e.g., extent of rurality, HPSA) in the ARF extract file. For population-based analyses, the data were linked based on the state and county of residence for Medicare beneficiaries; for facility-based analyses, the linkages were based on provider location. The geographic areas of interest were all counties not located within a metropolitan statistical area (called non-metropolitan counties).

SUMMARY OF FINDINGS

Characteristics and Provider Supply for Non-Metropolitan Counties

The non-metropolitan counties of the United States vary substantially in their population density, demographics, socioeconomic status, and supply of health care providers. Historically, classification methods have been less than successful in grouping rural areas by these characteristics to achieve relatively homogeneous groupings by "extent of rurality." The results of this descriptive analysis highlight this challenge.

- Although the non-metropolitan counties far outnumber the metropolitan counties (2,292 non-metropolitan compared to 834 urban counties), they contain only one-quarter of the Medicare population.

- Medicare beneficiaries represent larger shares of the total population in non-metropolitan counties, and the most remote counties have the largest shares of beneficiaries (20 percent of the population in 1997 compared to 16.3 percent for counties adjacent to an MSA and with a city of 10,000 or more).

- Large percentages of non-metropolitan counties have been designated as either whole-county or partial-county underserved areas (64.4 percent were HPSAs in 1997 and 65.5 percent were MUAs); 54.4 percent of non-metropolitan counties were designated as both HPSAs and MUAs, and only 9.6 percent were designated as neither.

- Physician-to-population ratios were substantially higher for metropolitan counties, but per capita ratios of hospitals and hospital beds, skilled nursing facilities, nursing homes, home health agencies, and rural health clinics were higher for non-metropolitan counties, especially the more remote county categories.

- Within the non-metropolitan counties, different patterns of provider supply were found for physicians and hospital beds. The ratios of physicians to population were highest in counties adjacent to an MSA and lowest for the most remote counties; ratios of hospital beds were higher for the more remote counties.

Special Payments for Rural Hospital Inpatient Services

A chronic issue for beneficiaries in the more remote areas of the country has been geographic access to hospital services. The most remote counties had the sparsest supplies of hospitals and certified hospital beds. The richest supplies were in counties with a city of at least 10,000 population, especially those adjacent to MSAs. Beneficiaries residing in the more remote counties tended to have *higher rates of inpatient stays* than those in more urbanized non-metropolitan counties, despite the generally longer distances to hospital locations. The *average Medicare payment per inpatient stay*, however, tended to be lower for beneficiaries in remote counties. Whereas beneficiaries in frontier counties had the lowest rates of inpatient stays per 1,000 beneficiaries, the average Medicare spending per inpatient stay was higher than for any of the other remote counties.

There was a gradual decline from 1992 to 1998 in the numbers of Medicare-certified hospitals serving non-metropolitan counties, with a total decrease of 5.5 percent between 1992 and 1998. The declining trends varied across geographic areas, and those hospitals that remained in operation showed encouraging signs of viability:

- The greatest losses of hospitals for non-metropolitan county categories were in the most remote rural counties (8.3 percent decline) and frontier counties (9.5 percent decline).

- Loss of non-metropolitan hospitals was greatest in the New York region designated by the HHS, and also was large in the Kansas City and Denver HHS regions.

- There was an increase in the number of non-metropolitan counties that had no hospitals, and a decrease in the number of hospitals in counties with more than one hospital.

- Growing numbers of hospitals in non-metropolitan counties offered home care (18.1 percent increase), hospice services (39.0 percent increase), and organized psychiatric inpatient units (42.1 percent increase), which should enhance access to care for Medicare beneficiaries.

- As the number of hospitals declined, increasing percentages of the non-metropolitan hospitals were owned by independent hospital districts or authorities, while ownership by local municipal governments decreased.

- The percentage of hospitals that had for-profit ownership increased in some categories of non-metropolitan counties but decreased in others, with little overall change in for-profit ownership across all non-metropolitan counties.

There were changes in the mix of hospitals designated for Medicare special payment provisions or reclassified for wage indexes for higher payments. The overall percentage of non-metropolitan hospitals with special payment designations decreased from 54.8 percent in 1992 to 38.2 percent in 1998, with a subsequent increase to 60.9 percent in 2000 as BBA provisions went into effect.

- Most of the overall reduction in special designations was due to discontinuation of Medicare-dependent hospitals after 1993; numbers increased when this designation was reactivated in 1997 by the BBA.

- The number of sole community hospitals increased somewhat from 1992 through 1998, whereas the number of rural referral centers decreased through 1998 and then increased by 2000.

- The percentage of hospitals reclassified for wage index declined from 25.8 percent in 1992 to 12.7 percent in 1998.

- Hospitals designated as rural referral centers were consistently much larger, on average, than other non-metropolitan hospitals, and they provided a greater diversity of services. The rural referral centers also were much more likely than the sole community hospitals to elect wage index reclassification.

We looked at changes in inpatient utilization and spending from two perspectives: (1) services provided by non-metropolitan hospitals and (2) services utilized by beneficiaries residing in non-metropolitan counties regardless of hospital location. From 1992 to 1998, the total number of Medicare inpatient stays in non-metropolitan hospitals increased by 12 percent, even as the number of hospitals declined. Differing trends were found by type of hospital designation.

- Percentages of total inpatient stays increased between 1992 and 1998 for sole community hospitals (from 15.0 percent to 20.6 percent) and for hospitals with no special payment designation (from 41.1 percent to 56.5 percent), whereas the percentage declined for rural referral centers (from 26.8 percent to 15.0 percent). These trends reflect trends in the number of hospitals—increasing numbers of SCHs and declining numbers of RRCs.

- In general, sole community hospitals had the largest shares of the Medicare inpatient stays provided by hospitals in the more remote counties, whereas rural referral centers had the largest shares of stays among hospitals in counties with a city of 10,000 population or greater (either adjacent to an MSA or remote), where many of them are located.

- Rural referral centers had much higher case mixes than other non-metropolitan hospitals, as reflected in the average DRG weights for inpatient stays at these hospitals.

- All groups of hospitals with special payment designations had higher average standardized payments (based on a DRG weight equal to 1.0) than those for other non-metropolitan hospitals, reflecting the higher payments provided under these designations.

- The average Medicare payment per stay for rural referral centers was higher than payments for other types of hospitals. After standardizing the payments to control for the higher case mix at rural referral centers, the average payments for rural referral centers and sole community hospitals were more similar.

- Metropolitan hospitals represented 31 percent of inpatient stays for beneficiaries residing in non-metropolitan counties and more than 45 percent of total Medicare spending on their inpatient care. The average payment per stay for metropolitan hospitals was much larger than the average payment per stay at non-metropolitan hospitals, because of a combination of a higher case mix and higher payment rates for urban facilities.

Rural Health Clinics and Federally Qualified Health Centers

The supply of RHCs and non-metropolitan FQHCs increased substantially between 1992 and 1998, and the mix of facility types changed.

- According to the POS files, 248 provider-based RHCs operated in 1992 and 1,860 in 1998. This growth represented an average annual increase of 100 percent, although the fastest rates of growth occurred early in the decade. The number of independent RHCs increased at a somewhat lower rate from 824 clinics in 1992 to 1,905 clinics in 1998 (58 percent annually).

- The number of independent RHCs increased faster in the more urbanized non-metropolitan counties, whereas growth in the provider-based RHCs tended to be in more remote counties with smaller towns.

- Non-metropolitan FQHCs increased from 364 facilities in 1992 to 795 facilities in 1998 (20 percent annual growth). The greatest growth in FQHCs tended to occur in counties adjacent to metropolitan areas and in remote counties with a city of at least 10,000 population.

- For the provider-based RHCs, for-profit ownership declined from 23.0 percent in 1992 to 18.9 percent in 1998. The opposite trend was found for independent RHCs, with for-profit ownership increasing from 45.4 percent in 1992 to 65.3 percent in 1998.

With greater numbers of FQHCs and RHCs delivering primary care services to Medicare beneficiaries across rural areas, Medicare utilization and spending for these services increased accordingly. Judging by data from provider claims for the 5 percent beneficiary sample, Medicare spending for all FQHC and RHC services (for rural and urban beneficiaries) was an estimated $54.5 million in 1991. Spending more than tripled to $175.8 million in 1994 and doubled again to $390.3 million in 1998.

- As of 1991, beneficiaries in the most remote counties (with no town of at least 2,500) were the most likely to use FQHCs and RHCs (e.g., 8.5 percent used FQHCs compared to 0.5 percent of all non-metropolitan beneficiaries). These areas are of special policy interest for access to care. The percentage of beneficiaries using FQHCs and RHCs increased through 1998 for remote counties with small towns and with no towns.

- Despite the increase in numbers of FQHCs and both types of RHCs in the most remote counties, facilities in these counties represented a declining share of the total number of facilities in non-metropolitan areas from 1991 to 1998 because the number of facilities grew faster in other county categories.

- Medicare spent an estimated $28.8 million in 1991 for RHC and FQHC services to beneficiaries living in non-metropolitan counties (52.9 percent of the total for these services), which increased to $276.3 million in 1998 (70.8 percent of the total).

- The distribution of spending shifted toward payments for provider-based RHC services during the 1990s. As of 1998, 28.8 percent of spending was for provider-based RHCs (up from 6.2 percent in 1991), 37.3 percent for independent RHCs (down from 47.1 percent in 1991), and 33.9 percent for FQHCs (down from 46.7 percent in 1991). Even with this shift in shares, the amounts of spending increased for all three types of facilities during this time.

- The average Medicare spending per beneficiary increased more than sixfold (from $1.54 per beneficiary in 1991 to $10.16 in 1998), indicating that all but a small portion of the increased spending was due to growth in the amount of services per beneficiary rather than to the size of the beneficiary population. (Inflation contributed a small share of the total spending increase.)

Physician Bonus Payments

Medicare spending for physician services to non-metropolitan beneficiaries increased steadily during the 1990s, but this trend did not translate into the same growth pattern for bonus payments. As expected, bonus payments were made predominantly for services to beneficiaries residing in non-metropolitan HPSAs, but some also were made for those residing in non-HPSA locations. These findings suggest that bonus payments may have contributed to access on a broader geographical scale than the strict limits of the HPSA boundaries, possibly reflecting the distances that rural beneficiaries often travel for care.

- After substantial increases during the first half of the decade, total bonus payments to physicians began to level off between 1994 and 1996 and then declined by 13.3 percent between 1996 and 1998.

- Bonus payments measured as a percentage of basic Medicare payments to physicians were 0.5 percent of basic payments in 1992, 0.7 percent in 1994, 0.6 percent in 1996, and 0.5 percent in 1998. These percentages reflect the flat trend in bonus payments, and they also highlight that bonus payments are an extremely small share of total Medicare costs for physician services to non-metropolitan beneficiaries.

- For each of the four years studied, close to an estimated 60 percent of bonus payments were made for physician services to beneficiaries residing in whole-county HPSAs, and 30 percent were for beneficiaries in partial-county HPSAs, including those residing outside the HPSA portion of the county.

- A relatively substantial balance of 10 percent of bonus payments was attributable to services for beneficiaries residing in non-HPSA counties.

We found that bonus payments had targeted primary care. Different trends were found for bonus payments for primary care physicians and for primary care services.

- An estimated 55.9 percent of total bonus payments in 1992 was paid to primary care physicians, although their shares decreased steadily over time to reach 49.7 percent in 1998.

- In 1992, payments for primary care services represented 14.0 percent of total basic Medicare payments for physician services and 29.7 percent of total bonus payments for beneficiaries in non-metropolitan counties. By 1998, these shares had grown to 18.6 percent of basic Medicare payments and 37.0 percent of total bonus payments.

The analysis of Medicare payments for non-physician practitioner services indicates that NPP services billed directly to Medicare were a very small but growing fraction of Medicare payments for physician/NPP services (sum of physician and NPP services) provided to Medicare beneficiaries in non-metropolitan areas. These findings may reflect a situation where both physicians and NPPs had a financial incentive to bill Medicare for NPP services through physicians' practices rather than through independent billing by the NPPs, to obtain payment at the full fee schedule rates rather than 75 percent (85 percent as of 1998). Anecdotal information indicates that physicians have been submitting Medicare claims and paying NPPs from payments received. Medicare regulations allow for such arrangements if the NPP is practicing under the active supervision of the physician. As a result, the Medicare claims for services directly billed by NPPs represent a small fraction of Medicare spending for NPP services, especially when considering services by NPPs employed in clinics or group practices, RHCs, FQHCs, or C/MHCs, for which the clinics bill Medicare.

Trends in AAPCC Rates

The AAPCC comparisons in this report document the well-known differences between metropolitan and non-metropolitan counties in their profiles of provider supply and mix as well as Medicare spending levels for its fee-for-service beneficiaries. We consider the average AAPCC rates, their volatility over time, and the share attributable to Part A costs. We defined relative volatility as the four-year average of absolute differences between a reference year and two years before and after it, measured as a percentage of the average AAPCC for the five years. Differences between metropolitan and non-metropolitan counties in AAPCC levels and volatility persisted over the past decade.

- AAPCC levels for metropolitan counties ($493 per month in 1997) were substantially higher than those for non-metropolitan counties ($386 per month), and relative volatility was somewhat lower (9.5 percent for 1995 compared to 10.7 percent for 1990)

- The gap between rates for metropolitan and non-metropolitan counties was reduced somewhat between 1990 and 1997 as a result of relatively higher annual increases in the AAPCC rates for non-metropolitan counties.

- At the same time, AAPCC relative volatility declined for all categories of counties except the most remote counties with no town. This decline was smaller for more remote counties than for metropolitan counties or counties adjacent to an MSA.

- The Part A AAPCC increased from an estimated 61 percent of the total AAPCC in 1990 to 66 percent in 1997. This trend reflects the net effect of reduced spending on hospital inpatient services and increased spending on home health and skilled nursing services.

- The Part A AAPCC as a percentage of total AAPCC was lower for metropolitan counties than for non-metropolitan counties (60 percent compared to 63 percent) in 1990, but this difference all but disappeared by 1997.

- Beneficiaries in non-metropolitan counties had much less access to Medicare health plans. In 1997 only 36.7 percent of counties had at least one health plan (compared to 84.1 percent of metropolitan counties) and only 6.5 percent of beneficiaries in those counties were enrolled (compared to 19.9 percent for metropolitan counties with plans).

- Non-metropolitan counties with at least one Medicare health plan had higher monthly AAPCC rates than counties without a plan available ($403 compared to $388).

The results of our regression models highlight the contrasts in AAPCCs between metropolitan and non-metropolitan counties. The models for all counties and for non-metropolitan counties explained a large percentage of the variation in AAPCC rates across counties, but the model for non-metropolitan counties explained much less. In addition, many factors for the models for all counties and for metropolitan counties had significant effects on AAPCC rates, but fewer factors were significant in the model for non-metropolitan counties.

These results could be interpreted in two ways. Other factors exist that we did not measure but that are predictors of AAPCC rates in non-metropolitan areas (e.g., patient characteristics and health status). On the other hand, the county-level AAPCC rates in non-metropolitan areas may be the net result of such a diversity of local service use patterns within each county that it may be impossible to explain much more of the variation in county rates than our models capture. For example, some remote non-metropolitan counties may have many small urbanized locations (communities or cities) within them, each of which has enough providers to support the demand for primary health care, but others may have only one or two urbanized locations that make access more difficult for beneficiaries living outside those locations. These two counties could have similar county-level averages of provider supply but different rates of utilization (and resulting AAPCC rates).

The models also showed positive associations between AAPCC rates and the supply of physicians and hospitals, but negative associations for SNFs, nursing homes, and home health agencies. Although these effects on AAPCCs were small, they do suggest that the mix of acute care and post-acute care services in non-metropolitan counties may be an important factor in access to care for Medicare beneficiaries and resulting service utilization and costs.

HPSAs and MUAs are, by definition, underserved areas. Therefore, there should be lower utilization rates by Medicare beneficiaries in these areas, which would be observable in lower AAPCC rates. The absence of strong relationships between AAPCC rates and either MUAs or HPSAs may reflect flaws in the criteria for these designation, such that the designated areas are not truly the most underserved areas, or there are enough other underserved areas that were not designated to dilute observed differences in AAPCC rates between the two groups. Alternatively, beneficiaries residing in these areas might have gone outside them for care, or we could hypothesize that these designations indeed had accomplished what was intended—increasing access to care for residents of the designated areas.

Effects of Rural Hospital Special Payments on Part A Costs

In considering the effects of the Medicare special payments for rural hospitals on Medicare Part A spending, we first examined the effects of these payments on hospital payments per inpatient stay, then looked at effects on payments per beneficiary for hospital inpatient services, and finally extended the analysis to effects on total Medicare Part A spending. This stepped approach allowed us to develop an understanding of the factors contributing to the ultimate effects of these payment provisions on Part A spending for non-metropolitan beneficiaries, including the costs per stay, rates of hospital inpatient utilizations, and the share of Part A spending that was for hospital inpatient services. Variations across counties in these factors also were examined in the analysis.

The three-year average data for 1996 through 1998 showed that, overall, the special payments for rural hospitals represented 2.6 percent of the actual payments for Medicare beneficiaries, with some variation in percentages across county categories.

- The percentage of inpatient stays at special payment hospitals differed by county category, and the average payment per stay differed by type of hospitals.

- Almost half the non-metropolitan counties would have less than a 1 percent reduction in average payment per stay as a result of removing the special payment component, whereas 17 percent would have a 5 percent reduction or greater.

- The percentages of total payments for inpatient stays attributable to special payment provisions were highest for beneficiaries in the more remote non-metropolitan counties and frontier counties.

- The shares of total inpatient payments for sole community hospitals, rural referral centers, and Medicare-dependent hospitals were larger in the more remote non-metropolitan counties and the frontier counties, thus explaining the larger reduction in payments for those counties.

Although the special payment provisions have had a relatively small overall effect on Medicare spending for inpatient services, these provisions have been important for the rural hospitals qualified for the payments. Without the special payment components, these hospitals would be paid an estimated 9 to 11 percent less per Medicare inpatient stay, on average, which could have a substantial effect on their financial viability.

The 2.6 percent reduction in Medicare payment per beneficiary for inpatient services would translate to an average 1.9 percent reduction in Medicare payments for all Part A services for non-metropolitan counties. Effects on Part A payments varied across categories of counties, and the greatest reductions would occur in the most remote counties and frontier counties.

ISSUES AND IMPLICATIONS

This study covered a broad range of topics and issues involved in the Medicare payment policies for rural health care providers and their effects on Medicare costs. The special payment policies for rural hospitals appear to have had the largest effects on Medicare spending and also may have contributed to retaining viable providers in the more remote rural areas. Payments for RHCs and FQHCs and bonus payments for physicians represented quite small portions of total per capita costs for Medicare beneficiaries. The decreased spending for physician bonus payments in the later years of the decade is a signal that the program may not be of value to physicians and, therefore, may not be achieving its goal of attracting and retaining physicians in rural locations. Physicians may have been using the RHC option rather than bonus payments to enhance their payments from Medicare. The extent to which payments for RHCs and FQHCs are contributing toward that goal is not clear, but it would be useful to develop further information on this question.

The sheer complexity of the Medicare policies for rural provider payments, which are revealed in this research, poses a challenge for the Congress and CMS with respect to policy changes they may contemplate. For example, this type of research cannot document whether a payment policy may be preventing erosion of provider supply in rural areas. If a decision were made to eliminate a particular policy, an "invisible" effect could become observable in the form of loss of providers. Furthermore, there appears to be a need to establish a coordinated payment policy framework that addresses rural providers as a system of care for beneficiaries residing in rural areas, with goals to support the achievement of such a system approach. This framework should pay attention to which roles are appropriate for both rural and urban providers of health care for rural beneficiaries.

We summarize a number of the policy issues that surfaced from these analyses in Section 9, and we discuss implications for future Medicare policy decisions. In addition, we present recommendations for future research in two general areas: (1) to continue to track service use and costs as Medicare payment policies change (as a result of the BBA, BBRA, and subsequent legislation) and (2) to explore in more depth issues identified in this research.

The report is organized to first describe the study background and the methods and data used in the analyses, followed by presentation of results for each research component. Section 1 presents background on rural issues and Medicare payment methods. In Section 2, we describe the methods and data we used for the trend analyses. The demographic and service supply profiles of urban and rural counties are presented in Section 3. Results of the four analyses are in subsequent chapters: rural hospitals in Section 4, RHC/FQHC payments in Section 5, physician bonus payments in Section 6, and the AAPCC rates in Section 7. Section 8 presents the county-level analysis of effects of special hospital payments on estimated Part A per capita costs for Medicare beneficiaries. Section 9 considers implications of our findings for future Medicare policy and research, including specific issues identified and tracking of effects of changes made by the BBA and subsequent legislation.

ACKNOWLEDGMENTS

This report contains an enormous amount of trend information about utilization and payments under three distinct Medicare special payment systems for rural providers, as well as about capitation payments based on the Medicare adjusted average per capita costs. The challenge we faced was to present our results in a consistent manner across these analyses and to synthesize the findings to allow a cohesive policy discussion of implications for future Medicare payment policies and research. We wish to thank the contribution made to this effort by our RAND colleagues Elizabeth Sloss and Barbara Wynn, who reviewed an earlier draft of the report. Their thoughtful comments helped to strengthen both the presentation of technical content and consideration of policy implications.

The CMS project officer, William Buczko, provided valuable assistance and guidance that supported our research activities. We thank him for his active involvement throughout the project. His efforts and Medicare expertise ensured our access to the large amounts of Medicare enrollment and claims data required for the research and also helped to inform our analyses and presentation of research results.

ACRONYMS

AAPCC	Adjusted Average per Capita Costs
AHA	American Hospital Association
AMA	American Medical Association
ARF	Area Resource File
BBA	Balanced Budget Act (1997)
BBRA	Balanced Budget Refinement Act (1999)
CAH	Critical Access Hospital
CFR	Code of Federal Regulations
C/MHC	Community/Mental Health Center
CMS	Centers for Medicare and Medicaid Services
COLA	Cost of Living Adjustment
CPT	Current Procedural Terminology
DRG	Diagnosis-Related Group
DSH	Disproportionate Share
EACH	Essential Access Community Hospital
ERS	Economic Research Service
ESRD	End Stage Renal Disease
FFHC	Federally Funded Health Center
FQHC	Federally Qualified Health Center
FTE	Full-time equivalent
GAO	Government Accounting Office
HCFA	Health Care Financing Administration (now the CMS)
HCPCS	HCFA's Common Procedure Coding System
HCPP	Health Care Prepayment Plan
HHS	Health and Human Services
HMO	Health Maintenance Organization
HPSA	Health Professional Shortage Area
HRSA	Health Resources and Services Administration
MAF	Medical Assistance Facility
MDH	Medicare-Dependent Hospital
MEDPAR	Medicare Provider Analysis and Review
MEI	Medicare Economic Index
MSA	Metropolitan Statistical Area
MUA/P	Medically Underserved Area/Population
NP	Nurse Practitioner
NPP	Non-Physician Providers
OBRA	Omnibus Budget Reconciliation Act
OIG	Office of the HHS Inspector General
OMB	Office of Management and Budget
PA	Physician Assistant
PC	Professional Component
PHS	Public Health Service
POS	Provider of Service

PPRC	Physician Payment Review Commission
PPS	Prospective Payment System
ProPAC	Prospective Payment Assessment Commission
PSF	Provider Specific File
RHC	Rural Health Clinic
RPCH	Rural Primary Care Hospital
RRC	Rural Referral Center
RUCA	Rural-Urban Commuting Area
RUCC	Rural-Urban Continuum Code
SCH	Sole Community Hospital
SNF	Skilled Nursing Facility
SSA	Social Security Administration
SSI	Supplemental Security Income
TC	Technical Component
UA	Urbanized Area
UIC	Urban Influence Code
USDA	U.S. Department of Agriculture
US GAO	U.S. Government Accounting Office

1. INTRODUCTION

The Centers for Medicare and Medicaid Services (CMS, formerly the Health Care Financing Administration) contracted with RAND to analyze special payments that Medicare has been making to rural providers and the implications for access and costs of care for rural Medicare beneficiaries. Although the special payment provisions are diverse, they all are intended to support the rural health care infrastructure to help ensure access to care for Medicare beneficiaries residing in rural areas. These provisions were introduced at various times during the past decade or earlier. CMS is interested in developing information for use in formulating future Medicare policy for rural health care services and payments.

The purpose of this research was to provide a comprehensive overview of Medicare special payments to rural providers over the last decade, including documentation of the supply of providers, trends in payments made by Medicare, and resulting Medicare costs per beneficiary. One focus of the study was on services in geographic areas designated by the Health Resources and Services Administration (HRSA) as either Health Professional Shortage Areas (HPSAs) or Medically Underserved Areas/Populations (MUA/Ps). The special payment provisions examined were:

- Special payments for Sole Community Hospitals (SCHs), Medicare-dependent hospitals (MDHs), and Rural Referral Centers (RRCs);

- Reimbursements to Rural Health Clinics (RHCs) and Federally Qualified Health Centers (FQHCs);

- Bonus payments to physicians in rural HPSAs; and

- Capitation payments in rural counties, especially in underserved areas.

In addition to the trend analyses, we estimated the relative contribution of special payments for rural hospitals to the Medicare per capita costs in rural counties, which are the basis for capitation rates. Similar analyses were not performed for RHC/FQHC services or for physician bonus payments because the trend analyses showed that both of these payment provisions had quite small effects on Medicare costs per beneficiary.

BACKGROUND

The ability of the rural elderly to access health care services has been a continuing source of concern for policymakers. This concern is driven by a number of factors that combine to make the rural elderly population more vulnerable and service delivery organizations less stable compared to their non-rural counterparts. (Many of these issues also affect the Medicare disabled population.) Elderly people live in rural areas in disproportionate numbers (Rogers et al., 1993). Second, although the incidence of acute conditions among the elderly does not appear to be any greater, a larger proportion of them (41 percent versus 36 percent) suffer from activity-limiting chronic diseases, such as diabetes and arthritis (Schlenker and Shaughnessy, 1996). Third, rural elderly people travel farther and wait longer for outpatient care and use fewer preventive services than their non-rural counterparts (Taylor et al., 1993; Van Nostrand et al., 1993).

The supply and financial viability of rural providers has been a chronic problem. Rural communities face difficulties recruiting and retaining physicians, because they are reluctant to locate in rural areas (PPRC, 1991). Low patient volumes in sparsely populated areas with relatively large numbers of uninsured make it difficult for service delivery organizations to be financially stable (ProPAC, 1991). Between 1990 and 1996, the number of rural hospitals decreased by 8.6 percent, from 2,383 to 2,177 hospitals. Rural hospitals tend to be small and offer a more limited range of services than their counterparts in more densely populated regions. In 1996, 72 percent of hospitals outside Metropolitan Statistical Areas (MSAs) had 100 or fewer staffed beds and 47 percent had fewer than 50 staffed beds.[1] Rural hospitals with fewer than 100 beds are less likely to offer a range of services considered standard in more densely populated regions. Instead, they provide proportionately more outpatient and long-term care services than urban hospitals do, and these services have been growing components of their total services during the 1990s (Moscovice et al., 1999).

Provisions contained in the Omnibus Reconciliation Acts of 1987 and 1989, and subsequent revisions to hospital and physician payment rules, influenced Medicare payments to rural providers throughout the 1990s. More recently, the 1997 Balanced Budget Act (BBA), as well as follow-up legislation in subsequent years, contained a number of provisions with important implications for the financing and delivery of Medicare-funded services in rural areas. Some provisions addressed fee-for-service payments for rural hospitals, skilled nursing facilities (SNFs), and home health agencies, which can be anticipated to have complex effects for rural providers. Some changes also were made in payment provisions for RHCs and FQHCs. Other provisions established a new methodology for capitation payments for the new Medicare+Choice organizations, including provisions to encourage plans to serve rural areas.

DESIGNATIONS FOR UNDERSERVED AREAS

Eligibility for many of the rural programs and payments being investigated in this report requires that service providers operate in underserved areas, which are so designated by Congressional provisions for MUA/Ps and HPSAs. These areas are designated by HRSA through its regulatory process. HRSA first designated MUA/Ps in 1973 and has added new MUA/P designations periodically through the 1990s. HPSAs were first designated in 1978 (HRSA, 1998; Goldsmith and Ricketts, 1999). HRSA reviews HPSA designations every three years, adding or deleting area designations as appropriate.

A major difference between MUAs and HPSAs is that a shortage of health care providers is the primary measure for designating a HPSA, whereas MUAs are identified using other factors as well (US GAO, 1995). To be designated a primary care HPSA, the geographic area must be rational for delivery of health services; must have a population-to-provider (primary care physician) ratio of at least 3,500 to 1 (or 3,000 to 1 under certain circumstances); and must be adjacent to areas with provider resources that are overused, more than 30 minutes travel time away, or otherwise inaccessible. To qualify for MUA designation, an area must meet four factors of health service need: primary care physician-to-population ratio, infant mortality rate,

---

[1]   By comparison, Medicare-certified hospitals in MSAs had an average of 265 certified beds in 1998, and an estimated 25 percent had fewer than 100 beds, showing the difference between the licensed capacity and the actual operating capacity of hospitals.

percentage of population with incomes below poverty level, and percentage of population aged 65 or older.

In 1997, roughly 64 percent of counties outside MSAs contained at least one region officially designated as a HPSA and roughly 10 percent of non-MSA counties had no active primary care physician (NC-RHRPAC, 1998). HRSA also has added new MUA/P designations periodically through the 1990s, but no existing MUA designations have been deleted.

In response to requirements of the Health Centers Consolidation Act of 1996, HRSA is revising the criteria and procedures for designating MUA/Ps and HPSAs. Earlier proposed changes provided for HPSAs to be a subset of the MUA/Ps and use of a consistent set of criteria to determine the two designations (HRSA, 1998). In response to extensive comments received on these proposed rules, HRSA is making substantial changes to the methodology, with plans to publish a revised proposed rule in the near future.

RURAL HOSPITALS

Rural communities face challenges in protecting the stability of the institutional providers that historically have served their residents. During the 1990s, in particular the first half of the decade, many rural hospitals discontinued operation (Office of the HHS Inspector General, 1992, 1994, 1996, 2000; Moscovice et al., 1999). Trends of hospital closures reported by the Office of the HHS Inspector General showed that rural hospital closures were highest in 1987 through 1989, peaking in 1988. Hospital representatives reported to that office that they closed because of a combination of "lagging revenues, declining occupancy, and rising costs" (Office of the HHS Inspector General, 1993a). The annual number of closures declined gradually, ebbing in 1994, and relatively small numbers of closures continued to occur in later years. Rural hospitals that closed were smaller and had lower occupancy, on average, than other rural hospitals. Neither Medicare nor Medicaid utilization for closed hospitals was consistently higher or lower than for the remaining hospitals (Office of the HHS Inspector General, 1992, 1994, 1996, 2000).

Studies of hospital utilization by rural residents found that a substantial share of inpatient stays for rural residents are in urban hospitals. Williamson et al. (1993) found that 44 percent of rural residents in the state of Washington went to urban hospitals when they were hospitalized for surgery. Although the presence of surgical providers increased use of local hospitals, a substantial proportion of patients getting basic surgical procedures bypassed available local services in favor of urban hospitals. Another study of a nationwide sample of rural residents found that they chose to use urban hospitals for an average of one-third of their hospital stays, and residents with higher incomes were more likely to do so. Therefore, low-income rural residents appear to be more vulnerable to access problems when local hospital closures, mergers, and consolidations reduce the level of local service provision (McNamara, 1998). This concern is reinforced by findings that medical admissions decreased significantly in areas with hospital closures, and patients in closure areas were more likely to be admitted to urban teaching hospitals following the closure of their local hospital. Physician services were not found to substitute for inpatient services following a closure (Rosenbach and Dayhoff, 1995).

As described above, a variety of federal laws governing Medicare provisions for rural hospitals were passed during the late 1980s and the 1990s. Table 1.1 presents highlights of this legislative history.

Table 1.1
Chronological History of Medicare Payment Policies for Rural Hospitals

Year	Program Characteristics
1984	Enactment of the Medicare PPS, including special payment provisions for sole community hospitals (SCHs) and RRCs
1987	Separate outlier pools established for urban and rural hospitals
1988	RRCs paid on the basis of standardized amount for urban areas
	Higher updates established for rural hospitals to improve financial performance
1989	OBRA 89 authorizes Medicare payments for Essential Access Community Hospital/Rural Primary Care Hospital (EACH/RPCH) demonstrations in seven states for inpatient and outpatient services
1990	More rural hospitals become eligible for DSH adjustment
	More generous payments made to SCHs
	Special payment rules established for Medicare-dependent hospitals (MDHs) whereby MDHs were paid as SCHs
1991	Rural hospitals again granted higher payment updates to phase in elimination of the differential in standardized amounts for urban and rural hospitals by 1995
1992	Program initiated that allows reclassification of rural hospitals adjacent to metropolitan areas to obtain higher urban payments and wage indices
1993	First RPCH is certified by Medicare; by 1997, 38 RPCHs operated in six states
1997	BBA contained many provisions affecting fee-for-service Medicare and Medicare managed care in rural areas; these provisions are being phased in at differing rates over several years, beginning in 1998

The Medicare Prospective Payment System (PPS), enacted in the early 1980s, was designed to create efficiency incentives while compensating hospitals for reasonable costs of care for Medicare beneficiaries. PPS payments are based on the expected cost of care for a patient stay within Diagnosis-Related Groups (DRGs). Poor financial performance of rural hospitals under PPS, relative to their urban counterparts, raised concerns about the adequacy of rural payments. In a 1991 report to Congress, ProPAC traced the poor financial performance of rural hospitals under PPS to three main factors: (1) declining patient volume that reduced revenues, (2) lower rural standardized amounts on which PPS payments are based, and (3) low patient volume that increased the relative share of fixed costs. A number of other technical issues also hurt rural hospitals, such as outlier payment pools, wage indices, and payment policy for transfer cases. PPS modifications include phase-in of larger updates for rural standardized amounts to bring them closer to urban rates, accompanied by elimination of the rural outlier payment pool; allowances for reclassification of rural hospitals in areas adjacent to urban areas to allow them to be paid using the higher urban standardized amounts and wage indices; and adjustments to disproportionate share (DSH) payments for rural hospitals.

Congress has created several new categories of rural hospitals with more favorable payment provisions to improve their financial performance. These special payment provisions are described in Appendix A. The scope and history of the Medicare special payment policies for inpatient services by rural hospitals reflect the diversity of issues faced by rural hospitals serving Medicare beneficiaries. Because each special payment designation responded to a unique set of issues, both the eligibility criteria and payment methodologies differ substantially. SCHs were designated early in the 1980s using criteria to ensure access for Medicare beneficiaries residing in non-metropolitan counties. SCHs are paid the higher of the federal rate or a hospital-specific rate based on historical costs. RRCs are larger rural hospitals with a range of services that serve as specialty referral resources for other rural hospitals. RRCs are given special treatment for geographic reclassification and related payment adjustments. Small rural MDHs were designated from April 1990 through October 1, 1994, and they were reactivated in 1997 by the BBA. To be designated an MDH, a hospital had to have fewer than 100 beds and be dependent on Medicare for at least 60 percent of its inpatient days or discharges. These hospitals are paid by a blend of the federal payment rate and a hospital-specific rate.

Two demonstrations were in operation during the 1990s to test alternative models for limited-service rural hospitals that refer to larger, full-service facilities. In 1988, the Montana Medical Assistance Facility (MAF) demonstration began, which designated small, limited-service hospitals within the state. In 1989, Congress authorized a demonstration of the EACH program in seven states. Beginning in 1991, this demonstration tested another rural hospital network model, with the purpose of improving the quality and efficiency of underutilized rural hospitals. Each network consisted of an EACH as the full-service referral hospital, plus one or more RPCHs that provided emergency care, basic inpatient treatment (with a limit of six beds), and primary care services on an outpatient basis. More complex cases are referred to a full-service EACH in its network. EACHs are paid as sole community hospitals, and RPCHs are reimbursed on the basis of costs. By 1997, networks were operating in six states with a total of 38 RPCHs (US GAO, 1998). The MAFs and RPCHs transitioned to Critical Access Hospitals (CAHs) after passage of the BBA.

An overview of the hospital supply in counties outside Metropolitan Statistical Areas for the year 2000 is presented in Table 1.2, including the total number of hospitals, distribution by bed size, and distribution by special designation category. We refer to these hospitals as "non-metropolitan" rather than "rural" because rural location is not the same as location in counties that are not in an MSA. Some hospitals located within an MSA serve rural populations in the less urbanized portions of the MSA. Similarly, some hospitals in non-MSA counties are in cities and serve urbanized populations.

Of the 2,136 Medicare-certified, non-metropolitan hospitals existing in the year 1999, 57.7 percent had fewer than 50 beds and only 3.2 percent had 200 or more beds. Hospitals with no special designation were only 39.1 percent of the total, indicating the importance of special Medicare payments for non-metropolitan hospitals. In our trend analysis, we track changes in the total numbers of hospitals during the 1990s, as well as designations for special payments and wage index reclassifications.

Table 1.2
Profile of Non-Metropolitan Hospitals, by Size and Special Designation Status, 1999

Hospital Category	Number	% of Total
All non-metropolitan hospitals	2,136	100.0%
Distribution by bed size		
0–49 beds	1,233	57.7
50–99 beds	535	25.0
100–149 beds	219	10.3
150–199 beds	81	3.8
200 or more beds	68	3.2
Distribution by special designation		
No special designation	835	39.1
Rural Referral Center	150	7.0
Sole Community Hospital	661	30.9
Medicare-dependent hospital	352	16.5
SCH and RRC	57	2.7
Other	81	3.8
Reclassified hospitals (2000)	426	19.9

SOURCE: Table II in *Final Rule: Medicare Program; Changes to the Hospital Inpatient Prospective Payment Systems and Fiscal Year 2001 Rates*, 65 FR 47196, August 1, 2000.

RURAL HEALTH CLINICS AND FEDERALLY QUALIFIED HEALTH CENTERS

Despite their differing histories, Rural Health Clinics and Federally Qualified Health Centers are treated similarly in the Medicare program in many ways (for example, in certification requirements and reimbursement methods). In rural areas, Medicare payment mechanisms for both RHCs and FQHCs provide additional financial support intended to protect the financial stability (and therefore availability) of rural health care providers.

Rural health clinics were created by the Rural Health Clinics Act (P.L. 95-210) of 1977. At the time, there were concerns that the health needs of rural Medicare and Medicaid beneficiaries were not being met, particularly those living in HPSAs or in medically underserved areas meeting other such criteria. One objective was to create a cost-based reimbursement mechanism for rural providers to encourage service provision to these rural beneficiaries (HRSA, 1995). Also, existing rural clinics staffed by nurse practitioners or physician assistants had not been eligible for Medicare reimbursement without immediate supervision of a physician, posing an additional financial barrier to practices in rural locations (US GAO, 1996). Thus, a second objective was to encourage the use of mid-level practitioners by allowing reimbursement for services when a physician was not present (HRSA, 1995).

The Omnibus Budget Reconciliation Act (OBRA) of 1989 created the FQHC program to establish cost-based reimbursement for services provided to Medicaid beneficiaries by federally funded community health centers. OBRA 1990 extended FQHC reimbursement to also cover services provided to Medicare beneficiaries. For several decades, the community health centers have served populations with reduced financial or geographical access to care in both urban and rural locations. FQHC status offered these centers additional sources of revenue to help support their financial solvency. In addition, clinics that meet the requirements to be a community health center but do not receive federal support also are qualified for FQHC designation. Both urban and rural health centers are eligible to apply for designation as FQHCs, and the scope of services the clinics are required to provide is broader than those required for RHCs.

Overview of RHC and FQHC Requirements

Table 1.3 summarizes the basic provisions for designation as RHCs or FQHCs and for reimbursement under the Medicare program, including the types of facilities designated, eligibility to qualify, type of ownership and required location, scope of outpatient services provided, reimbursement rules, and beneficiary cost sharing. The information is presented side by side to allow ready comparison of similarities and differences in these programs.

RHCs and FQHCs provide services for underserved areas. For RHCs, the facility must be in a non-urbanized area designated as a HPSA or an MUA, as specified in the Public Health Service (PHS) Act. RHCs have an additional designation option—location in an area designated as underserved by a state's governor and approved by HHS. Practices in non-urban locations with unmet primary health care needs, but without any of these shortage area designations, may be eligible for RHC status, but this provision is rarely invoked by CMS, according to the Office of Rural Health Policy (HRSA, 1995). An FQHC is required to serve populations in an MUA but does not have to be physically located in such a designated area (HRSA, 1995). A facility serving a HPSA or other designated area that does not have MUA status does not qualify for FQHC status.

An FQHC can convert to an RHC (or vice versa), but a facility cannot have concurrent status as both within Medicare or Medicaid. However, a facility may be an RHC for Medicare and at the same time an FQHC for Medicaid. It also is possible to have multiple facilities with different designations within a network. As noted by the GAO (1997), the financial incentive to become an RHC or FQHC is the cost-based reimbursement, where other providers must operate within the constraints of prospectively defined Medicare fee schedules that may pay them less than their costs.

Two major changes made by the BBA of 1997 addressed requirements for clinic location and payment rules. Both RHCs and FQHCs may be organized as either provider-based clinics or independent facilities. A provider-based clinic is part of a larger facility such as a hospital, home health agency, or skilled nursing facility. Payment rules historically differed for provider-based and independent facilities, but the BBA eliminated those differences. The BBA also tightened up the allowance for continuation of RHCs after their areas lost designation as a shortage area. Additional details of the BBA changes are discussed below.

Table 1.3
Federal Provisions for Rural Health Clinics and Federally Qualified Health Centers
Before Implementation of the BBA of 1997

Rural Health Clinics	Federally Qualified Health Centers
Types of facilities designated	
Provider-based and independent	Provider-based and freestanding
Eligibility to qualify	
Determined by the secretary of the HHS to meet requirements of the Social Security Act	Receives a grant under section 329, 330, or 340 of the PHS Act
Filed an agreement with the Secretary to provide RHC services	Recommended by PHS as meeting requirements of the PHS Act (called "look alike")
	Was a comprehensive FFHC as of January 1, 1990
	Outpatient facility operated by a tribe or tribal organization under the Indian Self-Determination Act or the Indian Health Care Improvement Act
Types of ownership allowed	
All types	Only private nonprofit or public ownership
Clinic locations required to qualify	
Rural area (outside Census Bureau urbanized areas)	Rural or urban location
Located in a HPSA, MUA, or shortage area designated by the state's governor	Located in an MUA
RHC designation can continue if its area later loses a shortage area designation	Serve residents of shortage areas if not located in such an area
Outpatient services required to be provided	
Physician services	Physician services
Nurse practitioner (NP), physician assistant (PA), or nurse-midwife services	NP, PA, or nurse-midwife services
Clinical psychologist and clinical social worker services	Clinical psychologist and clinical social worker services
Services and supplies incident to professional services provided	Services and supplies incident to professional services provided
Visiting nurse services for homebound patients	Visiting nurse services for homebound patients
Basic laboratory services essential to the immediate diagnosis and treatment of the patient	Preventive primary services
Payment for clinics	
For provider-based clinics, reimbursement of reasonable costs per 42 CFR 413	For provider-based clinics, reimbursement of reasonable costs per 42 CFR 413
For independent clinics, all-inclusive rate based on total allowable costs divided by estimated total visits	For freestanding clinics, all-inclusive rate based on total allowable costs divided by estimated total visits
Cap on all-inclusive rate for independent clinics	Cap on all-inclusive rate for freestanding clinics
Medicare pays 80 percent of allowed costs or all-inclusive rate after deductible has been met	Medicare pays 80 percent of allowed costs or all-inclusive rate
Year-end reconciliation of reimbursable costs	Year-end reconciliation of reimbursable costs
Beneficiaries served, cost sharing	
No requirement to serve those unable to pay	Must take all patients and have a sliding fee schedule based on ability to pay
Annual deductibles of the first $100 for services plus expenses for the first three pints of blood	No annual deductible
20 percent of remaining reimbursable costs	20 percent of reimbursable costs

SOURCE: *Medicare Provider Manual for Rural Health Clinics and Federally Qualified Health Centers,* 42 CFR Section 405, Subpart X.

Evolution of the RHCs and FQHCs

The rules and regulations governing RHCs and FQHCs changed periodically during the 1980s and 1990s. The most rapid growth in numbers of FQHCs occurred in the first few years following the enabling legislation. However, initial response to the RHC enabling legislation was weaker than expected, and program growth was slow. Reported reasons for this slow growth included caps on reimbursement rates that were considered low, restrictive state laws regarding independent practice for mid-level practitioners, a burdensome certification process, and concerns by states regarding cost impacts of RHC status on state-operated Medicaid programs (HRSA, 1995). Summarized here are key program changes during the 1980s and early 1990s, as compiled by the Office of Rural Health Policy (HRSA, 1995).

OBRA 1987

- Increased reimbursement cap for RHCs;
- Mandated annual increases in the RHC cap based on the Medicare Economic Index (MEI); and
- Added services of clinical psychologists to core services for RHCs.

OBRA 1989

- Reduced full-time equivalent (FTE) time of mid-level practitioner in RHC from 60 percent to 50 percent of operating hours;
- Added certified nurse midwives to definition of mid-level practitioners for RHCs;
- Added clinical social work services to core services of RHCs; and
- Provided governors the option of designating areas with a shortage of personal health services, and expanded shortage area eligibility to areas with a designated population group and high migrant areas for RHCs.

OBRA 1990

- Expedited the approval timeframe for RHC certification; and
- Modified productivity screens.

1992 legislation

- Excluded all diagnostic tests (except selected clinical laboratory services) from the all-inclusive reimbursement rate, thus permitting reimbursement of these services beyond the cost-based payment for RHCs and FQHCs.

OBRA 1993

- Clarified FQHC eligibility of outpatient programs operated by tribes and tribal organizations.

Beginning in the early 1990s, there was a substantial increase in the number of new RHC certifications. Some were concerned that the criteria for presence in an underserved area were too inclusive and that RHCs were located in areas that did not have sufficient need. The regulations governing RHCs essentially "grandfathered" RHC eligibility once the criteria had been met, with the objective of ensuring that RHCs would be able to attract health professionals to the rural area by creating greater stability in terms of ongoing eligibility. There were also concerns that cost reimbursement did not encourage efficiency and was not the most effective use of public funds for expanding health care access to rural Medicare beneficiaries.

Various recommendations have been offered by different agencies and institutional reports during the mid-1990s addressing these issues, including the following:

Certification
- Create specific underserved designation criteria (US GAO,1995), reevaluate designations periodically, or establish new criteria other than rural and underserved (Office of the HHS Inspector General, 1996); and

- Eliminate concentrations of RHCs by requiring documentation of need, creating geographic limits for locations, and involving state officials in certification (Office of the HHS Inspector General, 1996).

Reimbursement
- Require Medicare billing itemized by the service provided, rather than as an encounter, for independent RHCs (as provider-based RHCs reimbursed on charges currently do) (Office of the HHS Inspector General, 1996);

- Require that provider-based RHCs also submit the cost report worksheets submitted by independent RHCs (Office of the HHS Inspector General, 1996);

- Implement caps on provider-based RHCs along with focused audits (Office of the HHS Inspector General, 1996);

- Implement standardization of itemized billing and definitions of an encounter (Office of the HHS Inspector General, 1996); and

- Determine what proportion of independent RHCs are reimbursed at the capped rate, and consider a flat rate with itemized billing and annual adjustments (Office of the HHS Inspector General, 1996).

Interest in these issues culminated in legislative changes made by the 1997 BBA. The provisions of the BBA included the following:
- Refinement of the definition of what constitutes a qualifying rural shortage area for RHC eligibility;

- Establishment of criteria for determining which clinics may continue as approved Medicare RHCs in areas that lose designation as shortage areas;

- Limitations on waivers of some non-physician staffing requirements;

- Extension of the all-inclusive rate and related payment limits to provider-based RHCs except in hospitals with fewer than 50 beds;

- Rules to prevent "commingling" of RHC and non-RHC resources; and

- Establishment of a quality assurance program (HCFA, 2000).

Medicare Provisions for RHC/FQHC Payments

We provide here an overview of the Medicare cost-based reimbursement provisions for RHC and FQHC services that were in effect through 1997.[2] The payment methods are the same for RHCs and FQHCs, except that beneficiaries pay deductible amounts for RHC services but not for FQHC services. The methods differ for provider-based facilities and independent facilities; independent facilities are reimbursed an all-inclusive rate for a bundled package of core services, which is subject to a maximum limit (cap) set each year. Provider-based facilities are reimbursed reasonable costs for the individual services provided (unbundled), which are not subject to a cap. Other services provided by the facilities, such as radiology or therapy services, are paid under the Physician Fee Schedule or Medicare payment provisions for institutional outpatient services.

For each provider-based RHC or FQHC, an interim payment is calculated at the beginning of each year based on the facility's estimate of what its costs will be during the year for the core services provided. This payment is adjusted periodically during the year to reflect actual experience. There is a reconciliation of allowable costs at the end of each year, using standard Medicare methods for cost estimation (per Section 413 of the CFR) and claims for services provided. If the total costs are greater than the sum of the all-inclusive rate payments made during the year, Medicare pays the balance to the facility; if there are overpayments, the facility must return the excess funds to Medicare. Payments for provider-based facilities are not subject to any payment limits.

The all-inclusive rates for independent RHCs and freestanding FQHCs are calculated by CMS at the beginning of each year, and the rates are updated periodically during the year to achieve total reimbursements close to total allowable costs for the year. A separate rate is calculated for each RHC or FQHC as the total allowable costs for core services to Medicare beneficiaries, divided by the total number of outpatient encounters for these beneficiaries. Like the provider-based facilities, total costs are reconciled at the end of each year, with adjustments paid by either Medicare or the facility as needed.

The payment caps for the all-inclusive rates paid to independent facilities were initially established by legislation and are updated each calendar year by the percentage increase in the MEI applicable to primary care physician services. The payment caps for RHCs, urban FQHCs, and rural FQHCs for 1988 through 1997 are listed in Table 1.4. As shown, the limits are higher for the rural FQHCs than for the RHCs, reflecting the broader set of services covered by the FQHCs reimbursements. In addition, the limits for urban FQHCs are higher than those for rural FQHCs. Between 1992 and 1996, the percentage adjustments were higher for the FQHCs than for the RHCs because they included adjustments both for MEI and for general increases in family practice payments resulting from transition to the new physician fee schedule.[3] Both RHCs and FQHCs had the same 2.0 percent adjustment in 1997.

---

[2]   The source of this information is the *Medicare Provider Manual for Rural Health Clinics and Federally Qualified Health Centers*, Chapter 5, "Payment." Modifications to these provisions by the BBA went into effect in September 1997.

[3]   This reason for the additional increase in caps for FQHCs was reported in the *Medicare Provider Manual for Rural Health Clinics and Federally Qualified Health Centers*, Chapter 5, "Payment."

Table 1.4
Payment Limits for the Medicare All-Inclusive Rates
for Independent RHCs and FQHCs, 1988, 1990–1997

Year	Payment Limit per Clinic Encounter			% Annual Adjustment	
	RHCs	Rural FQHCs	Urban FQHCs	RHCs	FQHCs
1988	$46.00	—	—	—	—
1990	49.37	—	—	4.2%	—
1991	50.36	$62.25	$72.39	2.0	—
1992	51.77	63.99	74.42	2.8	2.8%
1993	53.17	65.72	76.43	2.7	2.7
1994	54.39	69.65	81.00	2.3	5.98
1995	55.53	72.63	84.47	2.1	4.28
1996	56.64	75.60	87.93	2.0	4.09
1997	57.77	77.11	89.69	2.0	2.0

SOURCE: *Medicare Provider Manual for Rural Health Clinics and Federally Qualified Health Centers*, Chapter 5, "Payment."

NOTE: The 1992–1996 annual adjustments for FQHCs include additional adjustments for the general increase in family practice physician payments with transition to the physician fee schedule.

Earlier Studies of RHC/FQHC Program Impact

In 1997, the GAO conducted detailed site visits in four states with RHCs (Alabama, New Hampshire, Kansas, and Washington) and examined national statistics to evaluate the locations of Rural Health Clinics, the volume of Medicare and Medicaid beneficiaries served, the reimbursement costs, and service patterns between 1992 and 1994. A detailed analysis of several selected locations was performed to characterize RHC location, applying mapping software to determine the extent of RHC collocation and average distance from clinic to beneficiaries. Approximately 5 percent of RHCs were described by the GAO report as existing in areas with fewer than 2,000 residents within 15 miles, whereas 19 percent of RHCs had more than 50,000 residents within 15 miles of the clinic (US GAO, 1996). The report noted that nationally, "37 percent of the 2,599 RHCs certified near the end of fiscal year 1995 were located in the same community as other RHCs or FQHCs, with 74 cities having 3 to 6 RHCs" (data source not cited). A review of Medicare and Medicaid claims data for the four study states shows that approximately 73 percent of the beneficiaries in the GAO sample had earlier obtained care from a provider in their city of residence, or in the city where the RHC was located.

From its evaluation of converted physician practices in the study states, the GAO report concluded that the RHC payments benefit clinics in suburban and rural locations, and that many RHCs were established through conversion of existing physician practices that would have continued to operate in the absence of the special RHC reimbursement provisions (US GAO, 1997). The GAO also noted the problems with the grandfathering provision allowing RHCs to continue cost-based reimbursement, even after the areas they served no longer were deemed to be medically underserved.

A Mathematica study published in 1997 evaluated the effects of the recent growth in Rural Health Clinics on access to care and on costs for the Medicare and Medicaid programs (Cheh and Thompson, 1997). The study examined 18 RHCs in six states that were designated in

1992–1993, including both independent and provider-based clinics. Site visits were conducted to collect detailed information on the clinics, and pre-post comparisons (1991 and 1994) were performed of utilization of outpatient and emergency services, the number of health care professionals per capita, and costs for services. They found evidence of improved access to care, including increases in clinic staffing, increased levels of service per capita, and reduced utilization of emergency room services. The majority of Medicare cost increases was found to be due to use of cost reimbursement, rather than increased service volume, and costs per encounter were higher for hospital-based clinics than for the independent clinics.

Krein (1999) studied rural hospital proclivity to adopt a provider-based RHC during the 1990s. The purpose of this study was to identify factors associated with decisions by rural hospitals to establish a provider-based RHC. Discrete-time logit models were used to test the effects of factors such as distance from other hospitals, hospital market share, physician supply, state non-physician provider (NPP) regulation, hospital financial performance, and measures of innovativeness. Few of the dimensions predicted by traditional economic theory (e.g., competitiveness of market, physician supply) were found to be associated with rural hospitals' decisions to establish an RHC. Rather, hospitals appeared to be responding to institutional pressure related to establishment of RHCs by other hospitals, i.e., imitating the strategies of others, perhaps because of uncertainty or limited ability to evaluate strategic options.

More recently, Project HOPE is performing a study entitled "Importance of Provider-Based Rural Health Clinics for Parent Hospitals and Local Access to Care" to assess the importance to hospitals of establishing an RHC (Walsh Center for Rural Health, 2001). This study is designed to examine the potential effect on rural hospitals and RHCs of the new cap on Medicare payment to provider-based RHCs imposed by the BBA of 1997 (excluding hospitals having fewer than 50 beds). Effects being examined include parent hospitals' financial performance and potential effects on access to local care if these hospitals or their RHCs are forced to close. According to unpublished information from that study, only 10 percent of hospital-based RHCs have the same address as the hospital, and two-thirds of these RHCs are in a different town from the hospital.

PHYSICIAN BONUS PAYMENTS

Physicians providing services to beneficiaries in the Medicare fee-for-service sector are paid for those services through the Medicare Part B program (supplementary medical insurance). Medicare Part B carriers are CMS contractors that process claims submitted by physicians for reimbursement. Beginning in 1992, the Physician Fee Schedule was implemented to establish payment amounts for all physicians' services based on the relative value for the service (the amount of resources required to provide the service, relative to other services), a conversion factor (a national payment amount or dollar multiplier established to achieve target budgets for Medicare), and geographic adjustment factors (to reflect variations across the country in physicians' costs for service inputs, e.g., staff salaries).

Before the Physician Fee Schedule was developed, Medicare reimbursement was determined by the physician's historical usual and customary charges. This resulted in some high-technology services provided by specialists receiving higher reimbursement than the diagnostic and care management services provided by primary care physicians. The implementation of the fee schedule yielded greater parity in reimbursement across physician specialties and geographic regions (PPRC, 1992). During the period under study, the introduction to the new fee schedule involved continuing changes in medical practices that influenced payments attributable to practice operating expenses and subsequent payment rates.

Each fall, CMS provides every Part B carrier with an updated Medicare Physician Fee Schedule Database that determines reimbursement for physicians' services and select other provider services. The database defines:

- Services paid under the Physician Fee Schedule;

- Global diagnostic services that have both professional and technical components;

- Diagnostic services considered professional or technical only;

- Services payable to an assistant surgeon;

- Code status (updating providers on changes to procedure codes and modifiers);

- Surgical procedures qualifying for multiple, bilateral, team, or co-surgery payment; and

- Payable medical supplies (Wisconsin Physician Service, 2000).

Rules for Bonus Payments

The legislation that established the physician bonus payment program states that *physician services* are eligible for a bonus payment if they are provided in a HPSA and the patient served is covered by Medicare Part B. Physician services that comply with these requirements will be paid an amount equal to 10 percent of the amount paid by Medicare for the service provided. Bonus payments are not included with the physician's reimbursement for the services provided, but are paid separately by the carriers on a quarterly basis. This program is paid for out of the Federal Supplemental Medical Insurance Trust Fund (42*USC*13951).

Health care providers eligible to receive Medicare bonus payments include medical doctors, doctors of osteopathy, dentists, podiatrists, licensed chiropractors, and optometrists. NPPs are not eligible for the bonus payment program. "Physician services" refers to professional services performed by physicians, including home, office, or institutional visits; surgery; consultation; and interpretation of laboratory or radiology tests. Bonuses are not paid for services reimbursed through Hospital Insurance (Part A) or provided by managed care contracts. It is not required that the physician's practice be located in a HPSA or that the Medicare beneficiary reside in a HPSA, only that the service be provided in a HPSA.

Of significance, the bonus payment is based on the amount that Medicare pays rather than the total payment allowed by Medicare (allowed charge). The bonus payment program was designed to not burden the Medicare beneficiary who receives services in a HPSA—if the bonus payment were based on the total allowed amount, the beneficiary would then be responsible for paying some of that bonus to the provider.

How Bonus Payments Are Made

The Part B carriers are responsible for administering the physician bonus payment program. To our knowledge, no regulations were written with respect to the implementation and administration of the program. Rules for identifying claims eligible for the bonus and for distributing bonus payments are found in the *Medicare Carrier's Manual*, which instructs carriers regarding all reimbursement issues related to Medicare. With respect to the bonus payment program, carriers are responsible for

- Informing the physician community of the provisions of the Medicare Incentive Payment Program;

- Identifying HPSA locations to interested physicians and the proper manner in which to code claims to qualify for the incentive payment;

- Modifying their claims processing system to recognize and appropriately handle eligible claims;

- Paying physicians the bonus payments; and

- Performing post-payment review samples of paid claims to ensure that they were eligible for the bonus payment (*CMS Carrier's Manual*, on CMS web site at http://www.hcfa.gov/pubforms/htmltoc.htm).

Physicians are required to indicate that the services they provided are eligible for the bonus payment by including a modifier to the CMS Common Procedure Coding System (HCPCS) codes.[4] The modifier identifying services provided in a rural HPSA is "QB" and the modifier for services provided in an urban HPSA is "QU." When one of these modifiers is present, the carrier calculates the bonus payment as 10 percent of the amount paid by Medicare.[5]

Services provided by physicians, reflected in the HCPCS codes, may include both professional and technical components billed globally, professional services only, or technical services only. Only the professional component of a physician's service is eligible for a bonus payment. The Professional Component/Technical Component (PC/TC) indicator field of the Medicare Physician Fee Schedule Database defines professional services eligible for bonus payments. Claims with a PC/TC indicator of "0" (Physician Service) are automatically eligible for the bonus payment. For a globally billed service (PC/TC indicator equals "1") to be eligible for a bonus payment, it must include both the bonus payment modifier and a modifier indicating that the professional component of the service is being billed for in the claim (modifier code "26"). Globally billed claims with no supplemental modifier or a technical component modifier ("TC") are ineligible for a bonus payment. If a HCPCS code reflecting a professional service only is unavailable for the service provided, the global HCPCS code must include the professional component modifier to be eligible for a bonus payment.

Carriers are responsible for reviewing claims for which a bonus was paid to identify incorrectly awarded payments. The carrier must identify physicians who received a bonus payment and rank them from highest to lowest according to the total bonus amounts they received for the quarter. The top 25 percent of physicians are selected for review. Five claims for each of these physicians are randomly selected and examined for compliance with the program rules. This process is repeated quarterly, skipping physicians previously found to be in

---

[4]   The HCPCS is a collection of codes representing procedures, supplies, products and services provided to Medicare beneficiaries. The codes are divided into three levels: (I) Current Procedural Terminology (CPT) codes from the American Medical Association (AMA); (II) primarily non-physician codes or physician codes not represented in the level I codes defined by CMS and other entities; (III) codes developed by local Medicare carriers.

[5]   Generally 80 percent of the allowed charge as defined by the Medicare Physician Fee Schedule.

compliance. Incorrectly claimed bonus payments are supposed to be pursued with the physician's billing staff. All findings are then reported to CMS within 75 days following the close of the reporting quarter.

Historical Performance of the Bonus Payment Program

Total bonus payments grew from $2 million in 1989 to $106 million in 1996, followed by a decline to $77 million in 1998. Table 1.5 summarizes trends in bonus payments for physician services in rural and urban HPSAs by calendar year. The large increase in bonus payments between 1990 and 1991 reflects not only increased usage of bonus payments, but also the legislative changes that increased the bonus payment from 5 percent to 10 percent of the amount paid by Medicare and expanded the program to urban HPSAs. After several years of growth, bonus payments declined between 1996 and 1998, with payments to urban physicians declining more rapidly than those to rural physicians.

Several federal entities have been scrutinizing the effects of these payments on improving access (Office of the HHS Inspector General, 1993b; PPRC, 1994a; US GAO, 1999). The Office of the HHS Inspector General surveyed physician attitudes regarding the bonus payments in 1993. Approximately one-quarter of all surveyed physicians described the bonus payments as extremely or very important to their decisions about where to practice. Still, another one-third said the bonus payments were not at all important (Office of the HHS Inspector General, 1993b).

Another early study of the bonus payment program was performed by PPRC, reporting data from 1992. The commission's critique of the program was tentative because of the relative infancy of the program. In addition, the Medicare Physician Fee Schedule was being phased in at the same time, making it difficult to distinguish the effects of the bonus payments from other physician payment reforms. Although long-term goals of retaining and recruiting physicians to rural regions could not be evaluated with this early program evaluation, intermediate goals were assessed (PPRC, 1994a).

Table 1.5
Health Professional Shortage Area Total Bonus Payments, by Selected Calendar Years

Year	Total, All HPSAs	Urban HPSAs		Rural HPSAs	
		Amount	% of Total	Amount	% of Total
1989	$1,951,267	—	—	$1,951,268	100.0
1990	4,061,006	—	—	4,061,006	100.0
1991	31,600,448	$13,164,458	41.7	18,435,990	58.3
1992	63,198,974	33,543,986	53.1	29,654,966	46.9
1996	105,797,754	58,353,215	55.2	47,444,539	44.8
1997	98,164,161	52,623,749	53.6	45,540,412	46.4
1998	77,177,972	37,744,513	48.9	39,433,459	51.1

SOURCE: Health Care Financing Administration (HCFA), unpublished quarterly report, 1993 (for years 1989–1992) and HCFA, unpublished quarterly report, 1999 (for years 1996–1998).

NOTE: Bonus payments for urban HPSAs did not begin until January 1, 1991.

In addition to documenting the general growth in the program (both in total payments and in number of participating physicians), the PPRC report demonstrated that a large portion of the bonus payments was being targeted at primary care physicians and primary care services. Tables 1.6 and 1.7 present data from the PPRC report showing the distribution of bonus payments by specialty and by service type. In 1992, about half of all bonus payments went to primary care physicians whose practices were in a HPSA, compared to one-quarter of bonus payments for physicians whose practices were outside a HPSA (see Table 1.6).[6] Bonus payments in rural HPSAs were more likely to be paid to primary care physicians, constituting 63.6 percent of all rural HPSA bonus payments. Family practice physicians received the largest share of the payments. As shown in Table 1.7, only 34 percent of bonus payments were paid to physicians providing primary care services in all HPSAs combined. However, a much higher percentage of bonus payments was paid for primary care services in rural HPSAs (41 percent) than in urban HPSAs (only 26 percent).

Table 1.6
Distribution of Bonus Payments for Health Professional Shortage Areas
and Other Areas, by Specialty, 1992

	Total Non-HPSA	HPSA		
Type of Specialty		Total	Urban	Rural
Primary care specialties	25.0%	49.0%	33.9%	63.6%
Internal medicine	16.6	20.1	21.7	18.6
Family practice	5.4	19.7	7.7	31.3
General practice	3.0	9.2	4.5	13.7
Other specialties	75.0	51.0	66.1	36.4

SOURCE: PPRC (1994b).

Table 1.7
Distribution of Bonus Payments for Health Professional Shortage Areas
and Other Areas, by Service, 1992

	Total Non-HPSA	HPSA		
Type of Service		Total	Urban	HPSA
Primary care services	20%	34%	26%	41%
Other services	80	66	74	59

SOURCE: PPRC (1994b).

The GAO published a report in 1999 that illustrated further growth in bonus payments to both rural and urban HPSAs. This growth, however, could not be directly linked to improved

---

6 It is not a requirement of the program that a physician's practice be physically located in a HPSA; the only requirement is that the service be provided in a HPSA.

access to care. In 1996, $35 million in bonus payments was paid to specialists for specialty care provided in urban HPSAs where specialty care was not necessarily in short supply (US GAO, 1999). The GAO staff was unable to find any direct evidence that the bonus payments contributed to physicians' decisions to stay in a particular community.

GAO staff analyzed the 1996 Medicare Current Beneficiary Survey and identified fewer than one million out of 29 million rural Medicare beneficiaries who had trouble obtaining health care. Only a fraction (estimated to be between 14,448 and 57,442) cited the inability to find a physician who would accept Medicare as the source of their trouble in getting access to needed services (US GAO, 1999). These analyses did not focus on services provided in HPSAs, however.

Similar findings were reported by Stearns et al. (2000). The authors examined not only self-reported satisfaction with and access to health care but went further to study rural/urban differences in preventive care received by a sample of Medicare beneficiaries. They found that rural beneficiaries received preventive care at rates similar to those in urban areas with the exception of preventive cancer screening for women and dental care.

MEDICARE CAPITATION PAYMENT RATES

Since 1983, Medicare has contracted with health maintenance organizations (HMOs) to provide Medicare-covered services on a capitated basis. The base capitation rates were county-level rates established at 95 percent of the adjusted average per capita cost (AAPCC) for fee-for-service beneficiaries living in each county. HMOs received a monthly payment for each enrollee that was the product of the base capitation rate for the enrollee's county of residence and a demographic (risk) adjustment factor. The published AAPCC rates consist of separate 95 percent rates for Medicare Part A and Part B services. The total base county AAPCC rate for health plan payments is the sum of the county's Part A and Part B rates.

There have been substantial problems with the AAPCC rates for rural counties. Rural AAPCCs have been low on average, and they have been more volatile than rates for urban counties, because service levels for small rural beneficiary populations fluctuate more from year to year than those for larger urban populations do. Given these payment issues and rural provider supply problems, few HMOs have contracted to serve Medicare beneficiaries in rural areas (PPRC, 1995). The BBA introduced a new capitation payment formula, effective January 1998, which stabilized and increase rural capitation rates. The 1997 AAPCC rates were the baseline rates for this new payment formula.

In the counties where beneficiaries are using providers that receive the special payments, the AAPCC rates will be larger than they would be without the special payment amounts. Medicare payment policies to enhance access for rural beneficiaries may be classified into three broad categories: (1) payments to health care professionals practicing in designated areas, (2) payments to special categories of service delivery organizations in designated areas, and (3) special payment provisions to lessen the negative effect on rural hospitals of national payment policies. All of the fee-for-service payments made to providers for services to beneficiaries residing in any given county are rolled into the AAPCC rates for that county. However, the size of this effect on the AAPCC rates is not known. One goal of this research project was to estimate the contribution of to the Medicare average per capita cost of each special payment policy alone as well as the aggregate effects of the combination of policies.

ORGANIZATION OF THIS REPORT

The remainder of this report presents the findings from our trend analyses of special payments for providers serving rural Medicare beneficiaries. In Section 2, we describe the methods and data we used for these trend analyses. The demographic and service supply profiles of urban and rural counties are presented in Section 3. Results of each of the four analyses are in subsequent chapters: rural hospitals in Section 4, RHC/FQHC payments in Section 5, physician bonus payments in Section 6, and the AAPCC rates in Section 7. Section 8 presents the county-level analysis of the effects of special hospital payments on estimated Part A per capita costs for Medicare beneficiaries.

2. METHODS AND DATA

The trend analysis results presented in this report encompass six distinct areas of research. The general research strategy was to analyze trends in Medicare payments during the 1990s under special payment provisions for rural hospitals, RHCs and FQHCs, and physicians. The methods and data used for these analyses are described in this section. The following specific analyses were performed, the results of which are presented in Sections 3 through 8 of this report:

- Descriptive profiles of the U.S. counties, categorized as urban, rural, or frontier, which generated baseline information on county characteristics for use in the trend analyses (Section 3);

- Trends in supply and Medicare payments for rural hospitals, with a focus on those with designations for Medicare special payments (Section 4);

- Trends in supply and Medicare payments for Rural Health Clinics and Federally Qualified Health Centers (Section 5);

- Trends in Medicare bonus payments made for physician services in HPSAs in non-metropolitan counties (Section 6);

- Trends in AAPCC capitation rates with comparisons for metropolitan and non-metropolitan counties (Section 7); and

- Effects of special payment provisions for rural hospitals on Medicare costs per beneficiary for Part A services (Section 8).

The first methodological step was to define the areas that would serve as the geographic basis for this research. We used counties as the unit of analysis because most data are or can be aggregated at the county level. Further, the Medicare AAPCCs, which are the estimates of Medicare costs per capita that are examined in this study, are calculated at the county level. The other important geographic areas are the designated underserved areas for which two measures have been established: HPSAs and MUAs. These also were recorded at the county level in the data files we used. The next research steps were to perform the four trend analyses and the estimation of the effects of special payment provisions on Medicare per capita costs for rural beneficiaries. Each analysis involved use of measures and methods specific to the respective topic area. Below we describe the data used in the analyses, the analytic methods, and the measures we used to categorize counties based on extent of rurality. Finally, we define the key variables used in the analyses.

MEASURES OF RURALITY

The method we used to define rural locations was based on whether a county is part of an MSA, as defined by the Office of Management and Budget. All counties outside an MSA were considered to be rural for purposes of this analysis. This definition is consistent with the geographic boundaries used in Medicare payment schedules for many provider services. However, county boundaries obscure a wide range of local characteristics because each county contains a mix of urbanized and more truly rural locations. Counties that are not in MSAs have fewer and smaller urbanized locations than MSA counties do, but they are not uniformly rural in nature. Therefore, we refer to these counties as "non-metropolitan" counties rather than "rural."

Categories by Urban Influence Codes

We defined categories of rural and urban counties to help characterize the rural or urban nature of each county. Urban and rural categories were established using values of the Urban Influence Codes (UICs) developed by the U.S. Department of Agriculture, which classify counties using values from 1 through 9 (Ghelfi and Parker, 1995). (Refer to Appendix B for additional discussion of coding systems.) Codes 1 and 2 define large and small counties in the MSAs established by the Census Bureau, and codes 3 through 9 define categories of counties outside the MSAs (non-metropolitan counties). The UICs classify non-metropolitan counties on two dimensions: (1) the size of the largest town in the county and (2) adjacency to a metropolitan county. Thus, the UICs do not yield a monotonic scale of rurality, but should be considered as a matrix with each dimension serving as an axis. UICs have not been updated since their publication in 1993. Consequently, the stratification of counties using these codes may not reflect the actual rural designation that would be assigned to a county based on data for later years of the study period. The advantage for the analysis is that consistent classification of counties avoids confounding study results with changes in county designations.

For our categories of rural counties, we used the two UICs for metropolitan counties and collapsed the UICs for non-metropolitan counties from the original seven categories into five categories.

Metropolitan categories

- Central and fringe counties in metropolitan areas of one million population or more (UIC 1); and

- Counties in metropolitan areas of fewer than one million population (UIC 2).

Non-metropolitan categories

- Counties adjacent to an MSA with a city of at least 10,000 population (UICs 3 and 5);

- Counties adjacent to an MSA without a city of at least 10,000 population (UICs 4 and 6);

- Remote counties not adjacent to an MSA with city of at least 10,000 population (UIC 7);

- Remote counties not adjacent to an MSA with town of 2,500–9,999 population (UIC 8); and

- Remote counties not adjacent to an MSA with no town of 2,500 population (UIC 9).

There is some consensus among rural health experts that the UICs are imperfect in capturing variations in characteristics among rural counties because they are based on county boundaries (Ricketts et al., 1998). Many rural counties have large land areas, and within a given rural county, there may be large local variations in population density, demographics, and health care provider supply that become lost in the larger county aggregates. Health service areas are not necessarily contiguous with county lines, and those health service areas within a given county can vary widely in the degree of rurality. In addition, many large metropolitan counties (mostly in the West) contain large rural areas.

Despite these limitations, the UICs are the preferred measure of rurality when compared to alternative measures, the most well known of which are the urban continuum codes. The Rural-Urban Continuum Codes (RUCCs) are based on the total urbanized population in a county, rather than the size of the largest city. Given the need for a "critical mass" of urban population to establish a local health care infrastructure, most analysts prefer the UICs as better representing this capability because they are based on the presence of a city of at least 10,000 population (Ricketts et al., 1998). A new classification system, called the Rural-Urban Commuting Area (RUCA) codes, was still under development at the time this research began, so it could not be used. The RUCA codes are expected to yield classifications that capture differences in extent of rurality more precisely than the existing systems do. (See Appendix B.)

Frontier Counties

Another important descriptive characteristic of rural services is location in frontier counties, which are remote, sparsely populated rural areas. Counties were classified as frontier if they were located in a western state and had a population density of six persons per square mile or fewer based on 1990 census data on population and county land area. Only a small number of counties in the eastern portion of the country had such low population densities, and they were omitted from the frontier county definition because residents in these counties had much better access to urbanized areas than those in the western frontier counties. We also tested the extent to which frontier county classifications would change if they were based on more recent (1997) population estimates. Only 18 counties had different classifications based on the 1997 population data, with 12 counties losing the frontier classification and six counties becoming frontier counties.

DATA SOURCES

The various analyses of trends in special payments for rural providers and AAPCC payments involved linking data from several sources, most of which were Medicare data files obtained from CMS. The following files were used, all of which were obtained from CMS except where noted otherwise:

1. Annual Medicare Provider of Service (POS) files for calendar years 1992 through 1998, which identified the hospitals, RHCs, and FQHCs serving Medicare beneficiaries and provided information on their location, characteristics and certification status;

2. Annual Provider Specific Files (PSFs) for calendar years 1992 through 1998, and Impact Files for 1996 through 1998, which provided data used to calculate Medicare payments for the hospitals and codes for special payment designation;

3. An extract of the 1997 HRSA Area Resource File (ARF extract), which provided county-level information on UICs, provider supply, population, and other environmental variables;

4. Quarterly Summary Files generated by CMS, containing county-level counts of Medicare beneficiaries and Medicare health plan enrollees for 1992 through 1998;

5. Annual Medicare 100 percent Denominator Files for the full Medicare population for calendar years 1996 through 1998, which provided data on the months and type of eligibility of beneficiaries;

6. County-level files of AAPCC capitation rates for calendar years 1990 through 1997;

7. Files of Medicare DRG code numbers, names, and weights for 1994 through 1998;

8. Medicare Provider Analysis and Review (MEDPAR) claims for short-term inpatient hospital services for the 100 percent sample of Medicare beneficiaries for calendar years 1992 through 1998, subset to include all claims for beneficiaries residing in non-metropolitan counties or hospitals located in these counties;

9. Medicare institutional outpatient claims from RHCs and FQHCs for the 5 percent sample of Medicare beneficiaries for calendar years 1991, 1992, 1994, 1996, and 1998; and

10. Medicare Part B claims for physicians' services for the 5 percent sample of beneficiaries for calendar years 1992, 1994, 1996, and 1998.

We used SSA state and county codes to link provider-level data or Medicare claims to county-level measures (e.g., extent of rurality, HPSA) in the ARF extract file. For population-based analyses, the data were linked based on the state and county of residence for Medicare beneficiaries; for facility-based analyses, the linkages were based on provider location.

The availability of certain county-level ARF data influenced the sets of counties we were able to include in each analysis. The Medicare program recognizes a larger set of counties (or other similar geographic jurisdictions) than those included in the ARF, which is reflected in the set of counties for which AAPCCs have been established historically. The ARF contains only one record for the entire state of Alaska, even though SSA county codes exist for a number of Alaskan boroughs. A discrepancy also existed for a set of independent cities in Virginia, which the state separates legally from historical county boundaries to form their own jurisdictions. These independent cities are recognized by Medicare. We added new records for the Alaska boroughs and the Virginia independent cities to our analysis file, for which we obtained data on the 1990 population, UICs, Metropolitan Statistical Areas, and Medicare beneficiary counts.

We could not obtain data for the new Alaska or Virginia independent cities on HPSAs, MUAs, or other county characteristics that were on the ARF. For any analyses that used these variables, we worked with the smaller set of counties for which we had the full set of data. Alaska counties were dropped from these analyses, and the Virginia independent cities were re-combined with the counties from which they were extracted.

ANALYSES PERFORMED

Trends in Rural Hospital Services

To examine trends from 1992 through 1998 for the supply of rural hospitals and utilization of inpatient services, we used a combination of facility-level data on rural hospitals and MEDPAR data on inpatient utilization and spending. Using POS files and PSFs for these years, combined with geographic data from the ARF, we identified all Medicare-certified, short-term hospitals in non-metropolitan counties, and we classified them according to county location based on Urban Influence Codes, as well as by special status under Medicare payment policies. Characteristics of these hospitals were profiled using data from the Medicare POS files and PSFs.

For the rural hospitals with special designations for Medicare payments, our analyses focused on sole community hospitals, rural referral centers, those designated as both, and Medicare-dependent hospitals. We also report descriptive information for MAFs, EACH/RPCHs and Indian Health Service hospitals in some tables to provide context regarding the relative numbers of special designation hospitals. We do not include the EACH/RPCHs or Indian Health Service hospitals in subsequent analyses, however, because there are so few of them compared to the other four groups of hospitals and they represent a very small fraction of total inpatient stays and payments.

We analyzed Medicare hospital inpatient utilization and expenditures, using MEDPAR claims data for the 100 percent beneficiary sample, taking two distinct approaches. First, we analyzed trends in utilization and Medicare spending for *services provided by rural hospitals*, by type of special payment status and by hospital location. Then we analyzed trends in utilization and spending on hospital inpatient services *used by Medicare beneficiaries* residing in rural areas, by beneficiary county of residence. Overall standardized average payments also were estimated for a standard DRG mix of patients, to decompose payment effects versus case mix effects across hospitals.

The analytic database for each year in our study period included only short-term hospitals in non-metropolitan counties that were certified in Medicare in any given year. Using merged data from the POS file and PSF for each year, we retained all hospitals that (1) were in the PSF, which indicated they were being paid by Medicare according to the provisions of the PPS, and (2) had current Medicare certification during the year, as defined by either not having a termination date or having a termination date later than January 5. These criteria eliminated all hospital units exempt from PPS (e.g., rehabilitation units), hospitals that served Medicare beneficiaries on an emergency basis (e.g., military hospitals or hospitals in Canada or Mexico), and hospitals that discontinued Medicare participation (e.g., for loss of certification or closure) before the year of interest.

We note that this approach relied on the certification data in the POS file, and to the extent that terminations are not correctly recorded in the POS, we have included some hospitals that should not be in our study population. This data problem would affect results from our analyses of provider supply but would not affect the analyses that use the MEDPAR claims, because the claims represent services actually provided by hospitals to Medicare beneficiaries, which presumes Medicare certification or status as emergency or other types of hospitals.

The MEDPAR claims for the 100 percent beneficiary sample identify the Medicare beneficiaries who use hospital inpatient services each year. From these files, we extracted all claims for non-metropolitan hospitals or for beneficiaries with counties of residence in the non-metropolitan counties, which included claims for services provided by both metropolitan and non-metropolitan hospitals. We used files from CMS with summary counts of all beneficiaries residing in each county to establish county-level data on the total beneficiary population for the analysis.

Trends in RHC/FQHC Payments

Two aspects of trends for RHCs and FQHCs from 1991 to 1998 were examined in this study: (1) trends in the numbers and geographic distribution of facilities and (2) trends in clinic utilization by Medicare beneficiaries and related costs. The facilities included were all RHCs as well as FQHCs in non-metropolitan counties. The Rural Health Clinics included some clinics in metropolitan counties, which were designated based on location in a non-urbanized area. They were included to document their numbers, and information for these facilities is reported separately in some analyses.

RHCs and FQHCs were included in the analysis for each year if they had current Medicare certification that year, defined by either not having a termination date or having a termination date later than January 5. These data on RHCs and FQHCs rely on the accuracy of POS data on certification.

The first set of analyses describes trends in the numbers of RHCs and FQHCs from 1992 through 1998, working with data in the Provider of Service files. Counts were developed separately for provider-based and independent RHCs. Facilities were profiled based on ownership status and staffing characteristics. We analyzed collocation of facilities to assess the extent to which beneficiaries in non-metropolitan counties had access to a clinic or to more than one clinic. Finally, we described the distribution of RHCs and FQHCs across county categories based on the UICs, for frontier counties, by HHS region, and by the two types of underserved areas (MUAs and HPSAs).

To analyze clinic collocation, we first created a set of mutually exclusive categories and classified each clinic by whether it was located in a county with no other clinics; with one or more FQHCs; with one or more RHCs (either provider-based or independent); or with a combination of clinic types (at least one FQHC and one RHC, in addition to the index clinic). Then we did a county-level analysis to determine how many counties with at least one clinic had at least one FQHC, one provider-based RHC, one independent RHC, or a combination of RHCs.

We note a limitation that a county-level analysis of collocation does not account for: (1) RHCs that are located near each other but are in separate counties or (2) RHCs that are located in the same county but are far apart. We recognize that most counties contain multiple primary care service areas, and many primary care service areas straddle county lines. With a county-level analysis, it was not feasible to perform geographically detailed analyses of facility locations within primary care service areas. Therefore, the presence of two or more clinics in a county cannot be interpreted as evidence that beneficiaries residing in the county have ready access to more than one clinic.

The second set of analyses estimated utilization rates and costs for services provided by RHCs and FQHCs for beneficiaries residing in non-metropolitan counties, working with the Medicare institutional outpatient claims for RHC and FQHC services for the 5 percent beneficiary sample. These estimates were developed on the basis of beneficiary residence by category of non-metropolitan counties, in frontier counties, and in underserved areas. This population-based analysis offered useful information regarding use of RHCs and FQHCs by this population of interest. However, the 5 percent sample data could not be used to perform facility-level analyses of Medicare use and costs for RHCs and non-metropolitan FQHCs because some facilities serving Medicare beneficiaries would not have served individuals in this sample. Such an analysis would require use of claims for the 100 percent beneficiary sample, which was beyond the project resources.

Trends in Physician Bonus Payments in Rural Areas

As reported in Section 1, studies by the Physician Payment Review Commission and the General Accounting Office have documented trends in bonus payments made to HPSAs (PPRC, 1992, 1994a; US GAO, 1999). We extended the information from those reports by examining trends in total Medicare payments and bonus payments for physician services provided to non-metropolitan beneficiaries for the years 1992, 1994, 1996, and 1998. We extracted physician claims from the Medicare physician/supplier claims data for the 5 percent beneficiary sample. We merged these claims with data from the ARF to identify services provided to beneficiaries in non-metropolitan counties, and to classify them by county category based on the Urban Influence Codes. We also examined bonus payments trends for primary care providers and primary care services.

An additional set of analyses was performed using claims for both physician and NPP services to examine the extent to which NPPs provided services for rural Medicare beneficiaries. We analyzed Medicare spending on NPP services as a share of total spending on physician and NPP services by HPSA designation and non-metropolitan county categories.

All trends in utilization and spending on health care services were analyzed for Medicare beneficiaries in non-metropolitan areas, *by beneficiary residence* rather than physician practice location or site of care. This is key to understanding and interpreting our results because bonus payments are paid based on location of care (in a HPSA) rather than location of residence. We chose this analytic approach for reasons of both policy emphasis and data requirements. The policy focus of these analyses is on access to care for rural beneficiaries, for which this analytic approach is appropriate. In addition, data requirements for establishing rural provider locations for four years of claims data would be substantial because we could not limit claims to those for beneficiaries residing in non-metropolitan counties. Furthermore, it was not possible to define county of service (and therefore rural or urban HPSA) because the physician/supplier claims data identify only the county of beneficiary residence and zip code of the provider's official location, which is not necessarily where the service was provided. Because the sample was selected from claims for the 5 percent sample based on beneficiary residence, we were not able to analyze the number or characteristics of physicians claiming the bonus payments.

Given the well-documented migration of Medicare beneficiaries across geographic boundaries for health care services (McNamara, 1998; also see hospital service use results in Section 4), this approach allowed us to capture basic Medicare payments and bonus payments for physician services that beneficiaries in non-metropolitan counties obtained in urban HPSAs. Conversely, claims for services provided in rural HPSAs for urban beneficiaries were lost to our analyses. We expect the loss of payments for the urban beneficiaries using rural services is equal to or smaller than the additional payments captured for rural beneficiaries using urban services.

Trends in AAPCC Capitation Rates

Issues regarding the wide variation in AAPCC rates across metropolitan and non-metropolitan counties, as well as their volatility in the more sparsely populated non-metropolitan areas, have been well documented (PPRC, 1995; McBride et al., 1997). The purpose of our analysis was to document trends in the AAPCC rates and related measures from 1990 through 1997, the last year the AAPCCs were calculated for Medicare health plan payments. We defined three measures (see the definitions below), which we compared over time between metropolitan and non-metropolitan counties, as well as across categories of non-metropolitan counties. The first measure was the average total AAPCC rates (the sum of the Part A and Part B rates established for each county). The second measure was the Part A AAPCC rate as a percentage of the total rate, and the third measure was the volatility of the AAPCC rates (i.e., the extent to which a county's AAPCC rate fluctuated from year to year).

Using the results of these descriptive analyses, we employed weighted linear regression methods to estimate models of the determinants of the AAPCC rates, with the county as the unit of observation. The dependent variable in the models was the 1997 AAPCC rate and the predictor variables included arrays of demographic variables (per capita income, percentage Medicare population), provider supply variables, HPSA and MUA designations, urban/rural categories, and frontier county status. The weights for the models were the county Medicare beneficiary populations for 1997.

The last component of the AAPCC analysis was a comparative analysis of enrollments in Medicare health plans by urban and rural county categories. For this analysis, we merged the data in our analysis file with CMS health plan enrollment data for 1993 and 1997. We examined the percentages of counties with health plans, average enrollments by county category, and average AAPCCs for counties with and without enrollees. Finally, we focused on the subset of health plans with enrollees who resided in rural counties to assess the urban/rural mix of enrollees in those plans.

Rural Hospital Payment Effects on Medicare Part A per Capita Costs

To analyze the effects of the Medicare special payment provisions on Part A costs per capita, it was necessary to simulate the payments that rural hospitals would receive in the absence of these special payment provisions. The effect on costs for hospital inpatient services was represented by the difference between the actual payments and adjusted payments from which components related to the special provisions were removed. Effects on total Part A costs were estimated by aggregating to the county level the actual and adjusted payments for hospital services and the costs for other Part A services. Actual and adjusted Part A costs were estimated by summing spending for other Part A services and the actual or adjusted inpatient payments, respectively. The difference between these two amounts represented the effects on Part A costs.

These estimates were developed for 1997, which was the last year the AAPCCs were used for capitation payments for Medicare health plans. We calculated three-year average payments using claims from calendar years 1996, 1997, and 1998 to smooth out volatility in payments for counties with small numbers of beneficiaries. The analysis included all claims for hospital inpatient stays for the 100 percent sample of beneficiaries residing in non-metropolitan counties. Data for the factors used to simulate adjusted payments were obtained from the annual PPS Impact Files for fiscal years 1996 through 1999, and these factors were applied to claims with dates of discharge in the relevant fiscal years. The resulting actual and adjusted payment amounts were analyzed on a calendar year basis.

We simulated adjusted PPS payments only for inpatient claims from hospitals with special payment designations, thus excluding any hospitals reclassified for wage index or standardized amount but not having a special designation. Adjusted payments were simulated for any inpatient stay that was:

- For a Medicare beneficiary residing in a non-metropolitan county;

- Provided by a hospital with special designation as a sole community hospital, rural referral center, both SCH and RRC, or Medicare-dependent hospital;

- Coded as a PPS service;

- A length of stay of greater than one day; and

- Paid by Medicare as primary payer.

To estimate adjusted Medicare payments for qualified claims, the basic payment amount for each claim was simulated, and then the amount paid by Medicare was calculated.[7] The "adjusted" payments for all other claims were set equal to the actual payments. Thus, the adjustments made in simulating payments for hospitals with special designations included removal of amounts attributable to any geographic reclassification that these hospitals had obtained. (These hospitals represented 55.4 percent of all hospitals reclassified for wage index in 1992 and 39.3 percent of those reclassified in 1998 (from Table 4.17).) The payments were calculated according to the following formulas:

$$M_i = P_{oij} + P_{cij} + L_i - BENECST_i + PCOST_{ij} \qquad (2.1)$$

$$P_{oij} = ((S_l * W_j) + S_n) * COLA * (1 + DSH_j) * DRGWT_i \qquad (2.2)$$

where:
M_i = Medicare payment amount for claim i;
P_{oij} = PPS operating DRG price for claim i in hospital j;
P_{cij} = PPS capital price for claim i in hospital j;
L_i = outlier amount for claim i;
$BENCST_i$ = beneficiary deductibles and coinsurance for claim i;
$PCOST_{ij}$ = pass-through amounts for claim i at hospital j;
S_l = standardized amount for rural/other urban areas—labor portion;
S_n = standardized amount for rural/other urban areas—non-labor portion;
W_j = hospital wage index for hospital j for actual location;
$COLA$ = cost of living adjustment (for Alaska and Hawaii);
DSH_j = disproportionate share adjustment for hospital j; and
$DRGWT_i$ = weight for the DRG coded for claim i.

The operating DRG price, P_{oij}, is the component subject to the special Medicare payment provisions for rural hospitals. We simulated this amount using Eq. (2.2), which is the standard formula for calculating the operating DRG price for a PPS inpatient stay. We then calculated the Medicare payment, M_i, using Eq. (2.1) and data from the claim for the actual values of the other payment components (capital price, outlier amounts, beneficiary costs, and pass-through amounts). Although the special payment provisions for disproportionate share also affect outlier payment amounts, L_i, we ignored this cost as a secondary effect because it would be small for any inpatient stay and only 7 percent of claims for rural hospitals with special designations had outlier payments. For the same reason, we did not compute an adjustment for indirect medical education. We also assumed that the beneficiary costs would not be affected by the adjustment of payments because neither the deductibles nor the coinsurance for long inpatient stays are proportional to the simulated operating DRG price.

---

[7]   We note that the actual amounts on the claims for SCHs and Medicare-dependent hospitals are interim payments, with the final payments determined through the cost report settlement process. Therefore, the actual differences between actual and adjusted payments can be determined only empirically, so the estimated difference derived from these simulations is an approximation of the effect of special payments for these facilities.

All payment amounts were calculated and reported as payments per beneficiary. Using data from the 100 percent denominator files for 1996 through 1998, we derived counts of beneficiaries for each county by summing the number of months of Medicare eligibility and dividing by 12 to obtain person-years of eligibility. Annual and three-year average counts were tabulated by county for all Medicare beneficiaries and for beneficiaries aged 65 or older (elderly beneficiaries) based on values of the Medicare status code on the denominator file records.

KEY VARIABLES

Several key variables were defined that we used throughout the analyses, and others were specific to each research area. We describe the variable definitions here, including discussion of relevant measurement or interpretation issues. These variables include measures of the extent of rurality, Health Professional Shortage Areas and Medically Underserved Areas, county-level supplies of health care providers, hospital inpatient utilization and payments, RHC/FQHC utilization and payments, physician bonus payments, and AAPCCs.

Measures of Underserved Areas

Designations of counties as underserved areas form an important basis for the analyses performed in this project because many of the Medicare payment policies were established specifically for providers serving these designated areas. The federal government has established MUAs and HPSAs as two distinct designations, although the rules for their designation processes differ (see Section 1 for specifics). For both MUAs and HPSAs, designations may be made for either whole-county or partial-county areas. The ARF contains variables for HPSA designations, including coding for the whole- or partial-county status. We worked with variables for primary care HPSA designations for 1991, 1993, 1995, 1996, and 1997, all of which were available on the ARF. A data file with the MUA designations was obtained from HRSA, and we merged these data into our county-level analytic file. The MUA designations were as of the current date, so we did not have data on historical trends in MUAs.

Region Groupings

We grouped the states into HHS regions, which we used because the CMS regional offices and Medicare program administration are organized that way. The states by HHS region are given in Table 2.1.

Table 2.1
Region Groupings

Region 1	Region 4	Region 6	Region 9
Maine	Kentucky	Arkansas	California
New Hampshire	North Carolina	Louisiana	Arizona
Massachusetts	South Carolina	New Mexico	Nevada
Vermont	Tennessee	Oklahoma	Hawaii
Rhode Island	Georgia	Texas	
Connecticut	Florida		**Region 10**
	Alabama	**Region 7**	Alaska
Region 2	Mississippi	Iowa	Idaho
New York		Missouri	Oregon
New Jersey	**Region 5**	Kansas	Washington
	Illinois	Nebraska	
Region 3	Indiana		
Pennsylvania	Michigan	**Region 8**	
Delaware	Minnesota	Montana	
Maryland	Ohio	North Dakota	
District of Columbia	Wisconsin	South Dakota	
Virginia		Colorado	
West Virginia		Utah	
		Wyoming	

Variables for County Provider Supply

The data for defining county-level variables for provider supplies were obtained from the ARF. We defined supply measures for the following providers at the county level:

- Patient care physicians, including primary care and specialty physicians;

- General short-term hospital facilities;

- General short-term hospital beds;

- Skilled nursing facilities;

- Skilled nursing facility beds;

- Nursing home facilities, other than skilled nursing;

- Nursing home beds;

- Home health agencies; and

- Rural health clinics.

ARF data for physicians and hospitals were available for several years during the 1990s, but data for skilled nursing facilities, nursing homes, home health agencies, and rural health clinics were available only for 1994. Guided by data availability, physician supply measures were established for 1990, 1993, and 1997, and hospital supply measures were established for 1990, 1993, and 1996.

For each provider supply measure (and year), we established two variables: (1) the number of providers in a county and (2) the ratios of providers per 100,000 population based on the total county population for the year for which the variable was calculated (obtained from the

ARF). The ratios are better measures than simple counts of the availability of providers to a county population. However, they are vulnerable to being inflated in counties with small populations that are the denominators for calculating the ratios. As a result, a rural county with few SNFs may have a much larger ratio of SNFs to population than an urban county with a much larger number of SNFs. We find this effect in our provider supply profiles reported below.

The ARF reports licensed beds, rather than staffed beds. Therefore, these measures overstate facilities' operational capacities, given the large number of hospitals that do not staff or use the full complement of beds they officially have. Similar issues may exist for SNF and nursing home beds, although to a lesser extent. The comparisons of bed capacities across county categories control somewhat for differences in staffed bed capacities because these capacities are related to their reported licensed capacities. However, these comparisons assume that all hospitals or other types of provider have the same ratio of staffed to licensed beds, which is not likely to be true. A frequently used methodological response to this issue is to use utilization measures such as inpatient census rather than the structural measures of supply. We do not take this approach because we intend these measures to represent the existence and capacity of providers as determinants of service use and costs.

Rural Hospital Characteristics

Ownership Status. The POS file defines eight ownership categories for hospitals based on survey data obtained for the Medicare certification application. These categories include for-profit ownership, three categories for non-profit ownership (church, private, or other), and four categories for government-owned facilities (federal, state, or local government, or independent hospital authority or district). We collapsed these categories into five: for-profit, non-profit, federal or state government, local government, or hospital district/authority.

Hospital Size and Capacity. The measures used to profile the sizes of Medicare-certified hospitals were the bed size and the total staffing, using data from the Medicare POS files. We measured beds as Medicare-certified beds rather than total beds, because this measure is more relevant to utilization by Medicare beneficiaries. The preferred bed size measure is staffed beds, which represent hospitals' actually operating capacities, but this variable was not available from the POS data. We used total staffing as an alternative measure of operating capacity, measuring it as the number of FTE staff for all categories of staff reported by the hospitals on their survey forms and contained in the POS file. We note that the POS data are only as current as the most recent recertification surveys, which typically are performed every three years and are less frequent for many rural hospitals. Resource constraints prevented us from using other sources of these data, such as hospital cost reports or American Hospital Association (AHA) survey data. We take these limitations into account when interpreting trends in capacity.

Mix of Services Offered. The POS file offers fairly rich information on specific types of services provided by hospitals, including identification of organized units for specialized inpatient services (e.g., psychiatric or physical rehabilitation), number of beds for specified services, and identification that a hospital offers specified services. We selected three measures of specific services that we used to profile hospitals in our analyses: offers home health services, offers hospice services, and has an organized psychiatric inpatient unit. Hospitals in both urban and rural locations moved increasingly into providing these services as traditional inpatient census declined during the 1990s, accompanied by substantial growth in utilization of all of these services by Medicare beneficiaries.

Rural Hospital Facility Type

The Provider Specific Files contain a variable that identifies the status of each hospital according to the Medicare special payment designations for rural hospitals. However, the codes used in this variable changed during the time period of the study, as payment policies were changed by Congress or regulations. We derived a new variable that collapsed the sets of codes used in the original variable into a smaller set of codes that were consistent across all years included in the study (1992 through 1998). We defined our new facility designation codes using the crosswalk shown in Table 2.2.[8]

Table 2.2
Facility Designation Codes

RAND Derived Code	Code in Provider Specific File
0 no special designation	00 or blank no special designation
1 sole community hospital	01 sole community provider 16 rebased sole community provider
2 rural referral center	07 rural referral center
3 Indian Health Service hospital	08 Indian Health Service hospital
4 SCH/rural referral center	11 SCH/rural referral center 17 rebased SCH/rural referral center
5 Medicare-dependent hospital	14 Medicare-dependent hospital
6 Medical Assistance Facility	18 Medical assistance facility
7 Essential access community hospital	21 Essential access community hospital
8 EACH/rural referral center	22 EACH/rural referral center
9 Rural primary care hospital	23 Rural primary care hospital
10 Critical access hospital	37 Critical access hospital
20 other designations for rural hospitals	All other provider type codes
30 urban hospitals	Located in county in an MSA
40 emergency hospitals[9]	In the POS file but not Provider Specific File

Inpatient Utilization and Spending

The variables for hospital inpatient utilization and spending were obtained from the MEDPAR claims, which provide detail on the reason for hospitalizations and payment amounts.

Utilization. We measured utilization using counts of short-term hospital inpatient admissions and the average length of stay. Length of stay was calculated as the number of days

---

[8] RPCHs and MAFs are additional categories of rural hospitals with special payment provisions, but we did not analyze them as separate hospital categories because there are so few of them (30 to 75 RPCHs and 4 to 12 MAFs) and they account for a very small share of total Medicare inpatient utilization.

[9] These hospitals are not certified by Medicare but are used on an emergency basis (e.g., military hospitals or hospitals in Canada or Mexico).

from the "first date" and "last date" variables on the MEDPAR file. We also used the DRG codes on the claims to measure case mix as the average of the DRG weights for the claims.

Spending for Inpatient Stays. The MEDPAR file provided data on the amounts that Medicare paid for each inpatient stay, as well as on payments by other primary payers and amounts to be paid by beneficiaries. We calculated the following two payment amounts using variables on the MEDPAR claims:

Medicare payment = DRG payment amount + cost pass-through amount.

Total payments =   Medicare payment + other primary payer payment + beneficiary service deductible + beneficiary blood deductible + beneficiary coinsurance.

We examine utilization and spending in the aggregate, and we also calculate inpatient use rates and spending per beneficiary (and in some cases per 100 or 1,000 beneficiaries). The denominator for the per beneficiary measures consisted of all beneficiaries residing in each non-metropolitan county, which included both fee-for-service beneficiaries and Medicare health plan enrollees, whereas the MEDPAR claims represent inpatient use only for fee-for-service beneficiaries. Using this denominator underestimated the use and spending rates, but the effect was quite small because Medicare health plan enrollment was very low in non-metropolitan counties. Only 1.6 percent of non-metropolitan beneficiaries were enrolled in Medicare health plans in 1993 and only 3.5 percent were enrolled in 1997 (see Table 7.10).

Rural Health Clinics and Federally Qualified Health Centers

Type of Facility. The type of clinic (FQHC, provider-based RHC, independent RHC) was determined from the provider identification numbers reported in the POS data, where these facilities were assigned numbers from within a specified range. Many FQHCs are funded as community health centers, migrant health centers, etc., which qualified them for designation as FQHCs (HRSA, 1995). These FQHCs were identified using a variable that codes for type of federal support under PHS provisions; other facilities were defined as the "look alike" providers that met requirements for federal support but did not receive funding. Our examination of these data indicated that receipt of federal program support was being underreported in the POS data.

The POS records are considered to be the "gold standard" with respect to total annual facility counts, but the ARF also includes a variable for the number of Rural Health Clinics in a county for the year 1994. We evaluated the level of agreement between clinic counts generated from the POS files and the aggregate variable in the ARF. This comparison showed that counts of clinics were somewhat higher from the 1994 POS files than from the ARF data. The POS file contained 827 provider-based RHCs and 1,318 independent RHCs, for a total of 2,145 clinics. In contrast, the ARF reported a national total of 2,032 RHCs for 1994.[10]

---

[10] This discrepancy may be due to overcounts in the POS files because not all facilities that have stopped operation are reported to CMS. Further, some organizations with multiple clinic locations have separate provider numbers for the individual clinics (personal communication with CMS staff). In addition, the criteria we used include all

The count of certified facilities also was compared to the counts of total Rural Health Clinics with one or more Medicare beneficiary visits, generated from the claims data. From the claims data, we tabulated the number of clinics that provided services to one or more Medicare beneficiaries in the 5 percent sample through the FQHC/RHC program. The claims for the 5 percent sample of beneficiaries underestimate the total number of facilities providing services as FQHCs or RHCs because some facilities did not serve any beneficiaries in the 5 percent sample even though they did serve other beneficiaries. Thus, our analyses of utilization and costs are limited to population-based measures, for which the sample is well suited.

Differences in facility counts obtained from the 1994 POS file and provider claims for the 5 percent sample are reported in Table 2.3. As expected, the total number of facilities identified as providing services to Medicare beneficiaries in the 1994 5 percent sample was smaller than the total number of certified facilities for that year. In 1994, 1,434 certified FQHCs were in the POS file, compared to 1,078 FQHCs identified as having one or more paid Medicare claims for the 5 percent beneficiary sample. This includes FQHCs in urban and in non-urban areas. Further analyses of the 100 percent claims files would be required to identify certified facilities that did not have any claims in 1994.

Clinic Ownership Status. The POS defines nine ownership categories for RHCs based on survey data obtained for the RHC application. These categories include both for-profit and non-profit ownership, which are subset to individual, corporation, and partnership categories, as well as three additional categories for government facilities (state, local, or federal). We collapsed these categories into three categories of for-profit, non-profit, and government (public) operated.

Table 2.3
Number of FQHCs and Rural Health Clinics, by Type and Data Source, 1994

Data Source	FQHCs[a]	Provider-based RHCs	Independent RHCs
Provider of Service file	1,434	827	1,318
Claims for 5 percent sample	1,078	727	1,098

NOTES: Claims were found in the 5 percent sample file for additional facilities not in the POS file.
[a]Includes all FQHCs in metropolitan and non-metropolitan counties.

Fewer ownership categories apply for FQHCs because for-profit facilities may not be designated as FQHCs. The full set of FQHC categories includes religious affiliated, private, other, proprietary, state/county government, and combined government and voluntary. We collapsed these categories into private (including religious affiliated, private, and proprietary), government (state-county and combined government and voluntary), and other.

---

facilities that were certified at some time during each year, which yields larger counts than a count taken at a point in time during the year.

RHC and FQHC Utilization and Costs

The utilization rate variables were the estimated number of beneficiaries residing in non-metropolitan counties with at least one claim for RHC or FQHC services, expressed as a percentage of the total beneficiaries residing in the counties in which users resided. The data on user counts and payments for RHC and FQHC services were obtained from the Medicare institutional outpatient claims for the 5 percent sample of beneficiaries. Therefore, we multiplied the counts of users by 20 before dividing by total beneficiary counts.

The two variables analyzed for our cost analysis were the Medicare payment amount and the total allowed payment. The total payment was calculated as the sum of the Medicare payment amount, amount paid by a primary payer, and payments by the beneficiary for service deductible, blood deductible, and coinsurance. Data for these payment components were extracted from the institutional outpatient claims.

Two different denominators were used to calculate per capita payments. The first was the counts of beneficiaries residing in counties of residence for clinic users from the CMS summary files, which is the same as the denominator used for the utilization variable. The second denominator, also derived from the CMS summary files, was the total number of beneficiaries residing in each category of counties for which the RHC and FQHC claims were aggregated in the analysis. This denominator allowed us to derive per capita payments that are normalized to the entire Medicare population, which we measured as payments per 100 beneficiaries. With this constant denominator, we could sum the per capita payments for the three types of clinics to obtain total costs per 100 beneficiaries across these facilities. Using all beneficiaries residing in a non-metropolitan county slightly underestimated the use and spending rates, as discussed above under hospital use rates, but the effect on estimates was small.

Physicians and Other Practitioners

Physicians Eligible for Bonus Payments. The enabling legislation for incentive payments authorizes bonus payments only for physician services, i.e., services provided by medical doctors, doctors of osteopathy, dentists, podiatrists, licensed chiropractors, and optometrists. This analysis used Medicare physician/supplier claims for the 5 percent sample of beneficiaries. We list in Table 2.4 all of the provider specialty codes used to identify claims for physician services that are potentially eligible for a bonus payment under the legislation (if provided in a HPSA). Only claims with one of these specialty codes were included in our analyses.

Primary Care Physicians and Other Specialties. One aim of this report is to replicate and extend analyses of the bonus payment program conducted by other studies, both to understand how those measures of program performance have changed over time and to validate our analyses. Both the PPRC (1994b) and the GAO (1999) examined the proportion of bonus payments distributed to physicians by specialty. In their analyses, they grouped physicians by whether their specialty was considered a primary care specialty or not. They included general practice (CMS specialty code "01"), family practice ("08"), and internal medicine ("11") in the category of primary care physician specialties. All other specialties were grouped together as "other" specialties.

Table 2.4
Medicare Specialty Codes Used to Identify Physician Claims
Eligible for the Medicare Bonus Payments

01 General Practice	25 Physical Medicine/	76 Peripheral Vascular Disease
02 General Surgery	Rehabilitation	77 Vascular Surgery
03 Allergy/Immunology	26 Psychiatry	78 Cardiac Surgery
04 Otolaryngology	28 Colorectal Surgery	79 Addiction Medicine
05 Anesthesiology	29 Pulmonary Diseases	81 Critical Care (Intensivists)
06 Cardiology	30 Diagnostic Radiology	82 Hematology
07 Dermatology	33 Thoracic Surgery	83 Hematology/Oncology
08 Family Practice	34 Urology	84 Preventive Medicine
10 Gastroenterology	35 Chiropractic	85 Maxillofacial Surgery
11 Internal Medicine	36 Nuclear Medicine	86 Neuropsychiatry
12 Osteopathic Manipulative	37 Pediatric Medicine	90 Medical Oncology
Therapy	38 Geriatric Medicine	91 Surgical Oncology
13 Neurology	39 Nephrology	92 Radiation Oncology
14 Neurosurgery	40 Hand Surgery	93 Emergency Medicine
16 Obstetrics/Gynecology	44 Infectious Disease	94 Interventional Radiology
18 Ophthalmology	46 Endocrinology	98 Oncology Gynecology
19 Oral Surgery (dentists only)	48 Podiatry	99 Unknown Physician
20 Orthopedic Surgery	66 Rheumatology	Specialty
22 Pathology	70 Clinic or Other Group	
24 Reconstructive Surgery	Practice	

SOURCE: Documentation for the Medicare Physician/Supplier File.

We examined trends in distributions of basic payments and bonus payments to physicians by this primary/other specialty care designation. We also looked separately at payments for each type of primary care specialty as well as for general surgeons, cardiologists, and gynecologists.

Non-Physician Practitioners. Although non-physician practitioners are not eligible for the bonus payment program, they are important providers of primary care services in underserved regions of the country. For these analyses, we used Medicare specialty codes to define non-physician practitioners to include physician assistants (specialty code "97"), nurse practitioners ("50"), certified nurse midwives ("42"), certified clinical nurse specialists ("89"), and certified nurse anesthetists ("43").

Primary Care Services

To examine the distributions of bonus payments according to the types of services being provided (as opposed to the type of provider), we coded each physician/supplier claim line item as a primary care service or other type of service. We identified primary care services using the definition of primary care services outlined in OBRA-87. The legislation defines primary care services as "physicians' services which constitute office medical services, emergency department services, home medical services, skilled nursing, intermediate care, and long-term care medical services, or nursing home, boarding home, domiciliary, or custodial care medical services." These services are categorized as Evaluation and Management services (AMA, 1997). Table 2.5 lists the services considered primary care and their corresponding HCPCS codes. These codes are found in the Level I HCPCS and those corresponding to the listed service types were identified in the claims data and coded as primary care services. All other physician claims were categorized as "other" services.

Table 2.5
HCPCS Codes Used to Define Primary Care Services for the Bonus Payment Analysis

Service Description	HCPCS Codes
Office or Other Outpatient Visit; New Patient	99201-99205
Office or Other Outpatient Visit; Established Patient	99211-99215
Emergency Department Visit	99281-99288
Comprehensive Nursing Facility Assessments	99301-99303
Subsequent Nursing Facility Care	99311-99313
Domiciliary, Rest Home (e.g., Boarding Home), or Custodial Care Services; New Patient	99321-99323
Domiciliary, Rest Home (e.g., Boarding Home), or Custodial Care Services; Established Patient	99331-99333
Home Services; New Patient	99341-99343
Home Services; Established Patient	99351-99353

SOURCE: AMA (1997).

Medicare Payments for Physicians

Basic Payments. Basic Medicare payments were defined as the amounts paid by Medicare, as reported in the line item payment amounts in the physician/supplier claims for 1992, 1994, 1996, and 1998. (The total allowed charges, also on the claim, included the coinsurance amount for which beneficiaries were liable.) Line item payments were summed across all physician claims for the 5 percent sample of beneficiaries and then multiplied by 20 to approximate the basic Medicare payments made to physicians for services provided to all rural beneficiaries. Because Medicare carriers are required to process bonus payments separately from claims, the physician claims do not include the bonus payment amounts.

Bonus Payments. For eligible physician services (i.e., provided in a HPSA), bonus payments are calculated as 10 percent of the Medicare payment amount. To be eligible for the bonus payment, a physician must include a HCPCS code modifier on the claim form to indicate the service was provided in a rural or urban HPSA (modifiers "QB" and "QU").[11] Therefore, to calculate the total bonus payments made in each year, we first identified all physician claims with the appropriate modifier in the physician/supplier claims. Then we multiplied the Medicare payment amount by 0.1 to estimate the bonus payment. These bonus payments were summed for the 5 percent sample of claims, and the sum was multiplied by 20 to estimate the total bonus payments made to all physicians providing services to beneficiaries residing in non-metropolitan counties.

---

[11] Beneficiaries in non-metropolitan counties obtained some services in urban HPSAs. As a result, somewhat less than 1 percent of the claims with a bonus payment modifier were coded for services provided in urban HPSAs. These payments are included in the total amounts examined in the analyses.

County Capitation Rates

We described and compared trends in Medicare AAPCC capitation rates for urban and rural counties, and among categories of rural counties. Each year through 1997, the CMS actuary calculated the county-level AAPCC rates at 95 percent of the adjusted average per capita cost for previous years (five-year averages) for Medicare fee-for-service beneficiaries residing in each county. We used the AAPCC rates that CMS established for Medicare Part A and Part B services for calendar years 1988 through 1997. To develop a comprehensive picture of how county AAPCC rates varied over time, and the extent to which trends differed for rural and urban counties, we examined the three measures described here.

Average Levels of the AAPCCs. A total AAPCC rate was calculated for each county as the sum of the county's Part A and Part B AAPCC rates. When calculating average AAPCCs for groups of counties, we weighted the averages by the number of Medicare beneficiaries residing in each county, because these beneficiaries were candidates for health plan enrollment (if a plan was offered). For the enrollment analysis, we also weighted some of the average AAPCC rates by the number of Medicare health plan enrollees in a county to compare the average rates for total beneficiaries and plan enrollees.

Part A Share of AAPCC Rates. The Part A AAPCC rate was measured as a percentage of total AAPCC. This measure was used to explore the extent to which the AAPCCs reflected shifts of service mix from inpatient to outpatient care that occurred during this past decade.

Volatility in Total AAPCC Rates. We defined absolute volatility as the four-year average of absolute differences between the reference year and two years before and after it, and relative volatility as this four-year average difference as a percentage of the average AAPCC for the five years. The measures of AAPCC volatility were calculated for each of the years 1990 through 1995 using Eq. (2.3):

$$\text{Relative volatility}_0 = \frac{\sum_i |A_i - A_0|/4}{\sum_i A_i/5} \qquad \text{for } i = -2, -1, 0, +1, +2 \qquad (2.3)$$

where: A_i = AAPCC rate for year i; and
A_0 = AAPCC rate for the reference year.

For example, AAPCCs for 1988 through 1992 were used to calculate the volatility measure for 1990. The numerator for the measure is the sum of the absolute deviations of the 1988, 1989, 1991, and 1992 AAPCCs from the five-year average AAPCC for 1988 through 1992. The denominator was the five-year average AAPCC. These standardized measures of relative volatility can be compared across years because they control for increases in the AAPCC levels over time. Averages of the AAPCC volatility measures are weighted by the number of Medicare beneficiaries residing in each county.

These AAPCC analyses applied and extended many of the techniques used by PPRC in its analyses of the Medicare AAPCCs, including calculation of indices of the five-year average volatility in the AAPCC rates for each year (PPRC, 1995). Our approach was to look independently at each year to assess the extent of financial risk for health plans related to uncertainty in the next year's AAPCC rates.

This measure of volatility differs from that used by McBride et al. (1997). They defined local volatility for the 1990 to 1997 time period as the nominal growth in AAPCC less the Consumer Price Index, that is, an inflation-adjusted measure of growth in per capita Medicare costs. They report the average absolute deviation in local volatility over the time period rather than fluctuations at specified points in time.

3. CHARACTERISTICS OF U.S. METROPOLITAN AND NON-METROPOLITAN COUNTIES

This section provides background information on the distributions of counties by the metropolitan and non-metropolitan categories used in this research and on their characteristics with respect to population size, designations of underserved areas, and supply of health care providers. This information provides context for the study, and a number of the measures presented also are used in analyses reported in subsequent sections. The analyses were designed to address the following research questions:

- To what extent do the non-metropolitan counties vary by extent of rurality, as measured by the UICs?

- What are the demographic and socioeconomic characteristics of non-metropolitan counties and how do these characteristics vary by county categories based on UICs?

- What proportion of non-metropolitan counties are underserved areas, designated as HPSAs or MUAs, by county category, and how do those designations differ?

- What is the supply of health care providers for non-metropolitan counties, and how does supply vary by county category?

PROFILES OF RURAL AND METROPOLITAN COUNTIES

County Distributions by Metropolitan and Rural Locations

As shown in Table 3.1, 73.3 percent of the U.S. counties are categorized as non-metropolitan based on the Urban Influence Codes. Non-metropolitan counties that do not contain a city of at least 10,000 population represent 57.8 percent of all counties (24.0 percent are adjacent to MSAs and 33.8 percent are remote counties). Large metropolitan counties are 9.9 percent of the total, and small metropolitan counties are another 16.8 percent of the total. However, the metropolitan counties have much larger total populations and Medicare populations than the non-metropolitan counties.

Counties that qualified as frontier counties because of low population densities represent 12.1 percent of the counties, as shown in Table 3.2. Of these frontier counties, 58.9 percent are classified as remote counties with no town, and the rest are other categories of non-metropolitan counties. The sole exception is Nye County, Nevada, which is a metropolitan county that qualified as a frontier county (a status that held for both the 1990 census population and the 1997 population estimates).

Table 3.1
Distribution of U.S. Counties, by Metropolitan and Non-Metropolitan County Categories,
Based on 1993 Urban Influence Codes

County Category	Number of Counties	% of Totals	
		All Counties	Metropolitan/ Non-Metropolitan
All counties	3,126	100.0	—
Metropolitan—all counties	834	26.7	100.0
Large counties	309	9.9	37.1
Small counties	525	16.8	62.9
Non-metropolitan—all counties	2,292	73.3	100.0
Adjacent, city 10,000+	251	8.0	11.0
Adjacent, no city 10,000+	749	24.0	32.6
Remote, city 10,000+	233	7.5	10.2
Remote, town 2,500–10,000	549	17.6	24.0
Remote, no town	510	16.2	22.2

SOURCE: Area Resource File for 1999 with relevant Medicare data added.

Table 3.2
Distribution of Frontier Counties, by Metropolitan and Non-Metropolitan County Categories,
Based on 1993 Urban Influence Codes and 1990 Population Census

County Category	Number of Counties	% of Counties	
		All Counties	Frontier Counties
Metropolitan—all counties	1	<0.1	0.3
Large counties	0	—	—
Small counties	1	<0.1	0.3
Non-metropolitan—all counties	376	12.1	99.7
Adjacent, city 10,000+	3	0.1	0.8
Adjacent, no city 10,000+	58	1.9	15.4
Remote, city 10,000+	5	0.2	1.3
Remote, town 2,500–10,000	88	2.8	23.3
Remote, no town	222	7.1	58.9
All frontier counties	377	12.1	100.0

SOURCE: Area Resource File for 1999 with relevant Medicare data added.
NOTE: The sole frontier county in a metropolitan area is Nye County, Nevada.

The distributions of the counties by metropolitan, non-metropolitan, and frontier status vary by HHS region, as shown in Table 3.3. In general, the eastern regions (1 through 5) have higher percentages of metropolitan counties than the western regions do (6 through 10). One eastern and two western regions stand out as having unique distributions of counties. Region 2 is predominantly an urban region, with 71.1 percent of its counties being classified as metropolitan.

By contrast, frontier counties represent 61.0 percent of the counties in Region 8, and only 8.6 of the region's counties are metropolitan (see Table 3.3). Region 9 has a balanced mix of metropolitan, non-metropolitan, and frontier counties, with 45.2 percent metropolitan, 32.3 percent non-frontier non-metropolitan, and 22.6 percent frontier counties. This distribution reflects the presence of Los Angeles and other large cities in California and other states, along with large areas of sparsely populated land outside of these cities. The distribution of counties by the metropolitan and non-metropolitan county categories is provided in Table 3.4.

Table 3.3
Distribution of Metropolitan, Non-Metropolitan, and Frontier Counties, by HHS Region

HHS Region	Number of Counties	% Metropolitan	% Non-Metro, Non-Frontier	% Frontier
All regions	3,126	26.6	61.3	12.1
1. Boston	67	44.8	55.2	0
2. New York	83	71.1	29.9	0
3. Philadelphia	284	43.3	56.7	0
4. Atlanta	736	27.6	72.4	0
5. Chicago	524	31.9	68.1	0
6. Dallas	502	22.5	61.2	16.3
7. Kansas City	412	11.4	73.5	15.1
8. Denver	290	8.6	30.3	61.1
9. San Francisco	93	45.2	32.3	22.6
10. Seattle	135	17.8	56.3	25.9

SOURCE: Area Resource File for 1999 with relevant Medicare data added.

Table 3.4
Percentage Distribution of Metropolitan and Non-Metropolitan Counties, by HHS Region

HHS Region	Metropolitan		Non-Metropolitan				
	Large	Small	Adjacent, City	Adjacent, No City	Remote, City	Remote, Town	Remote, No Town
All regions	9.9	16.8	8.1	24.0	7.5	17.6	16.3
1. Boston	14.9	29.9	13.4	16.4	7.5	11.9	6.0
2. New York	42.2	28.9	8.4	13.3	4.8	2.4	0
3. Philadelphia	19.4	23.9	6.0	27.1	3.2	11.6	8.8
4. Atlanta	6.5	21.1	7.5	29.9	6.5	15.2	13.3
5. Chicago	13.4	18.5	11.8	24.4	7.3	14.9	9.7
6. Dallas	6.6	15.9	10.6	28.5	7.6	19.9	11.0
7. Kansas City	4.4	7.0	4.9	19.4	9.5	24.5	30.3
8. Denver	3.1	5.5	1.7	15.9	9.7	22.1	42.1
9. San Francisco	23.7	22.6	10.8	17.2	5.4	16.1	4.3
10. Seattle	6.7	11.1	9.6	12.6	14.1	26.7	19.3

SOURCE: Area Resource File for 1999 with relevant Medicare data added.

NOTE: The percentages are for county types within region, summing across rows to 100 percent.

Populations and Demographics

The differences in average populations for metropolitan, non-metropolitan, and frontier counties and changes in levels over time reported in Table 3.5 are well known. The overall average metropolitan county population is 10 times that of the overall average non-metropolitan counties, and large metropolitan counties have much larger populations than small metropolitan counties. Similar contrasts are seen between non-metropolitan counties with and without cities of 10,000 or more. In addition, both larger and smaller counties adjacent to MSAs have larger populations than their more remote counterparts. The sparse populations in frontier counties also are seen clearly in these numbers. Annual compounded growth rates from 1990 to 1997 were slightly higher for metropolitan counties than for non-metropolitan counties. Two exceptions were adjacent non-metropolitan counties with no city of 10,000 or more and frontier counties, for both of which populations increased an average of 1.2 percent annually (similar to increases for metropolitan counties).

Table 3.5
Average Total Population by Metropolitan, Non-Metropolitan, and Frontier Counties, Selected Years

County Category	Average County Total Population			Annual % Change 1990–1997
	1990	1993	1997	
Metropolitan—all counties	242,100	251,400	261,200	1.1%
Large counties	407,500	421,900	437,700	1.0
Small counties	144,500	150,700	156,900	1.2
Non-metropolitan—all counties	22,300	23,000	23,800	0.9
Adjacent, city 10,000+	54,300	55,900	57,800	0.9
Adjacent, no city 10,000+	19,800	20,500	21,500	1.2
Remote, city 10,000+	42,400	43,700	44,800	0.8
Remote, town 2,500–10,000	17,500	17,900	18,400	0.7
Remote, no town	6,600	6,700	6,900	0.6
Frontier county status				
Frontier counties	6,000	6,200	6,500	1.2
Other non-metropolitan counties	25,600	26,300	27,300	0.9

SOURCE: Area Resource File for 1999 with relevant Medicare data added.

NOTE: Change in average county population is measured as average compounded annual percentage change from 1990 to 1997.

Contrasts in average per capita incomes for metropolitan and non-metropolitan counties are documented in Table 3.6. Residents of large metropolitan counties had the highest per capita incomes, with those for small metropolitan counties being somewhat smaller. Non-metropolitan residents had lower incomes than residents of either large or small metropolitan areas. Per capita incomes for larger non-metropolitan counties grew slightly more than 4 percent annually from 1990 to 1997, which was similar to the growth rate for metropolitan per capita income. Income increased more slowly for non-metropolitan counties without a city of 10,000 or more, with growth rates of 3.8 for counties adjacent to metropolitan areas, 3.9 percent for remote counties with a town, and 2.2 percent for counties with no town. Per capita incomes for frontier counties were reasonably high in 1990 but increased only 1.1 percent annually.

In Tables 3.7 and 3.8, we describe the sizes of the Medicare populations for metropolitan, non-metropolitan, and frontier counties. The average sizes of the Medicare populations by county categories, as shown in Table 3.7, mirror those of the total populations. Yet the numbers of Medicare beneficiaries have grown at faster rates than total populations have, and growth rates for non-metropolitan areas are similar to those for metropolitan areas. The greatest increase in Medicare populations of 2.0 percent annually occurred in small metropolitan counties. As shown in Table 3.8, Medicare beneficiaries are a larger share of non-metropolitan populations, compared to metropolitan populations, and the largest percentages are in the most remote counties with no towns.

Table 3.6
Average County per Capita Income, by Metropolitan, Non-Metropolitan,
and Frontier Counties, Selected Years

| County Category | Average County Total per Capital Income | | | Annual % Change |
	1990	1993	1996	1990–1996
Metropolitan				
Large counties	$19,290	$21,110	$25,020	4.4%
Small counties	16,090	18,100	21,160	4.7
Non-metropolitan				
Adjacent, city 10,000+	14,950	16,630	19,180	4.2
Adjacent, no city 10,000+	13,980	15,370	17,480	3.8
Remote, city 10,000+	14,710	16,490	19,130	4.5
Remote, town 2,500–10,000	14,250	15,780	17,930	3.9
Remote, no town	15,020	16,270	17,140	2.2
Frontier county status				
Frontier counties	16,550	17,940	17,660	1.1
Other non-metropolitan counties	14,040	15,520	17,910	4.1

SOURCE: Area Resource File for 1999 with relevant Medicare data added.

NOTE: Change in county per capita income is measured as average compounded annual percentage change from 1990 to 1996.

Table 3.7
Medicare Beneficiaries, by Metropolitan, Non-Metropolitan, and Frontier Counties, Selected Years

County Category	Average Number of Medicare Beneficiaries			Annual % Change 1990–1997
	1990	1993	1997	
Metropolitan				
Large counties	52,300	54,520	57,270	1.3%
Small counties	20,280	21,600	23,230	2.0
Non-metropolitan				
Adjacent, city 10,000+	8,530	8,940	9,420	1.4
Adjacent, no city 10,000+	3,360	3,540	3,760	1.6
Remote, city 10,000+	6,520	6,830	7,210	1.4
Remote, town 2,500–10,000	3,140	3,300	3,400	1.1
Remote, no town	1,270	1,300	1,400	1.4
Frontier county status				
Frontier counties	950	990	1,050	1.4
Other non-metropolitan counties	4,280	4,480	4,720	1.4

SOURCE: Area Resource File for 1999 with relevant Medicare data added.

NOTE: Change in average number of Medicare beneficiaries is measured as average compounded annual percentage change from 1990 to 1997.

Table 3.8
Medicare Beneficiaries as a Percentage of Total Population, by Metropolitan, Non-Metropolitan, and Frontier Counties, Selected Years

County Category	% of Total Population			Annual % Change 1990–1997
	1990	1993	1997	
Metropolitan				
Large counties	12.8%	12.9%	13.1%	0.3%
Small counties	14.0	14.3	14.8	0.8
Non-metropolitan				
Adjacent, city 10,000+	15.7	16.0	16.3	0.5
Adjacent, no city 10,000+	17.0	17.3	17.5	0.4
Remote, city 10,000+	15.4	15.6	16.1	0.6
Remote, town 2,500–10,000	17.9	18.2	18.5	0.4
Remote, no town	19.3	19.7	20.0	0.5
Frontier county status				
Frontier counties	15.7	16.1	16.2	0.4
Other non-metropolitan counties	16.7	17.0	17.3	0.5

SOURCE: Area Resource File for 1999 with relevant Medicare data added.

NOTE: Change in percentage Medicare population is measured as average compounded annual percentage change from 1990 to 1997.

DISTRIBUTION OF UNDERSERVED AREAS

We begin by examining the distribution of MUAs and HPSAs, which are designated based on demographic and provider supply factors. Table 3.9 shows that 46.3 percent of U.S.

counties are designated as whole-county MUAs and 33.3 percent are designated as partial-county MUAs in 1999. Smaller percentages are designated as HPSAs. As of 1997, 24.5 percent of counties were whole-county HPSAs and 38.9 percent were partial-county HPSAs. We see slight increases from 1991 to 1995 in the percentages of counties designated as HPSAs, followed by a decline in designations in 1997.

The percentages of MUA and HPSA designations vary across metropolitan, non-metropolitan, and frontier counties. In addition, HPSA designations for metropolitan counties increased steadily from 1991 to 1997, whereas designations in non-metropolitan areas increased markedly from 1991 to 1993 followed by only slight increases in subsequent years. Frontier counties have the largest percentages of both MUA and HPSA designations, with 72.8 percent of frontier counties designated as MUAs and 72.3 percent designated as HPSAs in 1997.

Within the non-metropolitan counties, MUA and HPSA designations varied with both adjacency to MSAs and the presence or absence of a city of 10,000 or more. The largest percentage of designations as MUAs or HPSAs was found for counties adjacent to an MSA without a city and for the most remote counties without a town. Non-metropolitan counties with a city had smaller percentages of designations than other non-metropolitan counties. Within the non-metropolitan counties with a city of 10,000 or more, the remote counties had relatively more HPSA designations than those adjacent to MSAs, and the differences grew over time. These differences have existed since the 1991 designations.

Table 3.9
Distribution of Medically Underserved Areas and Primary Care Health Professional Shortage Areas, by Metropolitan and Non-Metropolitan Counties, Selected Years

County Category	MUA Counties	Health Professional Shortage Area Counties			
		1991	1993	1995	1997
Number of counties	2,451	1,720	1,857	1,966	1,952
Percentage of all counties[a]					
Whole counties	46.3	22.7	25.2	25.4	24.5
Partial counties	33.3	33.1	35.2	39.4	38.9
Percentage of counties[b]					
Metropolitan—all counties	77.6	52.5	55.3	59.4	60.8
Large counties	69.0	45.9	49.8	54.8	56.4
Small counties	82.7	56.3	58.5	62.2	63.4
Non-metropolitan—all counties	65.5	57.1	62.2	65.5	64.4
Adjacent, city 10,000+	73.6	41.5	46.3	48.8	49.6
Adjacent, no city 10,000+	84.1	64.5	69.8	74.2	72.5
Remote, city 10,000+	71.3	41.3	48.3	51.7	51.3
Remote, town 2,500–10,000	78.2	52.2	55.7	60.6	61.1
Remote, no town	85.8	66.3	71.9	72.3	69.1
Frontier counties	72.8	69.3	75.2	72.8	72.3

SOURCE: Area Resource File for 1999 with relevant Medicare data added.

[a]Total of 3,078 counties excludes independent cities in Virginia and Alaska counties, for which this information was not available on the Area Resource File or other source files.

[b]The percentages of counties designated as MUAs or HPSAs is the sum of the percentages for whole-county and partial-county areas.

In Table 3.10, we show the extent of overlap between the MUA and HPSA designations, including both metropolitan and non-metropolitan counties. Overall, only 10.8 percent of the counties have no designation as either an MUA or a HPSA, and 53.9 percent of counties were designated as both an MUA and a HPSA. Another 35.3 percent of counties were either an MUA or a HPSA but not both. Larger percentages of non-metropolitan counties than metropolitan counties had at least one designation as underserved. For counties designated as both MUA and HPSA, 24.2 percent of the non-metropolitan counties were designated as whole-county areas and 10.9 percent were partial-county areas. By contrast, only 5.4 percent of metropolitan counties with both designations were whole-county areas but 36.5 of these counties were partial-county areas.

Table 3.10
Distribution of Medically Underserved Areas and Primary Care Health Professional Shortage Areas, by Metropolitan and Non-Metropolitan Counties, 1997 HPSAs

Type of Designation	All Counties		Non-Metropolitan Counties		Metropolitan Counties	
	Number	Percentage	Number	Percentage	Number	Percentage
All counties	3,078	100.0	2,262	100.0	816	100.0
Not MUA or HPSA	333	10.8	218	9.6	115	14.1
Mixed (one or other)	1,087	35.3	814	36.0	273	33.5
Both MUA and HPSA	1,658	53.9	1,230	54.4	428	52.5
Both whole county	592	19.2	548	24.2	44	5.4
Both partial county	545	17.7	247	10.9	298	36.5
Partial and whole	521	17.0	435	19.3	86	10.6

SOURCE: Area Resource File for 1999 with relevant Medicare data added. Counties with mixed designation were designated as either an MUA or a HPSA but not both.

SUPPLY OF PROVIDERS

An important factor in determining access to care and utilization rates by non-metropolitan beneficiaries is the local supply of providers. In this analysis, we use ARF data and HRSA data on MUA designations to describe provider supplies in metropolitan, non-metropolitan, and frontier areas. We summarize the total numbers of patient care physicians, hospitals, skilled nursing facilities, nursing homes, home health agencies, and rural health clinics, as reported in the Area Resource File.[12]

The well-known contrasts between metropolitan and non-metropolitan counties in the supplies of physicians and hospitals are documented in Table 3.11, with comparisons across the metropolitan, non-metropolitan, and frontier county categories. Using 1997 data for physicians and 1996 data for hospitals, provider supply is measured both as average counts of providers and as the number of providers per 100,000 total county population. Hospital supply is measured as number of hospitals as well as number of licensed hospital beds. The expected

---

[12] The data for skilled nursing facilities include only organized facilities reported in the ARF and do not reflect the swing beds in local hospitals that also provide skilled nursing care. Although many rural hospitals have swing beds, we did not have the data to allow us to estimate the proportion of SNF stays or days they provided.

metropolitan/non-metropolitan differences in counts of providers were found, with metropolitan counties having much larger numbers of physicians, hospitals, and hospital beds than non-metropolitan counties. Frontier counties had the smallest average numbers of providers per county.

We found quite different patterns for physician and hospital supplies when measured by the size of the populations served. For physicians, metropolitan counties had well over 200 physicians per 100,000 population, which was two to four times the ratio for non-metropolitan counties. Within non-metropolitan counties, the average physician supply ratio for counties with a city of at least 10,000 was twice that for the counties with smaller towns or no towns. The frontier county ratio was a low 54 physicians per 100,000 population, mirroring that of the most remote counties with no town.

By contrast, the ratios of hospitals per 100,000 population for non-metropolitan counties were consistently larger than those for metropolitan counties, and the ratios of hospital beds in non-metropolitan counties were equal to or larger than those for metropolitan counties. As discussed in Section 2, these ratios reflect the small populations in the denominators for these counties. Even though the numbers of institutional providers in non-metropolitan counties were small, they still represented substantial supply relative to the small resident population. The ratios of staffed hospital beds per 100,000 population would be smaller than the ratios reported here for licensed beds, and they would more accurately reflect operating capacity. We expect, however, that comparisons across county categories would not change substantially.

Table 3.11
Average Supply of Physicians and Hospitals, by Metropolitan, Non-Metropolitan, and Frontier Counties, 1996 or 1997

| | | | Short-Stay Hospital Services | | | |
| | Patient Care Physicians | | Facilities | | Beds | |
County Category	Average Number	Ratio[a]	Average Number	Ratio[a]	Average Number	Ratio[a]
Metropolitan						
Large counties	1,185	270	5.1	1.2	1,360	313
Small counties	347	221	2.5	1.6	558	359
Non-metropolitan						
Adjacent, city 10,000+	70	122	1.6	2.7	189	328
Adjacent, no city 10,000+	16	75	0.9	4.0	59	279
Remote, city 10,000+	76	170	1.5	3.3	193	432
Remote, town 2,500–10,000	17	91	1.1	6.1	73	396
Remote, no town	4	54	0.6	8.8	29	418
Frontier county status						
Frontier counties	5	54	0.7	12.3	32	546
Other non-metropolitan counties	29	91	1.1	4.4	94	393

SOURCE: Area Resource File for 1999 with relevant Medicare data added.

NOTES: 1997 data for physicians and 1996 data for hospitals in the Area Resource File. Under the frontier county groupings, the "non-metropolitan not-frontier" counties are all non-metropolitan counties that do not qualify as frontier.

[a]Ratio = number of providers, hospitals, beds per 100,000 total county population.

The supply patterns for SNFs, SNF beds, and home health agencies were similar to those observed for hospitals and hospital beds, although there were larger numbers of SNFs and home health agencies than hospitals.[13] As shown in Table 3.12, the numbers of SNF facilities and beds per county, as well as the numbers of home health agencies, were larger in metropolitan than non-metropolitan counties, and they were largest in the large metropolitan counties. The ratios per 100,000 population for SNFs and home health agencies were higher in non-metropolitan counties than the ratios for metropolitan counties, similar to the pattern found for hospitals. However, we see quite different supply patterns in non-metropolitan counties for SNF beds and hospital beds.

Table 3.12
Average Supply of Skilled Nursing and Home Health Providers, by Metropolitan, Non-Metropolitan, and Frontier Counties, 1994

| | Skilled Nursing Facilities | | | | Home Health Agencies | |
| | Facilities | | Beds | | | |
County Category	Average Number	Ratio[a]	Average Number	Ratio[a]	Average Number	Ratio[a]
Metropolitan						
Large counties	16.6	3.9	2,153	506	9.5	2.2
Small counties	7.3	4.8	847	555	4.7	3.1
Non-metropolitan						
Adjacent, city 10,000+	3.6	6.3	365	648	2.2	3.9
Adjacent, no city 10,000+	1.5	7.4	139	672	0.9	4.6
Remote, city 10,000+	2.9	6.6	283	641	2.2	5.0
Remote, town 2,500–10,000	1.4	8.0	283	678	1.4	7.5
Remote, no town	0.6	9.2	123	640	0.6	8.3
Frontier county status						
Frontier counties	0.6	9.6	37	596	0.6	9.5
Other non-metropolitan counties	1.9	7.1	176	661	1.3	5.1

SOURCE: Area Resource File for 1999 with relevant Medicare data added.
[a]Ratio = number of providers per 100,000 county population

Comparing counties adjacent to MSAs to the remote non-metropolitan counties, the adjacent counties had smaller ratios of hospital beds than remote counties, but the ratios of SNF beds were quite similar for the two county groups. In addition, within the non-metropolitan counties adjacent to MSAs, the counties without a city of at least 10,000 had smaller ratios of hospital beds but larger ratios of SNF beds than the other counties. The remote counties with a town of 2,500 were found to have the lowest ratio of hospital beds but the highest ratio of SNF beds. Both of these findings point to relatively greater supplies of SNF beds in non-metropolitan counties in 1994, especially in the counties without a city of 10,000. Of interest, frontier counties had the highest supply ratios for SNFs and home health agencies, but they had relatively

---

[13]   Skilled nursing services and other nursing home services differ in their goals and nature of care. Patients are given skilled nursing care to improve their health and functional status after an illness or health care event (e.g., after a stroke), whereas other nursing home services provide maintenance support for patients whose health status is not likely to improve.

fewer SNF beds than the non-metropolitan non-frontier counties (596 beds per 100,000 population compared to 661 beds for other non-metropolitan counties).

The remaining provider supplies we examined were nursing homes and rural health clinics, which are reported in Table 3.13. As expected, metropolitan counties had larger numbers of nursing homes and nursing home beds. However, the differences in the numbers were not as large as they were for hospitals or SNFs. Therefore, we find that non-metropolitan counties had substantially larger supplies of nursing homes and nursing home beds than metropolitan counties, relative to the sizes of their populations, when supplies are expressed as ratios per 100,000. Within the non-metropolitan counties, the counties adjacent to an MSA had lower ratios of both nursing homes and nursing home beds than the remote non-metropolitan counties, and frontier counties had ratios similar to those for the smaller remote non-metropolitan counties.

Table 3.13
Average Supply of Nursing Homes and Rural Health Clinics, by Metropolitan, Non-Metropolitan, and Frontier Counties, 1994

County Category	Nursing Home Services				Rural Health Clinics	
	Facilities		Beds			
	Average Number	Ratio[a]	Average Number	Ratio[a]	Average Number	Ratio[a]
Metropolitan						
Large counties	3.1	0.7	308	72	0.2	0.1
Small counties	2.0	1.3	200	131	0.5	0.3
Non-metropolitan						
Adjacent, city 10,000+	1.5	2.7	133	235	0.7	1.3
Adjacent, no city 10,000+	0.9	4.4	70	336	0.8	3.7
Remote, city 10,000+	1.4	3.2	124	281	0.8	1.7
Remote, town 2,500–10,000	1.0	5.4	73	406	0.8	4.6
Remote, no town	0.6	8.9	36	531	0.7	9.8
Frontier county status						
Frontier counties	0.4	6.7	21	343	0.6	9.2
Other non-metropolitan counties	1.1	4.1	86	323	0.8	3.0

SOURCE: Area Resource File for 1999 with relevant Medicare data added.

[a]Ratio = number of providers per 100,000 county population

By definition, RHCs are providers in underserved non-urbanized locations. Therefore, we expect to see the lower numbers and ratios of RHCs in metropolitan counties presented in Table 3.13. The fact that some RHCs are found in metropolitan counties reminds us that the geographic criterion for designation of these clinics is "located outside urbanized areas" rather than "in a non-metropolitan county." Non-metropolitan counties in all five categories had similar numbers of RHCs, averaging 0.8 RHCs per county. When expressed as ratios, the non-metropolitan counties without a city of 10,000 had higher ratios, with the highest ratio being 9.8 RHCs per 100,000 population for the most remote counties without a town. The frontier counties also had a high ratio of 9.2, which is consistent with the role of the RHCs to improve access to care for Medicare beneficiaries in remote areas.

ISSUES AND IMPLICATIONS

The analysis results reported in this section highlight the obvious differences between metropolitan and non-metropolitan counties in the characteristics of the local populations, Medicare beneficiaries, and provider supply, as well as the wide variation in these characteristics across non-metropolitan counties. For example, compared to metropolitan counties, the non-metropolitan counties had smaller and older populations as well as lower per capita incomes. Not surprisingly, the non-metropolitan counties that have at least one city of 10,000 population had higher per capita incomes than other non-metropolitan counties, and they also had richer supplies per capita of providers of all types. The frontier counties, with the most sparse populations, tended to have higher ratios of providers to population because of their very small populations. This measure, however, does not address the distance that people in frontier counties had to travel to get to those providers for care.

A substantial fraction of non-metropolitan counties was designated as HPSAs and MUAs, although these designations differed substantially across counties. An estimated 54.4 percent of the counties were designated as both HPSAs and MUAs, but the designations for these counties did not always agree with respect to whole- versus partial-county designation. Only 9.6 percent of the counties were not designated as either HPSA or MUA. Given these inconsistencies in definitions of underserved areas, we report distributions and trends according to both HPSA and MUA designations, to ensure that users have information that is as complete as possible.

4. PAYMENT TRENDS FOR NON-METROPOLITAN HOSPITALS

The analysis presented in this section describes trends during the 1990s in the distribution, characteristics, and utilization of both the total supply of hospitals in non-metropolitan counties and hospitals with special designations for payment purposes. In addition, we describe trends in utilization of inpatient services by Medicare beneficiaries residing in non-metropolitan counties, including examination of the extent to which they use urban or rural hospitals and differences in the types of admissions to each type of hospital. The analyses were designed to address the following research questions:

- How have the supply of Medicare-certified hospitals in rural areas and the mix of services they offer changed during the decade of the 1990s?

- How have service volumes and payments for Medicare inpatient services in rural hospitals changed during this time period?

- What are the trends in the levels and mix of service activity for Medicare beneficiaries and associated spending for sole community hospitals, rural referral centers, and Medicare dependent hospitals?

HOSPITAL SUPPLY AND CHARACTERISTICS

We examine here the supply of all Medicare-certified short-term acute care hospitals in non-metropolitan areas from 1992 through 1998, including their characteristics and location by type of rural county, as defined by the 1993 Urban Influence Codes. Detailed trend analyses were performed for all years from 1992 through 1998, but we found that most trends observed were gradual changes over time rather than abrupt changes occurring in specific years. Therefore, for ease in reading, we report data only for the years 1992, 1994, 1996, and 1998 unless there are specific reasons to use additional or different years.

Supply of Hospitals

The supply of hospitals in non-metropolitan counties declined slightly during the six years between 1992 and 1998. As shown in Table 4.1, the number of Medicare-certified hospitals in non-metropolitan counties decreased an estimated 5.5 percent, from 2,357 facilities in 1992 to 2,227 facilities in 1998. These declines followed earlier reductions in the supply of non-metropolitan hospitals during the 1980s, as well as extensive reengineering of service mix and operations, as the Medicare prospective payment system was introduced and other health system reform activities arose (ProPAC, 1991; Office of the HHS Inspector General, 1993a; Moscovice et al., 1999).

Table 4.1 also shows hospital locations during the 1990s according to the set of five categories of rurality we derived using the Urban Influence Codes (see the methods in Section 2). The table presents both the numbers of hospitals and percentage distributions by county category. The largest reduction in hospital supply during the 1990s was an 8.3 percent decline in the number of hospitals in the most remote rural counties that had no town of at least 2,500 population. Declines for the four other categories of non-metropolitan counties ranged from 4.3

percent to 5.6 percent. As a result of these trends, the most remote counties had a smaller share of total non-metropolitan hospitals in 1998 than they had in 1992, as shown by the percentage distributions for these two years.

Table 4.1
Distribution of All Short-Term Hospitals in Non-Metropolitan Counties,
by County Category, Selected Years

County Category	1992	1994	1996	1998	% Change 1992–1998
All hospitals	2,357	2,303	2,288	2,227	–5.5%
By county category					
Number of hospitals					
Adjacent, city 10,000+	394	382	381	372	–5.6
Adjacent, no city 10,000+	668	653	650	632	–5.4
Remote, city 10,000+	350	340	335	331	–5.4
Remote, town 2,500–10,000	633	620	616	606	–4.3
Remote, no town	312	308	306	286	–8.3
Percentage of hospitals					
Adjacent, city 10,000+	16.7%	16.6%	16.7%	16.7%	0.0
Adjacent, no city 10,000+	28.3	28.4	28.4	28.4	0.4
Remote, city 10,000+	14.8	14.8	14.6	14.9	0.7
Remote, town 2,500–10,000	26.9	26.9	26.9	27.2	1.1
Remote, no town	13.2	13.4	13.4	12.8	–3.0
Frontier counties					
Number of hospitals	283	277	276	256	–9.5
Percentage of non-metropolitan hospitals	12.0%	12.0%	12.1%	11.5%	–4.2

SOURCES: Medicare Provider of Service Files, Medicare Provider Specific Files, Area Resource File.

A different perspective on hospital supply in non-metropolitan counties is offered in Table 4.2, which shows the distribution of counties according to the number of hospitals located in each county. An estimated 22.3 percent of the non-metropolitan counties had no hospitals in 1992, and the percentage increased slightly to 24.8 percent in 1998. The majority of counties had only one hospital, and these percentages remained stable over the six-year period (58.0 percent in 1992 and 57.7 percent in 1998). Reductions in the number of hospitals tended to occur in counties with more than one hospital, thus shifting the entire distribution of counties downward to smaller hospital supplies. The declines could be due to hospital closures or to consolidations, although even with consolidation, many hospitals retain separate Medicare provider numbers and therefore would be counted separately in these data.

These trends are consistent with findings of the Office of the HHS Inspector General, which indicated that access to care did not decline substantially as a result of hospital closures and that other inpatient and emergency services were within reasonable travel distances for most people. In many cases, the closed hospital facilities were being used for some other form of health care (Office of the HHS Inspector General, 1993a, 2000).

Table 4.2
Distribution of Non-Metropolitan Counties,
by the Number of Hospitals in the County, Selected Years

Number of Hospitals	1992	1994	1996	1998
0	22.3%	23.1%	23.4%	24.8%
1	58.0	58.2	58.0	57.7
2	15.8	15.0	15.1	14.2
3	2.9	2.8	2.8	2.7
4	0.7	0.6	0.4	0.4
5	0.2	0.2	0.2	0.2
6	<0.1	0	0	0

SOURCES: Medicare Provider of Service Files, Medicare Provider Specific Files, Area Resource File.
NOTE: These percentages are calculated for 2,300 non-metropolitan counties.

Reductions in non-metropolitan hospital supply varied widely by region of the country, ranging from a small 1.1 percent loss for the San Francisco region to a large 16.3 percent loss for the New York region, as reported in Table 4.3. Other regions with large losses were Denver (9.0 percent decline) and Kansas City (8.2 percent decline). No region experienced an increase in supply of non-metropolitan hospitals.

Table 4.3
Number of Short-Term Hospitals in Non-Metropolitan Counties,
by HHS Region, Selected Years

HHS Region	1992	1994	1996	1998	% Change 1992–1998
All regions	2,357	2,303	2,288	2,227	–5.5
1. Boston	65	64	64	62	–4.6
2. New York	43	39	39	36	–16.3
3. Philadelphia	132	133	132	125	–5.3
4. Atlanta	508	495	497	489	–3.7
5. Chicago	416	403	396	391	–6.0
6. Dallas	388	382	379	374	–3.6
7. Kansas City	354	348	344	325	–8.2
8. Denver	233	225	223	212	–9.0
9. San Francisco	89	88	88	88	–1.1
10. Seattle	129	126	126	125	–3.1

SOURCES: Medicare Provider of Service Files, Medicare Provider Specific Files, Area Resource File.

Characteristics of Non-Metropolitan Hospitals

As the supply of non-metropolitan hospitals declined gradually during the 1990s, the characteristics of the remaining hospitals also would be expected to shift. Such shifts could be due to differences in characteristics between the hospitals that closed and those that remained in operation, changes in the way the surviving hospitals provided health care, or a combination of these effects. The hospital characteristics we examined in this analysis were ownership, bed size, staffing, and whether a hospital offered each of three selected services (home health, hospice services, and inpatient psychiatric care units).

In Tables 4.4 and 4.5, we present trends in distributions of non-metropolitan hospitals by type of ownership. Table 4.4 compares ownership trends for all hospitals to those in frontier counties, and Table 4.5 compares trends by county category based on the UIC codes.

Overall, virtually half of non-metropolitan hospitals are not-for-profit institutions, and only about 7 percent are for-profit (see Table 4.4). The remainder are government-owned— either federal, state, or local government—or independent hospital district. Ownership mix shifted slightly between 1992 and 1998. The percentage of not-for-profit facilities increased 1.4 percent (47 more hospitals), and the remaining ownership categories declined (83 fewer hospitals), whereas the number of hospitals owned by hospital districts remained stable.

The trend in ownership mix for hospitals in frontier counties, also shown in Table 4.4, is quite distinct from the overall patterns for non-metropolitan hospitals. An estimated 60 percent of hospitals in frontier counties are government-owned (federal, state, or local governments or local hospital districts), compared with 46 percent or less for all non-metropolitan hospitals. Within government-owned facilities in frontier counties, there was a large increase (23.4 percent) in the percentage owned by hospital districts and a small increase (3.8 percent) in the percentage of facilities owned by federal or state governments. There were substantial declines in the percentage of hospitals owned by local governments (–13.4 percent) and for-profit hospitals (-11.1 percent), as well as a slight decline in the percentage of not-for-profit facilities (–4.0 percent). Fewer than 2 percent of the facilities in frontier counties had for-profit ownership in 1992, and this percentage declined slightly over the six-year period.

Table 4.4
Mix of Ownership for All Short-Term Hospitals in Non-Metropolitan Counties, for All Hospitals and Hospitals in Frontier Counties, Selected Years

Ownership Category	% of Hospitals by Type of Ownership				% Change 1992–1998
	1992	1994	1996	1998	
All hospitals	2,357	2,303	2,288	2,227	
Voluntary not-for-profit	48.4%	48.3%	48.6%	49.1%	1.4%
For-profit	7.2	7.3	7.1	7.0	–2.8
Government—federal, state	2.5	2.6	2.4	2.4	–4.0
Government—local	24.0	23.5	23.1	22.4	–6.7
Hospital district or authority	17.9	18.4	18.8	19.0	6.1
Frontier counties	283	277	276	256	
Voluntary not-for-profit	37.8%	37.2%	37.0%	36.3%	–4.0
For-profit	1.8	1.8	1.8	1.6	–11.1
Government—federal, state	5.3	5.8	5.4	5.5	3.8
Government—local	30.7	28.9	26.8	26.6	–13.4
Hospital district or authority	24.4	26.4	29.0	30.1	23.4

SOURCES: Medicare Provider of Service Files, Medicare Provider Specific Files, Area Resource File.

Distributions of hospital ownership by county category, given in Table 4.5, reveal some complex but interesting patterns. We list some highlights here:

- For non-metropolitan counties with a city of at least 10,000 population (either adjacent to an MSA or remote), percentages of for-profit and not-for-profit hospitals are greater than those for other categories of non-metropolitan counties.

- The most remote counties have a larger percentage of hospitals owned by local governments than other county categories.

- The percentages of hospitals owned by hospital districts were highest for remote counties with a town of 2,500 to 10,000 (but not the most remote counties) and for counties adjacent to an MSA without a city of 10,000 population higher.

- The most remote counties had the largest shift in hospital ownership mix between 1992 and 1998. The percentage of hospitals in these counties that were owned by hospital districts increased by 36.4 percent, from 15.4 percent in 1992 to 21.0 percent in 1998. The percentage owned by federal or state governments also increased by 10.3 percent, whereas the percentage decreased for not-for-profit hospitals (–11.3 percent change) and for-profit hospitals (–7.1 percent change).

- In remote counties that include a city of 10,000 population or more, the percentage of for-profit hospitals increased by 20.5 percent over time, from 8.3 percent of hospitals in 1992 to 10.0 percent in 1998.

Another important dimension of hospital supply is the capacity of each hospital to provide inpatient services for the community it serves. Drawing upon data from the Provider of Service files, we analyzed two measures of hospital capacity: the average number of Medicare-certified beds and average FTEs of total staffing. Certified bed counts are not the most useful measures of operating capacity because hospitals typically are staffed to operate a much smaller number of beds (we discuss our choice to use the two measures and the data limitations in more detail in Section 2). The staff FTE measure offers another view of actual service activity. We could not calculate average daily census or occupancy rates because we had data only for Medicare inpatient stays.

Non-metropolitan hospitals certified by Medicare had an average of 75 certified beds, as shown in Table 4.6, and there was no change in the average number of beds between 1992 and 1998. At the same time, however, average total staffing per hospital increased by 19.2 percent from 213 FTEs to 254 FTEs. These trends suggest that hospitals that discontinued operation during this period, on average, were operating at smaller capacities than the surviving hospitals, even though they reported having similar numbers of certified beds.

Both average bed counts and total staffing reflect variations in average hospital size across categories of non-metropolitan counties. The largest hospitals were clustered in the two categories of counties with a city of 10,000 population (adjacent to an MSA or remote). Hospitals in these counties had an average of 122 to 131 certified beds, depending on the county category and year, whereas hospitals in the other county categories had 60 beds or fewer. They also had average total staffing that was more than twice the staffing levels of hospitals in other county categories. Hospitals in the most remote counties and frontier counties had the smallest number of certified beds and staffing levels. In 1998, bed counts averaged 35 beds in the remote counties with no towns and 30 beds in frontier counties.[14]

Table 4.5
Mix of Ownership for All Short-Term Hospitals in Non-Metropolitan Counties,
by County Category, Selected Years

County Category	% of Hospitals by Type of Ownership				% Change 1992–1998
	1992	1994	1996	1998	
Adjacent, city 10,000+					
Number of hospitals	394	382	381	372	
Voluntary nonprofit	56.9%	57.3%	58.5%	58.9%	3.5%
For-profit	9.1	9.2	8.4	8.3	−8.8
Government—federal, state	2.5	2.1	2.1	2.2	−12.0
Government—local	14.2	13.9	13.4	12.1	−14.8
Hospital district, authority	17.3	17.5	17.6	18.6	7.5
Adjacent, no city 10,000+					
Number of hospitals	668	653	650	632	
Voluntary nonprofit	46.4%	46.9%	47.9%	48.9%	5.4
For-profit	7.5	8.0	7.4	7.3	−2.7
Government—federal, state	1.2	1.4	1.2	1.1	−8.3
Government—local	24.4	23.1	22.9	22.6	−7.4
Hospital district, authority	20.5	20.7	20.6	20.1	−2.0
Remote, city 10,000+					
Number of hospitals	350	340	335	331	
Voluntary nonprofit	55.4%	55.9%	55.2%	55.0%	−0.7
For-profit	8.3	8.5	9.9	10.0	20.5
Government—federal, state	5.4	5.0	4.8	4.8	−11.1
Government—local	18.9	18.8	18.2	18.1	−4.2
Hospital district, authority	12.0	11.8	11.9	12.1	0.8
Remote, town 2,500–10,000					
Number of hospitals	633	620	616	606	
Voluntary nonprofit	44.1%	44.7%	44.6%	45.5%	3.2
For-profit	6.5	6.1	6.2	5.9	−9.2
Government—federal, state	2.1	2.6	2.6	2.3	9.5
Government—local	27.2	26.1	25.7	25.3	−7.0
Hospital district, authority	20.2	20.5	20.9	21.0	4.0
Remote, no town					
Number of hospitals	312	308	306	286	
Voluntary nonprofit	42.6%	39.3%	38.9%	37.8%	−11.3
For-profit	4.2	4.2	3.6	3.9	−7.1
Government—federal, state	2.9	2.9	2.6	3.2	10.3
Government—local	34.9	36.0	35.6	34.3	−1.7
Hospital district, authority	15.4	17.5	19.3	21.0	36.4

SOURCES: Medicare Provider of Service Files, Medicare Provider Specific Files, Area Resource File.

---

[14] Within each county category, hospitals' bed sizes vary substantially, and there are some extremely small rural hospitals. Furthermore, average daily census for some of these hospitals is fewer than five patients.

There was little change in the average number of certified beds between 1992 and 1998 for hospitals in any of the categories of non-metropolitan counties, but rates of increase in average staffing did vary across county categories. Hospitals in the most remote counties had the largest increase in average total staffing, doubling from 66 FTEs in 1992 to 132 FTEs in 1998. Hospitals in counties adjacent to an MSA and having a city of 10,000 population had the smallest staffing increase of 11.7 percent.

Table 4.6
Average Number of Certified Beds and Staffing for Short-Term Hospitals
in Non-Metropolitan Counties, by County Category, Selected Years

County Category	1992	1994	1996	1998	% Change 1992–1998
Average number of beds					
All non-metropolitan hospitals	75	76	75	75	0.0%
By county category					
Adjacent, city 10,000+	122	124	121	122	0.0
Adjacent, no city 10,000+	59	59	58	58	−1.7
Remote, city 10,000+	129	131	131	129	0.0
Remote, town 2,500–10,000	55	56	55	55	0.0
Remote, no town	33	33	32	35	6.1
Frontier counties	29	29	29	30	3.4
Average total staff FTEs					
All non-metropolitan hospitals	213	227	241	254	19.2
By county category					
Adjacent, city 10,000+	366	380	398	409	11.7
Adjacent, no city 10,000+	153	161	168	176	15.0
Remote, city 10,000+	400	424	437	476	19.0
Remote, town 2,500–10,000	153	162	184	177	15.7
Remote, no town	66	95	98	132	100.0
Frontier counties	69	72	75	81	17.4

SOURCES: Medicare Provider of Service Files, Medicare Provider Specific Files, Area Resource File.
NOTES: Beds are Medicare-certified beds. FTEs are full-time equivalent staff employed by a hospital, as reported in the Provider of Service files.

In addition to looking at the raw counts of hospital supply for non-metropolitan counties, it was important to standardize the counts to the size of the markets the hospitals served. We examined two standardized measures of hospital bed supply for this analysis. A widely used measure is the ratio of a supply quantity to the size of the population being served (in this case the number of certified hospital beds per 100,000 population). Such a ratio may not perform well for rural areas, however, because a small rural population in the denominator may inflate the ratio. Therefore, in addition to using beds per population, we calculated beds per square mile as an independent measure of geographic access to inpatient services.

The two hospital supply ratios for non-metropolitan counties for the years 1993 and 1997 are summarized in Table 4.7, with comparisons across county category and for frontier counties. The ratios of hospital beds to population varied much less across county categories than the average numbers of hospital beds reported in Table 4.6, reflecting direct (i.e., positive) relationships between the number of beds and population size. The bed-to-population ratios declined between 1993 and 1997 for all county categories and for frontier counties because of growth in the county populations, closure of some hospitals, and stability in the bed size (on average) of the remaining hospitals. In addition, bed ratios varied more widely across county categories in 1993 than in 1997. This finding is consistent with the Office of the HHS Inspector General findings that the non-metropolitan hospitals that closed in the intervening years were located in areas with richer hospital supplies relative to their populations, such that bed supply ratios declined faster for those areas than ratios for other areas (Office of the HHS Inspector General, 1996).

Table 4.7
Average Hospital Bed Supply per Population and per Square Mile for Non-Metropolitan Hospitals, by County Category, 1993 and 1997

County Category	Bed Ratios by Year		% Change 1993–1997
	1993	1997	
Certified beds per 100,000 population			
All non-metropolitan hospitals	334	308	−7.8%
By county category			
Adjacent, city 10,000+	342	313	−8.5
Adjacent, no city 10,000+	252	228	−9.5
Remote, city 10,000+	439	319	−27.3
Remote, town 2,500–10,000	353	327	−7.4
Remote, no town	307	272	−11.4
Frontier counties	340	303	−10.9
Certified beds per 100 square miles			
All non-metropolitan hospitals	6.7	6.4	−4.5
By county category			
Adjacent, city 10,000+	20.6	19.4	−5.8
Adjacent, no city 10,000+	6.5	6.1	−6.2
Remote, city 10,000+	13.9	13.6	−2.2
Remote, town 2,500–10,000	4.4	4.2	−4.5
Remote, no town	1.5	1.3	−13.3
Frontier counties	9.3	9.3	0.0

SOURCES: Medicare Provider of Service Files, Medicare Provider Specific Files, Area Resource File.

NOTES: Ratios are measured as the number of Medicare-certified hospital beds per 100,000 total population or per 100 square miles in a county. Averages are summarized across county categories, weighting by the county population or size of county in square miles.

We found diverse trends in bed supply per population for the different categories of non-metropolitan counties. Counties adjacent to an MSA *with no city* of 10,000 population had the lowest ratios of beds to population of all county categories in both 1993 and 1997. Remote counties *containing a city* of 10,000 population had the highest average ratio of beds per population in 1993 (439 beds per 10,000 population), but these counties also had the largest declines in bed ratios by 1997. The resulting average ratio of 319 beds per 100,000 population for this category of county was similar to average ratios for the other categories in 1997. Remote counties containing a town of 2,500 to 10,000 population had the second highest average bed-to-population ratio in 1993 but the lowest rate of decline over time. As a result, these counties had 327 beds per 100,000 population in 1997, the highest of all the county categories. By contrast, the most remote counties had the lowest average bed-to-population ratios in both 1993 and 1997.

Variations across county categories in the number of certified beds per square mile highlight familiar issues regarding geographic access to hospital care for rural beneficiaries. In areas with lower ratios, patients must travel greater distances to obtain hospital care. The presence of a city of at least 10,000 population in a county appears to be an important factor for geographic access to hospital care. The two categories of non-metropolitan counties that contain at least one city of 10,000 population had much higher ratios of beds per square mile than the other three county categories did, although these beds probably are clustered in the city(s). Although frontier counties had fewer beds per square mile than counties with cities, the average ratios for frontier counties were noticeably higher than those for the more remote counties.

In addition to the generalized measures of bed supply and staffing, we measured trends in selected specific services offered by hospitals in non-metropolitan counties. We view information on these services as both (1) contributing to building profiles of hospitals in non-metropolitan counties and (2) serving as indicators of access to specific services for Medicare beneficiaries living in those areas. We chose to track home health care, hospice services, and psychiatric services because they are important services for Medicare beneficiaries and new Medicare payment rules for these services will affect hospitals providing them. In reviewing data in the POS files, we found clear trends of growth in the number of non-metropolitan hospitals offering these services.

We defined three dichotomous variables that measured whether a hospital offered home health care, offered hospice services, or had an organized inpatient psychiatric unit, and we summarized the percentages of hospitals providing each service in the years 1992 through 1998. As shown in Table 4.8, there was substantial growth between 1992 to 1998 in the percentage of non-metropolitan hospitals that offered each of these services. In 1992, an estimated 46.1 percent of hospitals offered home health care, 23.2 percent offered hospice services, and 12.0 percent had a psychiatric unit. By 1998, the percentages of hospitals had increased to 58.1 percent for home health, 36.1 percent for hospice, and 20.1 percent for psychiatric units.

Portions of these increases may be due to closure of hospitals that did not offer these services, but sizeable portions are related to hospitals' expansion into these services over time. The number of hospitals declined by only 5.5 percent during that time (see Table 4.1), and the percentages of growth for all these services exceed that 5.5 percent by large margins, reflecting the introduction of services between 1992 and 1998.

In 1992, hospitals in non-metropolitan counties containing a city of 10,000 population were considerably more likely to provide home health care, hospice services, or an inpatient psychiatric unit than hospitals in the three county categories without a city. Between 1992 and 1998, however, the percentages of hospitals in the other three categories that offered each service grew at high rates, resulting in a "closing of the gap" between hospitals in counties with cities and those in other categories of counties. Yet some differences still remain, most noticeably for the percentage of hospitals having psychiatric inpatient units.

The hospitals in frontier counties were similar to other non-metropolitan hospitals in the extent to which they offered home health care, but considerably smaller percentages of frontier

- 61 -

county hospitals offered hospice services or had inpatient psychiatric units. In particular, only 1.1 percent of hospitals in frontier counties had inpatient psychiatric units in 1992, and the percentage increased to only 1.6 percent by 1998. Only 7.8 percent of frontier county hospitals offered hospice services in 1992, but the percentage increased by 141.0 percent so that, by 1998, an estimated 18.8 percent of these hospitals offered hospice services.

Table 4.8
Non-Metropolitan Hospitals Offering Selected Services, by County Category, Selected Years

County Category	% of Hospitals Providing a Service				% Change 1992–1998
	1992	1994	1996	1998	
Home health care					
All non-metropolitan hospitals	46.1%	49.5%	53.9%	58.1%	26.0%
By non-metropolitan category					
Adjacent, city 10,000+	53.6	56.8	62.7	66.4	23.9
Adjacent, no city 10,000+	40.6	44.7	48.8	53.5	31.8
Remote, city 10,000+	52.9	56.2	58.5	61.3	15.9
Remote, town 2,500–10,000	45.7	49.5	53.7	57.6	26.0
Remote, no town	42.0	42.9	49.0	54.9	30.7
Frontier counties	41.3	43.0	51.8	57.8	40.0
Hospice services					
All non-metropolitan hospitals	23.2%	27.4%	33.0%	36.1%	55.6
By non-metropolitan category					
Adjacent, city 10,000+	34.8	39.0	42.8	43.8	25.9
Adjacent, no city 10,000+	20.7	26.0	33.4	36.2	74.9
Remote, city 10,000+	32.9	38.2	42.4	43.5	32.2
Remote, town 2,500–10,000	19.9	22.3	28.1	33.0	65.8
Remote, no town	9.9	14.6	19.9	23.4	136.4
Frontier counties	7.8	11.9	15.9	18.8	141.0
Inpatient psychiatric unit					
All non-metropolitan hospitals	12.0%	14.5%	17.4%	20.1%	67.5
By non-metropolitan category					
Adjacent, city 10,000+	24.6	30.1	33.1	37.1	50.8
Adjacent, no city 10,000+	7.0	8.9	12.2	13.8	97.1
Remote, city 10,000+	26.6	30.0	33.4	35.7	34.2
Remote, town 2,500–10,000	6.5	8.2	11.4	13.5	107.7
Remote, no town	1.9	2.9	3.6	7.7	305.3
Frontier counties	1.1	1.1	1.1	1.6	45.5

SOURCES: Medicare Provider of Service Files, Medicare Provider Specific Files, Area Resource File.

Hospitals in Rural Underserved Areas

In this discussion, we examine the distribution of non-metropolitan hospitals, and the services they provide, on the basis of location in areas with shortages of primary care providers, as defined by MUA and HPSA designations. Location in a designated shortage area is not required for hospitals to qualify for any of the Medicare special payment provisions for inpatient services. However, access to care for beneficiaries residing in shortage areas is affected by the extent to which hospitals are located in these areas and the mix of services they offer.

Counts of non-metropolitan hospitals by location in MUA and HPSA counties, reported in Table 4.9, reveal differences in the availability of hospitals in MUAs and HPSAs. In 1997, more than 45 percent of hospitals were in counties designated as whole-county MUAs, whereas only 19 percent of hospitals were in whole-county HPSAs. By comparison, 22 percent of hospitals were in counties with no MUA designation, while close to 40 percent were in counties with no HPSA designation.

Differences also are found in trends for the numbers of hospitals between 1993 and 1997. For MUAs, hospital supply in MUAs declined at rates similar to the decline in counties without MUA designation. For HPSAs, hospital supply in partial-county HPSAs increased by 3.5 percent whereas supply in both whole-county HPSAs and counties with no HPSA designation decreased (by 6.5 percent and 8.4 percent, respectively). The HPSA designations changed over time, and these results suggest that counties with partial-county HPSAs designated between 1993 and 1997 had more hospitals than did counties with previously existing partial-county HPSAs.

Table 4.9
Distribution of All Short-Term Hospitals in Non-Metropolitan Counties,
by Shortage Area Designation, 1993 and 1997

County Category	1993	1997	% Change 1993–1997
All non-metropolitan hospitals	2,319	2,238	−3.5%
By MUA designation			
Number of hospitals			
Not MUA	513	499	−2.7
Whole-county MUA	1,065	1,020	−4.2
Partial-county MUA	741	719	−3.0
Percentage of hospitals			
Not MUA	22.1%	22.3%	0.9
Whole-county MUA	45.9	45.6	−0.7
Partial-county MUA	32.0	32.1	0.3
By HPSA designation			
Number of hospitals			
Not HPSA	976	894	−8.4
Whole-county HPSA	462	432	−6.5
Partial-county HPSA	881	912	3.5
Percentage of hospitals			
Not HPSA	42.1%	39.9%	−5.2
Whole-county HPSA	19.9	19.3	−3.0
Partial-county HPSA	38.0	40.8	7.4

SOURCES: Medicare Provider of Service Files, Medicare Provider Specific Files, Area Resource File.

NOTE: Hospital counts differ from those for county categories because ARF data on MUA and HPSA designations were not available for some counties where hospitals are located, so a small number of hospitals had to be dropped from the analysis.

For both rural MUAs and HPSAs, hospitals in the whole-county shortage areas had substantially fewer beds, on average, than did hospitals in counties with partial-county shortage areas or hospitals in counties with no designation. As shown in Table 4.10, hospitals in whole-county MUAs had an average of 68 Medicare-certified beds in 1993, and they still had that level of certified beds in 1997. Bed sizes were yet smaller for whole-county HPSAs, where hospitals had an average of 52 certified beds in 1993, decreasing to 49 beds in 1997. Only hospitals in counties with partial-county HPSAs diverged from the overall trend of declining bed size between 1993 and 1997, increasing 8 percent from an average of 75 to 81 certified beds.

As discussed above, the average staffing of non-metropolitan hospitals increased visibly over time despite fairly stable levels of certified beds (see Table 4.6). Within the MUA designations, the highest rate of increase was an 11.1 percent increase in staff FTEs for hospitals in whole-county MUAs (see Table 4.10). For the HPSA designations, the highest rate was a 15.4 percent staffing increase for hospitals in counties with partial-county HPSAs. Staffing did not increase at hospitals in counties with no HPSA designation, although it increased by 7.5 percent for hospitals in non-MUA counties.

Table 4.10
Average Number of Certified Beds and Staffing for Short-Term Hospitals
in Non-Metropolitan Counties, by Shortage Area Designation, 1993 and 1997

County Category	1993	1997	% Change 1993–1997
Average number of beds			
All non-metropolitan hospitals	76	75	−1.3%
By MUA designation			
Not MUA	86	81	−5.8
Whole-county	68	68	0.0
Partial-county	92	90	−2.2
By HPSA designation			
Not HPSA	88	82	−6.8
Whole-county	52	49	−5.8
Partial-county	75	81	8.0
Average total staff FTEs			
All non-metropolitan hospitals	224	242	8.0
By MUA designation			
Not MUA	254	273	7.5
Whole-county	162	180	11.1
Partial-county	292	308	5.5
By HPSA designation			
Not HPSA	261	262	0.4
Whole-county	115	125	8.7
Partial-county	240	277	15.4

SOURCES: Medicare Provider of Service Files, Medicare Provider Specific Files, Area
Resource Files.

NOTES: Beds are Medicare-certified beds. FTEs are full-time equivalent staff
employed by a hospital, as reported in the Provider of Service files.

Hospitals in whole-county MUAs or whole-county HPSAs were less likely than other non-metropolitan hospitals to offer each of the selected services (home health, hospice, and organized inpatient psychiatric units), as shown in Table 4.11. From 1993 to 1997, the percentages of hospitals offering hospice services and psychiatric units grew more rapidly in the whole-county shortage areas than in counties with partial-county shortage areas or counties with no shortage designations, whereas the percentages offering home health care grew at similar rates. The growth from 1993 to 1997 was especially rapid for inpatient psychiatric units (78.6 percent for hospitals in whole-county MUAs and 163.5 percent for hospitals in whole-county HPSAs).

Table 4.11
Non-Metropolitan Hospitals Offering Selected Services,
by Shortage Area Designation, 1993 and 1997

County Category	% of Hospitals Providing a Service		% Change 1993–1997
	1993	1997	
Home health care			
All non-metropolitan hospitals	47.5%	56.1%	18.1%
By MUA designation			
Not MUA	54.2	63.9	17.9
Whole-county	43.0	50.8	18.1
Partial-county	49.3	58.3	18.3
By HPSA designation			
Not HPSA	52.3	62.8	20.1
Whole-county	41.6	48.1	15.6
Partial-county	45.3	53.4	17.9
Hospice services			
All non-metropolitan hospitals	25.1%	34.9%	39.0%
By MUA designation			
Not MUA	32.2	41.7	29.5
Whole-county	16.2	25.0	54.3
Partial-county	33.1	44.2	33.5
By HPSA designation			
Not HPSA	28.9	38.7	33.9
Whole-county	13.6	24.3	78.7
Partial-county	27.0	36.2	34.1
Inpatient psychiatric unit			
All non-metropolitan hospitals	13.3%	18.9	42.1%
By MUA designation			
Not MUA	16.8	20.2	20.2
Whole-county	9.8	17.5	78.6
Partial-county	15.9	19.9	25.2
By HPSA designation			
Not HPSA	16.1	19.4	20.5
Whole-county	5.2	13.7	163.5
Partial-county	14.4	20.9	45.1

SOURCES: Medicare Provider of Service Files, Medicare Provider Specific Files, Area
       Resource File.

RURAL HOSPITALS WITH SPECIAL MEDICARE PAYMENT PROVISIONS

Over the years, federal legislation established a number of special Medicare payment provisions for hospitals in rural areas, with the goal of helping to retain a supply of viable rural health care hospitals. The special Medicare payment methods reimburse specific types of hospitals more favorably for services to Medicare beneficiaries, where payments under the Prospective Payment System may not be sufficient to cover their costs. (Refer to Section 1 and Appendix A for a summary of eligibility requirements and payment methods for these special payment programs.)

We profile here the hospitals in non-metropolitan counties that have qualified for special payments during the 1990s, including the number of hospitals in each payment group, their characteristics, and the types of rural counties in which they are located. Table 4.12 gives basic information on the number of hospitals with each Medicare special payment designation for 1992 through 1998, as well as hospitals that are reclassified for an urban wage index for prospective payment calculation. The table also shows the rates of change during this period in the numbers of hospitals with each designation or reclassification. Indian Health Service hospitals are included in this list because the code that defines the special payment designations also identifies these facilities, but we do not focus on them in our comparative analyses.

Table 4.12
Number of Hospitals in Non-Metropolitan Counties,
by Medicare Special Payment Designation, Selected Years

Payment Designation	1992	1994	1996	1998	% Change 1992–1998
All non-metropolitan hospitals	2,357	2,303	2,288	2,227	
No special designation	1,066	1,485	1,423	1,377	29.2%
Sole community hospital	524	596	621	635	21.2
Rural referral center	189	144	103	95	−49.7
Indian Health Service hospital	33	36	35	35	6.1
SCH and RRC	43	36	39	37	−14.0
Medicare-dependent hospital	501	4	51	38	−92.4
EACH	na	na	4	9	na
EACH and RRC	na	na	4	1	na
Other	1	2	8	0	−100.0
Reclassified hospitals	609	691	265	282	−53.7

SOURCES: Medicare Provider of Service Files, Medicare Provider Specific Files, Area Resource File.

NOTES: Reclassified hospitals are hospitals paid under PPS using a wage index for a nearby MSA. Hospitals can also be reclassified for standardized amounts and those with reclassification may or may not also have a special designation.

Changes in the number of hospitals with each designation reflect legislative changes regarding each Medicare special payment provision. For example, special payments for Medicare dependent hospitals terminated after October 1, 1994, but were renewed in October 1997. These changes are not accurately reflected in counts of these facilities in 1994 and 1996 obtained from the PSF data. The data indicate a virtual absence of Medicare-dependent hospitals for 1994, when they were still in operation; similarly, hospitals are identified in 1996, when the program had not yet been reestablished by the BBA. The time of year when hospital status was coded in the PSF could have affected these counts, e.g., the 1994 counts of MDHs would be very low if the status was updated at the end of the year after the program terminated. Given these discrepancies, we report trend data only for 1992 and 1998 for the Medicare-dependent hospitals. In addition, the EACH/RPCH program became operational in the mid-1990s, so hospitals with EACH or EACH/rural referral center designations are found only in 1996 and 1998.

Hospitals with Special Payment Designations

Profiles of the characteristics of non-metropolitan hospitals that received special Medicare payment designations during the 1990s are explored in this analysis: ownership, service capacity as measured by bed counts and total staffing, and provision of selected services. Trends in hospital ownership mix by Medicare payment designation are presented in Table 4.13 for the major groups of special payment hospitals. Within each hospital group, we report the percentages of hospitals by type of ownership, which sum to 100 percent across each row in the table. We excluded EACHs and EACH/rural referral centers because there are few hospitals in these two groups. Indian Health Service hospitals also are excluded because they are federal government facilities that did not vary in ownership over time.

Substantial differences are found among the hospital special payment groups in mix of ownership. Overall, rural referral centers and SCH/rural referral centers have a similar ownership mix, which differs in several ways from the ownership of the other hospital groups. Larger percentages of hospitals in these two groups are not-for-profit facilities, and smaller percentages are owned by a local government or a hospital district or authority. Furthermore, these are the only groups for which the percentage of for-profit ownership increased between 1992 and 1998, accompanied by a marked decline in the percentage of hospitals owned by local governments. For the SCH/rural referral centers, the percentage of not-for-profit hospitals also declined.

As discussed above, growing percentages of non-metropolitan hospitals were owned by hospital districts or authorities during the 1990s. Judging by the information in Table 4.13, this ownership shift appeared to have occurred primarily for the sole community hospitals, SHC/rural referral centers, and Medicare-dependent hospitals.

Table 4.13
Distribution of Ownership of Non-Metropolitan Hospitals,
by Medicare Special Payment Designation, 1992, 1995, and 1998

Payment Designation and Year	% of Hospitals by Type of Ownership				
	Voluntary Nonprofit	For-profit	Government— Federal, State	Government— Local	Hospital District or Authority
No special payment hospitals					
1992	46.1	10.1	1.4	23.6	18.8
1995	48.4	9.3	1.1	23.0	18.2
1998	48.3	8.4	0.8	24.2	18.3
Sole community hospital					
1992	51.9	4.2	1.7	22.0	20.2
1995	48.9	3.5	1.7	22.3	23.6
1998	49.0	3.8	1.3	22.4	23.5
Rural referral center					
1992	69.8	6.9	0.5	14.3	8.5
1995	68.1	11.5	0.6	13.4	6.4
1998	67.4	12.6	1.1	10.5	8.4
SCHs and RRCs					
1992	76.7	4.7	0	11.6	7.0
1995	70.9	9.1	0	12.7	7.3
1998	70.3	10.8	0	8.1	10.8
Medicare-dependent hospital					
1992	42.3	4.6	0.2	33.5	19.4
1995	na	na	na	na	na
1998	47.4	2.6	0	26.3	23.7

SOURCES: Medicare Provider of Service Files, Medicare Provider Specific Files, Area Resource File.
NOTE: The percentages sum to 100 percent across each row.

Differences in hospital capacity across the hospital special payment groups, presented in Table 4.14, are consistent with the types of payment designations. Rural referral centers and SCH/rural referral centers have much larger capacities, measured by either the average number of certified beds or by total staffing, than other non-metropolitan hospitals including hospitals with no special designation (the "no special payment" group). Sole community hospitals, Indian Health Service hospitals, and Medicare-dependent hospitals have smaller capacities than hospitals with no special designation.

There was little change in average number of certified beds for any of the hospital groups between 1992 and 1998, but the groups varied in the size of increases in average total staff FTEs. The SCH/rural referral centers had a 38.5 percent increase in staffing, the largest increase of all the groups. By contrast, staffing at Indian Health Service hospitals rose by only 2.9 percent.

Table 4.14
Average Number of Certified Beds and Staffing for Short-Term Hospitals in Non-Metropolitan Counties, by Medicare Special Payment Designation, Selected Years

Payment Designation	1992	1994	1996	1998	% Change 1992–1998
Average number of beds					
No special designation	71	66	70	71	0.0%
Sole community hospital	54	56	56	58	7.4
Rural referral center	221	226	223	221	0.0
Indian Health Service hospital	42	41	41	41	–2.4
SCH and RRC	211	223	210	214	1.4
Medicare-dependent hospital	42	na	na	38	–9.5
EACH	na	na	115	121	—
Average total staff FTEs					
No special designation	184	179	208	215	16.8%
Sole community hospital	159	185	189	204	28.3
Rural referral center	744	772	797	925	24.3
Indian Health Service hospital	136	141	140	140	2.9
SCH and RRC	749	851	1,055	1,037	38.5
Medicare-dependent hospital	92	na	na	92	0.0
EACH	na	na	342	398	—

SOURCES: Medicare Provider of Service Files, Medicare Provider Specific Files, Area Resource File.

NOTES: Beds are certified beds. FTEs are full-time equivalent staff employed by a hospital, as reported in the Provider of Service files.

In addition to having substantial service capacity, the RRCs and SCH/rural referral centers were more likely than other non-metropolitan hospitals to offer home health care, hospice services, and inpatient psychiatric units during the 1990s, as reported in Table 4.15. The SCH/rural referral centers introduced home health and hospice services later than the RRCs that were not SCHs did, as shown by the noticeably higher percentages of RRCs offering these services in 1992. By 1998, the percentages offering the services were similar for the two groups. On the other hand, larger percentages of the SCH/rural referral centers than RRCs had inpatient psychiatric units in 1992. Percentages of hospitals with psychiatric units increased for both groups between 1992 and 1998 at similar rates, with the result that differences between them did not change over time.

For hospitals with no special payments and sole community hospitals, there was rapid growth in the percentage of hospitals providing home health care, hospice services, and inpatient psychiatric units between 1992 and 1998 (see Table 4.15). However, this growth only partially closed the gap with the percentages of RRCs offering these services. In particular, very small percentages of hospitals in these groups had psychiatric units in 1992, so that even after rapid rates of increase, the percentages with psychiatric units in 1998 were still modest.

Table 4.15
Non-Metropolitan Hospitals Offering Selected Services,
by Medicare Special Payment Designation, Selected Years

| Payment Designation | % of Hospitals Providing a Service | | | | % Change |
	1992	1994	1996	1998	1992–1998
Home health care					
No special designation	42.3%	46.1%	50.6%	55.3%	30.7%
Sole community hospital	49.4	53.3	58.4	62.8	27.1
Rural referral center	67.2	66.7	70.9	73.7	9.7
Indian Health Service hospital	39.4	36.1	37.1	37.1	–5.8
SCH and RRC	48.8	69.4	74.4	70.3	44.1
Medicare-dependent hospital	43.1	na	na	47.4	10.0
EACH	na	na	75.0	66.7	
Hospice services					
No special designation	22.9%	25.8%	32.9%	35.7%	55.9%
Sole community hospital	20.2	24.8	30.6	35.0	73.3
Rural referral center	49.2	53.5	51.5	57.9	17.7
Indian Health Service hospital	6.1	11.1	11.4	11.4	86.9
SCH and RRC	39.5	52.8	59.0	56.8	43.8
Medicare-dependent hospital	17.0	na	na	15.8	–7.1
EACH	na	na	0.0	33.3	
Psychiatric Unit					
No special designation	9.9%	11.4%	16.0%	19.2%	93.9%
Sole community hospital	8.4	10.2	12.1	13.9	65.5
Rural referral center	48.1	52.8	59.2	63.2	31.4
Indian Health Service hospital	0.0	0.0	0.0	0.0	0.0
SCH and RRC	55.8	75.0	69.2	73.0	30.8
Medicare-dependent hospital	3.8	na	na	15.8	315.8
EACH	na	na	25.0	11.1	

SOURCES: Medicare Provider of Service Files, Medicare Provider Specific Files, Area Resource File.

Hospitals Reclassified for Urban Wage Index

Reclassification of non-metropolitan hospitals to allow them to be paid on the basis of an urban wage index is another important special payment provision for these facilities.[15] According to data in the Provider Specific Files, 25.8 percent of all non-metropolitan hospitals were reclassified in 1992, and the percentages declined to 12.2 percent in 1995 and 12.7 percent in 1998, as shown in Table 4.16. By 2000, 19.9 percent of hospitals had wage index reclassifications (refer to Table 1.2), a substantial increase from the intervening years. The declines in reclassifications appear to be related to policy changes that established more structured criteria for reclassifications. Rates of wage index reclassifications vary by category of non-metropolitan county (see Table 4.16). As expected, given the design of the reclassification

---

[15] We did not perform a similar analysis for hospitals reclassified for standardized amounts because, as of FY1995, rural hospitals and "other urban" hospitals were paid the same standardized amount. However, according to CMS records (65 FR, August 1, 2000), some hospitals continued to be reclassified to "other urban" status to obtain higher DSH payments, and others sought to qualify for the higher urban standardized amount.

policy, the largest percentages of reclassified hospitals are in counties adjacent to MSAs and remote counties containing a city of 10,000 population. Only small percentages of hospitals in the more remote counties or frontier counties are reclassified.

Table 4.16
Non-Metropolitan Hospitals Reclassified for Urban Wage Index,
by County Category, 1992, 1995, and 1998

County Category	Number of Reclassified Hospitals			% of Hospitals in Category		
	1992	1995	1998	1992	1995	1998
All non-metropolitan hospitals	609	280	282	25.8%	12.2%	12.7%
By county category						
Adjacent, city 10,000+	192	105	105	48.7	27.3	28.2
Adjacent, no city 10,000+	193	71	59	28.9	10.9	9.3
Remote, city 10,000+	118	64	73	33.7	18.9	22.1
Remote, town 2,500–10,000	87	33	37	13.7	5.3	6.1
Remote, no town	19	7	8	6.1	2.3	2.8
Frontier counties	29	12	7	10.3	4.3	2.7

SOURCES: Medicare Provider of Service Files, Medicare Provider Specific Files, Area Resource File.
NOTES: Reclassified hospitals are hospitals paid under PPS using wage indices for a nearby MSA. These do not include hospitals that were reclassified for standardized amount.

The number and percentages of non-metropolitan hospitals with wage index reclassifications are reported in Table 4.17, listed by special payment designation. Declines in reclassification rates between 1992 and 1995 are found for all hospital groups. RRCs and SCH/rural referral centers had the largest percentages of reclassifications in 1992, 1995, and 1998. An estimated 70.9 percent of RRCs were reclassified in 1992, decreasing to 46.3 percent in 1998. Somewhat smaller percentages are found for the SCH/rural referral centers. For hospitals with no special designation, 25.4 percent had wage index reclassifications in 1992, declining to 12.4 percent in 1998. SCHs had a similar reclassification rate of 22.0 percent in 1992, but the percentage declined more sharply to 8.7 percent by 1998.

Table 4.17
Non-Metropolitan Hospitals Reclassified for Urban Wage Index,
by Medicare Special Payment Designation, 1992, 1995, and 1998

Payment Designation	Number of Reclassified Hospitals			% of Hospitals in Group		
	1992	1995	1998	1992	1995	1998
No special designation	271	139	170	25.4%	13.4%	12.4%
Sole community hospital	115	46	55	22.0	7.6	8.7
Rural referral center	134	60	44	70.9	38.2	46.3
SCH and RRC	27	18	11	62.8	32.7	29.7
Medicare-dependent hospital	61	na	0	12.2	na	0

SOURCES: Medicare Provider of Service Files, Medicare Provider Specific Files, Area Resource File.
NOTES: Reclassified hospitals are hospitals paid under PPS using wage indices for a nearby MSA. Reclassifications for EACHs and EACH/rural referral centers are not reported because the number of hospitals in each group is small.

Regional differences in wage index reclassifications for non-metropolitan hospitals wcrc moderate, as shown in Table 4.18. In 1992, reclassification rates ranged from 15.9 percent (Denver region) to 38.0 percent (Chicago region). Similar ranges in rates occurred in 1995 and 1998, although at substantially lower percentages of reclassification. The Boston and New York regions experienced the sharpest decline in reclassification rates between 1992 and 1998. By contrast, only the Denver region saw little decline in reclassification rates during that period.

Table 4.18
Non-Metropolitan Hospitals Reclassified for Urban Wage Index,
by HHS Region, 1992, 1995, and 1998

HHS Region	Number of Reclassified Hospitals			% of Hospitals in Group		
	1992	1995	1998	1992	1995	1998
1. Boston	18	4	4	27.7%	6.3%	6.5%
2. New York	16	5	3	37.2	12.8	8.3
3. Philadelphia	38	15	18	28.8	11.4	14.4
4. Atlanta	132	69	77	26.0	14.0	15.8
5. Chicago	158	64	63	38.0	16.0	16.1
6. Dallas	94	51	47	24.2	13.3	12.6
7. Kansas City	60	29	21	17.0	8.4	6.5
8. Denver	37	26	29	15.9	11.6	13.7
9. San Francisco	21	8	11	23.6	8.9	12.5
10. Seattle	35	9	9	27.1	7.1	7.2

SOURCES: Medicare Provider of Service Files, Medicare Provider Specific Files, Area Resource File.
NOTE: Reclassified hospitals are hospitals paid under PPS using wage indices for a nearby MSA.

INPATIENT USE AND SPENDING FOR NON-METROPOLITAN HOSPITALS

This subsection presents trends in Medicare fee-for-service inpatient stays for non-metropolitan hospitals, using MEDPAR claims data. We describe utilization and spending trends during the 1990s for inpatient hospital stays in non-metropolitan facilities. The number of inpatient stays, lengths of stay, total spending, and Medicare spending are tracked for selected calendar years. Distributions of inpatient stays for non-metropolitan hospitals also are provided by the most common DRGs, Medicare eligibility status, source of admission, and discharge destination. (Later in this section, we describe inpatient utilization for rural Medicare beneficiaries residing in non-metropolitan counties, and associated spending, including examination of use of rural and urban facilities and rural hospitals with special designations.)

Total Inpatient Stays

We begin by reporting the total Medicare inpatient stays for non-metropolitan hospitals and examining how those hospital stays are distributed by county category, by Medicare payment designation and by payment designation with county category. As shown in Table 4.19, non-metropolitan hospitals provided services for more than 2.1 million Medicare inpatient stays in 1992, which increased to 2.4 million stays in 1998. Approximately half of these stays were provided by hospitals in the two county categories adjacent to MSAs. Another quarter of the stays were provided by hospitals in remote counties that contained a city of 10,000 population. These distributions remained steady from 1992 to 1998.

Table 4.19
Distribution of Inpatient Stays for Non-Metropolitan Hospitals,
by County Category, Selected Years

County Category	1992	1994	1996	1998
All inpatient stays	2,139,863	2,246,213	2,346,815	2,397,450
By county category				
Adjacent, city 10,000+	28.5%	28.3%	28.4%	28.2%
Adjacent, no city 10,000+	21.7	21.7	21.7	21.4
Remote, city 10,000+	26.6	26.7	26.8	27.1
Remote, town 2,500–10,000	18.7	18.7	18.6	18.7
Remote, no town	4.5	4.5	4.5	4.6
Frontier counties	2.8	2.9	2.8	2.8

SOURCES: MEDPAR data for the 100 percent beneficiary population, Medicare Provider of Service Files, Medicare Provider Specific Files, Area Resource File.

From Table 4.20, we find that the distributions of Medicare inpatient stays at non-metropolitan hospitals shifted over time across hospital categories by special Medicare payment designation. Between 1992 and 1998, inpatient stays at hospitals without special payment designation increased from 41.1 percent to 56.5 percent of total stays, reflecting the decline in RRC and MDH designations. At the same time, the share of inpatient stays served by SCHs increased from 15.0 percent to 20.6 percent of total stays, whereas the share for RRCs declined from 26.8 percent to 15.0 percent. Hospitals that were designated as both SCHs and RRCs accounted for only 5.7 percent of the stays provided by non-metropolitan hospitals, a percentage that remained steady from 1992 to 1998.

Table 4.20
Distribution of Inpatient Stays for Non-Metropolitan Hospitals,
by Medicare Payment Designation, Selected Years

Payment Designation	1992	1994	1996	1998
All inpatient stays	2,139,863	2,246,213	2,346,815	2,397,450
By hospital payment designation				
No special designation	41.2%	54.8%	58.2%	56.6%
Sole community hospital	15.0	18.3	19.3	20.7
Rural referral center	26.9	21.6	15.9	15.0
Indian Health Service hospital	0.2	0.3	0.3	0.3
SCH and RRC	5.7	5.0	5.5	5.7
Medicare-dependent hospital	11.0	na	na	0.7
EACH	na	na	0.3	0.7
EACH and RRC	na	na	0.5	0.3

SOURCES: MEDPAR data for the 100 percent beneficiary population, Medicare Provider of Service Files, Medicare Provider Specific Files, Area Resource File.

The mix of types of non-metropolitan hospitals utilized by Medicare beneficiaries for inpatient services varied widely across categories of hospital county locations. Percentage distributions of inpatient stays by hospital payment designation and county category are reported in Table 4.21, presenting a separate distribution for each of the five county categories and for frontier counties. The most notable result is for frontier counties, where in 1992, sole community hospitals accounted for 68.3 percent of inpatient stays provided by hospitals located in frontier counties, and only 16.3 percent of stays were provided by hospitals with no special designation. Percentages for 1998 were similar.

Within the different categories of non-metropolitan counties, shifts in shares of inpatient stays between sole community providers and rural referral centers occurred between 1992 and 1998 (see Table 4.21). In 1992, SCHs accounted for larger percentages of total inpatient stays for hospitals in the more remote counties, but for much smaller shares of stays for hospitals in counties with cities or adjacent to an MSA. By contrast, RRCs had larger shares of inpatient stays among hospitals in counties that contained at least one city of 10,000 population. By 1998, use of SCHs had increased, relative to other types of hospitals, in all of the five county categories, as measured by the percentages of total inpatient stays provided by SCHs. At the same time, percentages declined for RRCs.

Table 4.21
Distribution of Inpatient Stays for Non-Metropolitan Hospitals,
by Hospital Location and Medicare Payment Designation, 1992 and 1998

Payment Designation	Non-Metropolitan Category for Hospital County Location					
	Adjacent, City	Adjacent, No City	Remote, City	Remote, Town	Remote, No Town	Frontier County
1992						
Nonspecial designation	42.9%	53.3%	25.5%	49.8%	33.2%	16.6%
Sole community hospital	8.6	14.1	12.1	25.0	34.9	68.4
Rural referral center	37.0	12.0	47.0	6.2	0	0
Indian Health Service hospital	0.2	0.1	0.3	0.3	1.0	2.7
SCH and RRC	6.5	1.9	11.6	1.6	0	2.5
Medicare-dependent hospital	4.8	18.6	3.5	17.1	30.9	9.8
1998						
Nonspecial designation	63.6	69.3	37.5	61.6	56.3	16.7
Sole community hospital	12.9	19.7	18.9	31.3	39.1	74.2
Rural referral center	17.9	9.3	26.9	3.7	0.0	0.0
Indian Health Service hospital	0.2	0.1	0.4	0.5	0.9	4.3
SCH and RRC	5.0	1.1	13.6	1.8	0.0	0.0
Medicare-dependent hospital	0.4	0.5	0.7	1.1	3.7	4.8

SOURCES: MEDPAR data for the 100 percent beneficiary population Medicare Provider of Service Files, Medicare Provider Specific Files, Area Resource File.

NOTE: Within each year, columns sum to 100 percent for each rural geographic designation and for frontier counties.

Individuals are eligible for Medicare benefits not only if they are aged 65 or older, but also if they are younger than 65 and permanently disabled or have end stage renal disease (ESRD). We examined the extent to which each of these groups is represented in the inpatient stays provided by non-metropolitan hospitals, the results of which are given in Table 4.22. Overall, for all non-metropolitan hospitals, the percentage of inpatient stays attributable to disabled beneficiaries increased from 9.8 percent in 1992 to 12.2 percent in 1998, and the percentage for ESRD beneficiaries went from 1.1 percent in 1992 to 1.3 percent in 1998.

Percentages of inpatient stays at RRCs were slightly larger for both disabled and ESRD beneficiaries, whereas percentages are slightly smaller for SCHs. These differences occur for all three years reported in the table.

Table 4.22
Distribution of Inpatient Stays at Non-Metropolitan Hospitals
for Disabled and ESRD Medicare Beneficiaries, by Medicare Payment Designation,
1992, 1995, and 1998

| | Stays as a Percentage of Total | | | | | |
| | 1992 | | 1995 | | 1998 | |
Payment Designation	Disabled	ESRD	Disabled	ESRD	Disabled	ESRD
All inpatient stays	9.8%	1.1%	11.3%	1.3%	12.2%	1.3%
By hospital payment designation						
No special designation	10.3	0.8	11.9	1.0	12.4	1.0
Sole community hospital	8.5	0.8	9.9	0.8	10.9	1.0
Rural referral center	10.8	2.0	12.2	2.4	13.0	2.4
Indian Health Service hospital	11.4	5.3	15.6	6.3	16.2	5.2
SCH and RRC	10.0	1.9	11.8	1.9	13.2	2.0
Medicare-dependent hospital	7.1	0.3	na	na	7.4	0.2
EACH	na	na	na	na	12.1	0.4
EACH and RRC	na	na	na	Na	12.5	2.1

SOURCES: MEDPAR data for the 100 percent beneficiary population, Medicare Provider of Service Files, Medicare Provider Specific Files, Area Resource File.

NOTE: ESRD category includes all ESRD beneficiaries, including those who also are aged or disabled.

Utilization by Type of Inpatient Stay

In the following tables, we explore how non-metropolitan hospitals with special Medicare payment designations may differ according to several measures of the delivery of inpatient services. First we compare the hospital groups according to source of admission, type of admission, and discharge destination.[16] Then we look at differences in case mix, as measured by the DRGs used to establish PPS payments for the inpatient services provided.

Percentage distributions of Medicare inpatient stays by source of admission for 1992 and 1998 are presented in Table 4.23, comparing hospitals with no special designation, sole community hospitals, rural referral centers, SCH/RRCs, and Medicare-dependent hospitals. Although some obvious differences in trends are observed for the different types of hospitals, we are cautious in interpreting these trends because they may be due to data accuracy and coding changes as much as (or more than) actual changes in practices.

---

[16] CMS staff caution that data for the sources and types of admissions on the MEDPAR claims are not as accurate as other data elements on these records, especially during the early 1990s. In addition, coding changes were made for these data elements during the time period of this study.

Table 4.23
Distribution of Inpatient Stays for Non-Metropolitan Hospitals,
by Source of Admission and Medicare Payment Designation, 1992 and 1998

Source of Admission	No Special Designation	Sole Community Hospital	Rural Referral Center	SCH and RRC	Medicare-Dependent Hospital
1992					
Physician referral	47.1%	44.4%	47.0%	46.7%	49.0%
Clinic referral	1.1	1.6	2.0	2.4	3.1
Transfer from another hospital	0.4	0.4	2.0	2.4	0.4
Emergency room	48.8	52.0	45.7	46.5	43.8
Other	2.2	1.5	2.8	1.4	3.6
Information not available	0.3	0.1	0.6	0.7	0.1
1998					
Physician referral	45.1	20.1	15.1	41.2	53.6
Clinic referral	1.5	14.5	22.0	1.5	2.3
Transfer from another hospital	1.0	13.0	31.1	3.2	0.3
Emergency room	50.6	53.2	47.2	51.9	40.1
Other	1.7	1.5	2.5	2.2	3.8
Information not available	0.1	<0.0	0.1	<0.0	<0.1

SOURCES: MEDPAR data for the 100 percent beneficiary population, Medicare Provider of Service
Files, Medicare Provider Specific Files, Area Resource File.

In 1992, physician referrals and the emergency room were the most important sources of admissions for all hospital designations, together accounting for greater than 95 percent of hospital stays (see Table 4.23). By 1998, however, the percentage of referrals from physicians appeared to decline for SCHs and RRCs, accompanied by increases for clinic referrals and transfers from other hospitals. In particular, for RRCs, reported transfers from other hospitals rose from 2.0 percent of total stays in 1992 to 31.1 percent of stays in 1998. It is not clear whether these differences are real or the result of changes in coding on the inpatient claims. Some of the change may be due to increased referrals to EACHs from RPCHs.

Modest differences are found in the mix of inpatient stays by type of admission for non-metropolitan hospitals with different payment designations, according to percentage distributions given in Table 4.24. In both 1992 and 1998, urgent admissions were the source of larger percentages of total inpatient stays for Medicare dependent hospitals than for hospitals with other designations. Within each payment designation category, there was little change in distributions of stays by type of admission between 1992 and 1998, with the exception of Medicare-dependent hospitals, for which the percentage of emergency admissions declined and the percentage of elective admissions increased.

Table 4.24
Distribution of Inpatient Stays for Non-Metropolitan Hospitals,
by Type of Admission and Medicare Payment Designation, 1992 and 1998

Type of Admission	No Special Designation	Sole Community Hospital	Rural Referral Center	SCH and RRC	Medicare-Dependent Hospital
1992					
Emergency	45.1%	43.8%	44.4%	45.2%	34.8%
Urgent	41.5	41.8	35.4	35.2	53.1
Elective	13.2	14.3	20.1	19.3	11.9
Not known	0.2	0.1	0.1	0.0	0.2
1998					
Emergency	45.1	43.9	42.0	44.9	20.4
Urgent	36.9	37.9	33.7	32.4	51.8
Elective	17.8	17.9	23.5	22.7	22.9
Not known	0.2	0.2	0.8	<0.1	5.0

SOURCES: MEDPAR data for the 100 percent beneficiary population, Medicare Provider of Service Files, Medicare Provider Specific Files, Area Resource File.

In Table 4.25, we present distributions of inpatient stays for non-metropolitan hospitals according to discharge destination, again comparing distributions for hospitals with different payment designations. The majority of discharges from hospitals with all designations in both 1992 and 1998 were to home or self care. However, a shift occurred between 1992 and 1998 toward larger percentages of inpatient stays discharged to a skilled nursing facility, and a similar but smaller shift was found for discharges to a home health agency. These changes cut across all hospital groups. Medicare-dependent hospitals differed from hospitals with other payment designations, in that relatively more of their discharges went to skilled nursing or intermediate care facilities.

Table 4.25
Distribution of Inpatient Stays for Non-Metropolitan Hospitals,
by Discharge Destination and Medicare Payment Designation, 1992 and 1998

Discharge Destination	No Special Designation	Sole Community Hospital	Rural Referral Center	SCH and RRC	Medicare-Dependent Hospital
1992					
Home/self care	62.3%	63.3%	66.9%	66.6%	57.2%
Other short-term hospital	6.1	6.4	3.5	3.8	7.1
Skilled nursing facility	10.1	10.6	8.4	8.8	11.7
Intermediate care facility	5.4	5.5	4.5	3.4	9.9
Another institution	1.8	1.5	2.4	2.5	1.5
Home health agency	8.1	6.5	8.1	8.8	6.3
Died	5.6	5.5	5.8	5.5	5.7
Other	0.6	0.6	0.6	0.6	0.5
1998					
Home/self care	56.9	57.5	58.8	60.4	53.3
Other short-term hospital	6.4	6.9	3.5	4.3	6.9
Skilled nursing facility	15.8	15.3	14.8	13.5	23.6
Intermediate care facility	5.1	4.9	3.5	3.0	9.8
Another institution	2.9	2.3	3.7	4.1	0.9
Home health agency	8.2	8.3	10.7	9.7	1.7
Died	4.4	4.3	4.6	4.4	3.7
Other	0.5	0.4	0.4	0.5	0.3

SOURCES: MEDPAR data for the 100 percent beneficiary population, Medicare Provider of Service Files, Medicare Provider Specific Files, Area Resource File.

In the next two tables, we summarize average DRG weights for inpatient stays at non-metropolitan hospitals, which are measures of the relative complexity and costliness of inpatient stays for Medicare beneficiaries. Table 4.26 gives average DRG weights for hospitals grouped by non-metropolitan county category. For comparison, the 1999 regional case mix indexes for urban hospitals ranged from 1.18 to 1.32. Hospitals in the two county categories with a city of 10,000 population had the highest average DRG weights, which exceeded 1.20 in all years. DRG weights were more moderate for hospitals in counties adjacent to an MSA without a city (1.13 in 1992) and in remote counties with a town (1.11 in 1992). Hospitals in the more remote counties and frontier counties had the lowest DRG weights (1.01 and 1.04 in 1992, respectively). DRG weights for all categories of non-metropolitan hospitals increased slightly between 1992 and 1998. Overall DRG weights for non-metropolitan hospitals remained steady from 1992 to 1998 at average weights ranging from 1.19 in 1992 to 1.23 in 1996 (see Table 4.26).

Case mix varied across hospitals with different Medicare payment designations, as shown in Table 4.27. Rural referral centers had the highest case mix, with average DRG weights of 1.32 in 1992 and 1.39 in 1998. Hospitals that were both SCHs and RRCs had similarly high average DRG weights. Sole community hospitals had average DRG weights similar to those for hospitals for no special designation. Medicare-dependent hospitals and Indian Health Service hospitals had the lowest average case mix. Average DRG weights increased slightly over time only for the RRCs and SCH/rural referral centers.

Table 4.26
Average DRG Weights for Non-Metropolitan Hospitals,
by County Category and Frontier County Status, Selected Years

County Category	1992	1994	1996	1998
All non-metropolitan hospitals	1.19	1.20	1.23	1.21
By county category				
Adjacent, city 10,000+	1.23	1.25	1.27	1.25
Adjacent, no city 10,000+	1.13	1.15	1.17	1.15
Remote, city 10,000+	1.27	1.29	1.33	1.31
Remote, town 2,500–10,000	1.11	1.12	1.15	1.12
Remote, no town	1.01	1.02	1.03	1.05
Frontier counties	1.04	1.05	1.07	1.06

SOURCES: MEDPAR data for the 100 percent beneficiary population and Medicare DRG weight files, Medicare Provider of Service Files, Medicare Provider Specific Files, Area Resource File.

Table 4.27
Average DRG Weights for Non-Metropolitan Hospitals,
by Medicare Payment Designation, Selected Years

Payment Designation	1992	1994	1996	1998
No special designation	1.14	1.15	1.19	1.17
Sole community hospital	1.14	1.15	1.18	1.16
Rural referral center	1.32	1.35	1.42	1.39
Indian Health Service hospital	0.98	0.97	0.98	0.99
SCH and RRC	1.31	1.33	1.34	1.33
Medicare-dependent hospital	1.07	na	na	1.06
EACH	na	na	1.14	1.14
EACH and RRC	na	na	1.31	1.26

SOURCES: MEDPAR data for the 100 percent beneficiary population and Medicare DRG weight files, Medicare Provider of Service Files, Medicare Provider Specific Files, Area Resource File.

Spending on Inpatient Care at Non-Metropolitan Hospitals

The utilization data discussed above translate into total spending and Medicare spending for inpatient care provided by non-metropolitan hospitals to Medicare beneficiaries. The total spending we report here is the amount received by a hospital, which is the sum of the amounts paid by Medicare, any primary payer, and the beneficiary for a hospital inpatient stay. The Medicare amount includes only the portion of the total payment for which Medicare was liable.

In Table 4.28, we report the average total spending and Medicare spending per inpatient stay for hospitals in non-metropolitan counties, comparing average payments across categories of counties. Overall, total spending increased from $4,624 per stay in 1992 to $5,087 per stay in 1998, a 10 percent increase. Medicare spending also increased over time from $4,034 in 1992 to $4,436 in 1998, remaining close to 87 percent of total spending in each year. Of note, there was a pronounced shift upward in average payments between 1994 and 1996, reflecting the final phase-out of a separate, lower standardized payment amount for hospitals in non-metropolitan counties.

Table 4.28
Average Total Spending and Medicare Spending per Inpatient Stay
for Beneficiaries at Non-Metropolitan Hospitals, by County Category, Selected Years

County Category	1992	1994	1996	1998
Total spending per stay				
All non-metropolitan hospitals	$4,624	$4,674	$5,040	$5,087
By county category				
Adjacent, city 10,000+	4,989	5,056	5,364	5,341
Adjacent, no city 10,000+	4,387	4,441	4,678	4,678
Remote, city 10,000+	5,044	5,124	5,604	5,714
Remote, town 2,500–10,000	4,023	4,013	4,438	4,434
Remote, no town	3,503	3,466	3,866	4,409
Frontier counties	4,060	4,124	4,417	4,542
Medicare spending per stay				
All non-metropolitan hospitals	4,034	4,065	4,415	4,436
By county category				
Adjacent, city 10,000+	4,384	4,429	4,720	4,675
Adjacent, no city 10,000+	3,825	3,855	4,077	4,068
Remote, city 10,000+	4,419	4,489	4,951	5,022
Remote, town 2,500–10,000	3,455	3,430	3,839	3,805
Remote, no town	2,980	2,919	3,306	3,809
Frontier counties	3,522	3,570	3,838	3,949

SOURCES: MEDPAR data for the 100 percent beneficiary population, Medicare
Provider of Service Files, Medicare Provider Specific Files, Area Resource
File.

Average Medicare spending per inpatient stay can be expected to vary across hospitals with different special payment designations because each type of hospital serves a unique role in delivering health care for rural areas. Actual Medicare spending per stay, reported in Table 4.29, is higher for RRCs and SCH/rural referral centers and lower for SCHs and Medicare-dependent hospitals. We also report estimates of average standardized spending per inpatient stay, based on a DRG weight equal to 1.0 (calculated as actual spending per stay divided by the average DRG weight). The overall standardized spending was lower than actual average spending, reflecting the downward adjustment from an average DRG weight for non-metropolitan hospitals of 1.20 to 1.00. Case mix was an important source of spending variation across hospital groups with special Medicare designations, as shown by the much smaller variation in standardized spending per stay compared to actual spending, as well as by the ratios in average spending relative to hospitals with no special designation.

Table 4.29
Average Medicare Spending per Inpatient Stay for Non-Metropolitan Hospitals,
Actual and Standardized for DRG Weight = 1, by Medicare Payment Designation, Selected Years

Payment Designation	Average Medicare Spending per Stay				Spending Ratios (1998)[a]
	1992	1994	1996	1998	
Actual spending per stay					
No special designation	$3,649	$3,663	$4,109	$4,130	1.00
Sole community hospital	3,887	3,966	4,303	4,358	1.06
Rural referral center	4,811	4,904	5,366	5,379	1.30
Indian Health Service hospital	3,861	4,210	4,441	4,582	1.11
SCH and RRC	5,034	5,216	5,383	5,439	1.32
Medicare-dependent hospital	3,258	na	na	3,623	0.88
All non-metropolitan hospitals	4,034	4,065	4,415	4,436	1.07
Standardized spending per stay (DRG weight = 1)					
No special designation	3,201	3,185	3,453	3,530	1.00
Sole community hospital	3,410	3,449	3,647	3,757	1.06
Rural referral center	3,645	3,633	3,779	3,815	1.08
Indian Health Service hospital	3,940	4,385	4,532	4,628	1.31
SCH and RRC	3,843	3,922	4,017	4,059	1.15
Medicare-dependent hospital	3,045	na	na	3,450	0.98
All non-metropolitan hospitals	3,390	3,388	3,589	3,666	1.04

SOURCES: MEDPAR data for the 100 percent beneficiary population, Medicare Provider of Service Files, Medicare Provider Specific Files, Area Resource File.

NOTE: Standardized Medicare spending per stay was calculated as a weighted average, where the weight was the inverse of the DRG weight for each stay.

[a]Ratio of 1998 average payment per stay for each hospital designation to "no special designation" hospitals.

INPATIENT USE AND SPENDING FOR RURAL MEDICARE BENEFICIARIES

All measures presented in this subsection are calculated on the basis of inpatient stays experienced by beneficiaries who lived in non-metropolitan counties. (Analyses in the above subsection focused on all inpatient stays in short-stay hospitals located in non-metropolitan counties.) This population-based approach is intended to gain a better understanding of the extent to which rural beneficiaries utilize inpatient services, where they obtain those services (hospital type, urban versus rural), and how utilization and spending vary across beneficiaries living in counties with differing levels of hospital supply in the county or nearby.

Rates of inpatient stays and average lengths of stay for beneficiaries in non-metropolitan counties are summarized in Table 4.30. Overall, there were 333 inpatient stays per 1,000 beneficiaries in 1992, which increased to 348 inpatient stays per 1,000 in 1998. On the other hand, average length of stay declined from 7.3 days to 5.6 days during this period.

Table 4.30
Hospitalization Rate and Average Length of Stay for Non-Metropolitan Beneficiaries, by County Category, Selected Years

County Category	1992 Stay Rate	1992 LOS	1994 Stay Rate	1994 LOS	1996 Stay Rate	1996 LOS	1998 Stay Rate	1998 LOS
All beneficiaries	333	7.3	343	6.6	345	5.9	348	5.6
By county category								
Adjacent, city 10,000+	323	7.6	331	6.8	335	6.0	335	5.7
Adjacent, no city 10,000+	335	7.4	341	6.7	344	5.9	345	5.6
Remote, city 10,000+	322	7.5	332	6.8	333	6.1	340	5.7
Remote, town 2,500–10,000	343	7.0	360	6.3	359	5.7	367	5.4
Remote, no town	352	6.9	367	6.2	370	5.6	374	5.3
Frontier counties	316	6.3	319	5.7	319	5.2	324	4.9

SOURCES: MEDPAR data for the 100 percent beneficiary population, Medicare Provider of Service Files, Medicare Provider Specific Files, Area Resource File.

NOTES: Hospital stay rates are measured as the number of inpatient stays per 1,000 Medicare beneficiaries residing in non-metropolitan counties. LOS is the average length of stay in days.

Hospitalization rates did not vary much across counties of differing degrees of rurality. For example, rates ranged from 322 to 352 inpatient stays per 1,000 beneficiaries in 1992 (a difference that is 9 percent of the average), and similar differences occurred in later years (see Table 4.30). Of note, beneficiaries living in the two categories of non-metropolitan counties with a city of 10,000 had somewhat lower inpatient use rates than those living in less urbanized counties.

The average total per capita spending for inpatient stays by beneficiaries in non-metropolitan counties, summarized in Table 4.31, increased from $1,881 per beneficiary in 1992 to $2,234 per beneficiary. Medicare spending per capita was a stable 89 percent of total spending for all years during the time period we examined. Differences in per capita spending for inpatient care across county categories were not large, nor were they consistent on the basis of their degree of rurality. For example, per capita spending for beneficiaries in the most remote non-metropolitan counties was lower than spending for beneficiaries in more urbanized counties in 1992, but it was higher in 1998.

Table 4.31
Total and Medicare Spending per Capita on Inpatient Hospital Services
for Non-Metropolitan Beneficiaries, by County Category, Selected Years

County Category	1992	1994	1996	1998
Total spending per stay				
All beneficiaries	$1,881	$1,993	$2,180	$2,234
By county category				
Adjacent, city 10,000+	1,931	2,047	2,210	2,224
Adjacent, no city 10,000+	1,919	2,017	2,209	2,255
Remote, city 10,000+	1,807	1,910	2,103	2,189
Remote, town 2,500–10,000	1,843	1,980	2,167	2,243
Remote, no town	1,842	1,956	2,190	2,265
Frontier counties	1,782	1,869	2,038	2,106
Medicare spending per stay				
All beneficiaries	1,667	1,766	1,948	1,989
By county category				
Adjacent, city 10,000+	1,718	1,820	1,979	1,986
Adjacent, no city 10,000+	1,704	1,791	1,979	2,014
Remote, city 10,000+	1,596	1,686	1,871	1,944
Remote, town 2,500–10,000	1,626	1,745	1,933	1,989
Remote, no town	1,629	1,727	1,952	2,015
Frontier counties	1,585	1,663	1,822	1,887

SOURCES: MEDPAR data for the 100 percent beneficiary population, Medicare Provider of Service Files, Medicare Provider Specific Files, Area Resource File.

NOTE: Spending is measured as total spending or Medicare spending per Medicare beneficiary residing in the relevant non-metropolitan counties.

Estimated spending per inpatient stay for beneficiaries in non-metropolitan counties is summarized in Table 4.32, including total spending and Medicare spending. Overall, total spending in 1992 for inpatient services to non-metropolitan beneficiaries was $5,657 per stay, which increased to $6,424 per stay in 1998. These amounts are larger than the average total spending per stay for services provided by non-metropolitan hospitals, which was $4,624 per stay in 1992 and $5,087 in 1998 (refer to Table 4.28). Thus, beneficiaries in non-metropolitan counties appear to be obtaining inpatient services from urban hospitals that are more costly than those provided by the local hospitals.

Table 4.32
Average Total and Medicare Spending per Inpatient Stay
for Non-Metropolitan Beneficiaries, by County Category, Selected Years

County Category	1992	1994	1996	1998
Total spending per stay				
All beneficiaries	$5,657	$5,817	$6,324	$6,424
By county category				
Adjacent, city 10,000+	5,977	6,176	6,598	6,644
Adjacent, no city 10,000+	5,735	5,918	6,415	6,534
Remote, city 10,000+	5,614	5,747	6,309	6,443
Remote, town 2,500–10,000	5,368	5,496	6,038	6,135
Remote, no town	5,233	5,324	5,924	6,052
Frontier counties	5,637	5,863	6,394	6,493
Medicare spending per stay				
All beneficiaries	5,015	5,153	5,651	5,721
By county category				
Adjacent, city 10,000+	5,320	5,493	5,907	5,933
Adjacent, no city 10,000+	5,096	5,257	5,747	5,836
Remote, city 10,000+	4,957	5,071	5,614	5,722
Remote, town 2,500–10,000	4,736	4,842	5,386	5,440
Remote, no town	4,628	4,700	5,280	5,382
Frontier counties	5,012	5,218	5,717	5,816

SOURCES: MEDPAR data for the 100 percent beneficiary population, Medicare Provider of Service Files, Medicare Provider Specific Files, Area Resource File.

Unlike the per capita spending for inpatient services, the average spending per stay was noticeably higher for beneficiaries living in counties adjacent to an MSA or containing a city of at least 10,000 population than for those in the more remote counties (see Table 4.32). However, total spending for beneficiaries in frontier counties was $5,637 per stay in 1992 and $6,493 in 1998, both of which were close to the overall average spending for all non-metropolitan beneficiaries. The Medicare spending per stay for non-metropolitan beneficiaries mirrors the total spending, at levels of 89 percent of total spending. Medicare spent $5,015 per stay for these beneficiaries in 1992 and $5,721 per stay in 1998.

In Table 4.33, we decompose the total hospitalization rates for non-metropolitan beneficiaries into the components attributable to hospitals with the various types of special Medicare payment designations. For example, of the 333 inpatient stays per 1,000 beneficiaries for 1992, 105 occurred in metropolitan hospitals, 93 occurred in non-metropolitan hospitals with no special payment designation, and 61 occurred in RRCs. Thus, in 1992, approximately 30 percent of hospital stays for non-metropolitan beneficiaries are in metropolitan hospitals, and 28 percent are in non-metropolitan hospitals with no special payment designation. The remaining 42 percent of stays were in hospitals with one or more special payment designations.

Table 4.33
Hospitalization Rates and Average Length of Stay for Non-Metropolitan Beneficiaries,
by Hospital Payment Designation, Selected Years

Payment Designation	1992	1994	1996	1998
Inpatient stays per 1,000				
All beneficiaries	333	343	345	348
By hospital designation				
No special designation	93	129	135	134
Sole community hospital	34	44	46	50
Rural referral center	61	51	38	36
Indian Health Service hospital	1	1	1	1
SCH and RRC	13	12	13	14
Medicare-dependent hospital	25	na	na	2
EACH	na	na	1	2
EACH and RRC	na	na	1	1
Non-certified rural hospital [a]	<1	<1	<1	1
Urban hospital	105	106	108	109
Average length of stay (days)				
All beneficiaries	7.3	6.6	5.9	5.6
By hospital designation				
No special designation	6.5	5.9	5.4	5.1
Sole community hospital	6.2	5.7	5.2	4.9
Rural referral center	7.7	7.0	6.2	5.8
Indian Health Service hospital	6.2	5.9	5.2	5.0
SCH and RRC	7.8	7.3	6.2	5.9
Medicare-dependent hospital	5.9	na	na	4.8
EACH	na	na	5.4	5.2
EACH and RRC	na	na	6.4	6.5
Non-certified rural hospital [a]	12.2	6.6	5.0	4.7
Metropolitan hospital	8.5	7.6	6.7	6.3

SOURCES: MEDPAR data for the 100 percent beneficiary population, Medicare Provider of Service Files, Medicare Provider Specific Files, Area Resource File.

NOTE: Hospitalization rate is the number of inpatient stays per 1,000 Medicare beneficiaries residing in non-metropolitan counties.

[a]The non-certified rural hospitals are not Medicare-certified but are used in emergencies.

The share of inpatient stays for beneficiaries in non-metropolitan areas that occurred in metropolitan hospitals did not change much between 1992 and 1998 (31 percent in 1998) (see Table 4.33). However, with the discontinuation of the designation of Medicare dependent hospitals by 1994, the percentage of inpatient stays in non-metropolitan hospitals with no special designations increased to greater than 38 percent and remained at that level through 1998.

The average length of stay for non-metropolitan beneficiaries who were hospitalized varied by the type of hospital in which the stays took place (see Table 4.33). Inpatient stays in urban hospitals were longer than those in non-metropolitan county hospitals. In addition, stays in rural referral centers were longer than those in other non-metropolitan hospitals. The inpatient stays shortened considerably between 1992 and 1998, a trend that affected all types of urban and rural hospitals.

The decomposition of Medicare spending per beneficiary, aggregated for all beneficiaries in non-metropolitan counties, is presented in Table 4.34. Although only 30 percent of inpatient stays took place in metropolitan hospitals (from Table 4.33), these stays accounted for 45.3 percent of Medicare spending for these beneficiaries in 1992 and 47.2 percent in 1998.[17] Medicare per capita spending for beneficiaries using non-metropolitan hospitals with no special designation also increased during the decade. For hospitals with special designations, spending for sole community hospitals increased, spending for SCH/RRCs did not change, and spending for rural referral centers declined. As a result, overall per capita spending for inpatient stays in these hospitals decreased from $570 per beneficiary in 1992 to $496 per beneficiary in 1998 (the sum of amounts is reported separately in Table 4.34).

Table 4.34
Average Medicare Spending per Capita on Inpatient Stays for Non-Metropolitan Beneficiaries, and Share of Spending, by Hospital Payment Designation, Selected Years

Payment Designation	1992		1994		1996		1998	
	Spending	%	Spending	%	Spending	%	Spending	%
All beneficiaries	$1,667	100.0	$1,766	100.0	$1,948	100.0	$1,989	100.0
By hospital designation								
No special designation	337	20.2	470	26.6	557	28.6	549	27.6
Sole community hospital	134	8.0	173	9.8	197	10.1	215	10.8
Rural referral center	290	17.4	247	14.0	201	10.3	191	9.6
Indian Health Service hospital	2	0.1	3	0.2	3	0.2	4	0.2
SCH and RRC	64	3.8	61	3.5	70	3.6	73	3.7
Medicare-dependent hospital	82	4.9	na	na	na	na	6	0.3
EACH	na	na	na	na	3	0.2	7	0.4
EACH and RRC	na	na	na	na	6	0.3	4	0.2
Other designation	2	0.1	<1	0.0	2	0.1	n/a	n/a
Non-certified rural	2	0.1	1	0.1	1	0.1	2	0.1
Metropolitan hospital	755	45.3	812	46.0	908	46.6	939	47.2

SOURCES: MEDPAR data for the 100 percent beneficiary population, Medicare Provider of Service Files, Medicare Provider Specific Files, Area Resource File.

NOTE: The non-certified rural hospitals are not Medicare-certified but are used in emergencies.

When we compare Medicare spending per inpatient stay versus spending per capita for beneficiaries in non-metropolitan areas, we observe quite distinct patterns of variations across types of hospital. Care provided by metropolitan hospitals clearly has increased the overall average spending per stay. As shown in Table 4.35, the average Medicare spending for inpatient stays in metropolitan hospitals is much higher than for stays in non-metropolitan hospitals,

---

[17] These results are consistent with other studies' finding that rural residents use urban hospitals for a substantial share of their inpatient care (Williamson et al., 1993; Rosenbach and Dayhoff, 1995; McNamara, 1998).

reflecting both higher case mix and urban payment provisions. Similarly, Medicare spending per stay at rural referral centers is higher than at other non-metropolitan hospitals. These patterns exist for each year between 1992 and 1998.

Table 4.35
Average Medicare Spending per Inpatient Stay for Non-Metropolitan Beneficiaries, by Hospital Payment Designation, Selected Years

Payment Designation	1992	1994	1996	1998
All inpatient stays	$5,015	$5,153	$5,651	$5,721
By hospital designation				
No special designation	3,622	3,627	4,083	4,092
Sole community hospital	3,877	3,965	4,311	4,343
Rural referral center	4,755	4,837	5,339	5,348
Indian Health Service hospital	3,804	4,155	4,382	4,476
SCH and RRC	5,007	5,188	5,365	5,416
Medicare-dependent hospital	3,241	na	na	3,614
EACH	na	na	3,679	3,945
EACH and RRC	na	na	5,267	5,260
Other designation	4,690	3,404	3,674	n/a
Non-certified rural hospital	3,665	3,281	3,497	3,573
Metropolitan hospital	7,221	7,651	8,401	8,585

SOURCES: MEDPAR data for the 100 percent beneficiary population, Medicare Provider of Service Files, Medicare Provider Specific Files, Area Resource File.

According to the results presented in Tables 4.9 through 4.11, the supply of hospitals and related services differed for whole-county MUAs and whole-county HPSAs. Whole-county MUAs had the largest supply of hospitals, but these hospitals were smaller and offered fewer services than hospitals in other counties did. Whole-county HPSAs had fewer and smaller hospitals. We examine here population-based measures of utilization of hospital inpatient services by Medicare beneficiaries residing in counties with shortages of primary care providers, identifying separately counties designated as either MUAs or HPSAs. Where differences are observed between inpatient utilization or spending for beneficiaries residing in shortage areas and beneficiaries in other non-metropolitan counties, such differences may be indicators of access issues. We examine trends in utilization first, followed by trends in spending per capita and spending per inpatient stay.

Some consistent variations in hospitalization rates are found for beneficiaries residing in shortage areas, and these differences are similar for MUAs and HPSAs. At the same time, average lengths of stay did not vary by category of shortage areas. As shown in Table 4.36, the 1993 hospitalization rates were 311 inpatient stays per 1,000 beneficiaries for beneficiaries in counties with no MUA designation, compared to 353 stays for those in whole-county MUAs and 318 stays for those in partial-county MUAs. A similar pattern was observed for HPSAs. Hospitalization rates increased for all beneficiaries between 1993 and 1997, regardless of shortage area designation, whereas average lengths of stay declined.

Table 4.36
Hospitalization Rate and Average Length of Stay for Non-Metropolitan Beneficiaries,
by Shortage Area, 1993, 1995, and 1997

Shortage Area	1993		1995		1997	
	Hospital Rate	LOS	Hospital Rate	LOS	Hospital Rate	LOS
All inpatient stays	332	7.0	343	6.2	351	5.7
By MUA designation						
Not MUA	311	6.8	316	6.0	321	5.5
Whole-county MUA	353	7.0	372	6.3	383	5.8
Partial-county MUA	318	7.0	324	6.2	329	5.7
By HPSA designation						
Not HPSA	336	7.0	344	6.2	359	5.7
Whole-county HPSA	354	7.0	372	6.3	378	5.8
Partial-county HPSA	316	7.0	329	6.2	333	5.7

SOURCES: MEDPAR data for the 100 percent beneficiary population, Medicare Provider of Service Files, Medicare Provider Specific Files, Area Resource File.

NOTES: Hospitalization rates are measured as number of inpatient stays per 1,000 Medicare beneficiaries residing in non-metropolitan counties. LOS is the average number of days per stay.

Trends in average total spending and Medicare spending per inpatient stay are reported in Table 4.37, with comparisons for beneficiaries residing in counties with shortage area designations and those in counties without such designation. For MUAs, spending per stay was lowest for beneficiaries in whole-county MUAs, and it was highest for those in counties without MUA designation. For HPSAs, spending also was lowest for beneficiaries in whole-county HPSAs. Lower spending per stay may be attributable to lower case mix, lower area wage index, fewer outlier cases, lower disproportionate share payments, fewer hospital with special Medicare payments, or combinations of these factors.

Per capita spending for inpatient services used by Medicare beneficiaries reflects the combined effects of hospitalization rates and spending per inpatient stay. Non-metropolitan counties designated as whole-county shortage areas had higher hospitalization rates than counties not designated as shortage areas, yet they also had lower spending per inpatient stay. These balancing effects are reflected in the average total spending and Medicare spending per beneficiary reported in Table 4.38, with shortage area comparisons. Compared with the higher hospitalization rates in whole-county MUAs and HPSAs, the differences in average per capita spending are smaller. Spending for beneficiaries in partial-county MUAs is virtually the same as that for beneficiaries in counties without MUA designation. The same is not true for partial-county HPSAs, however, where spending per beneficiary tends to be slightly lower than spending in counties without HPSA designation.

Table 4.37
Average Total and Medicare Spending per Inpatient Stay for Non-Metropolitan Beneficiaries, by Shortage Area, 1993, 1995, and 1997

Shortage Area	1993		1995		1997	
	Total	Medicare	Total	Medicare	Total	Medicare
All beneficiaries	$5,736	$5,074	$5,999	$5,330	$6,461	$5,782
By MUA designation						
Not MUA	5,938	5,261	6,254	5,572	6,754	6,052
Whole-county MUA	5,502	4,854	5,827	5,173	6,299	5,634
Partial-county MUA	5,938	5,266	6,093	5,412	6,523	5,837
By HPSA designation						
Not HPSA	5,718	5,055	5,957	5,290	6,398	5,715
Whole-county HPSA	5,520	4,872	5,832	5,179	6,379	5,720
Partial-county HPSA	5,879	5,211	6,125	5,446	6,554	5,869

SOURCES: MEDPAR data for the 100 percent beneficiary population, Medicare Provider of Service Files, Medicare Provider Specific Files, Area Resource File.

Table 4.38
Average Total and Medicare Spending per Capita on Inpatient Services for Non-Metropolitan Beneficiaries, by Shortage Area, 1993, 1995, and 1997

Shortage Area	1993		1995		1997	
	Total	Medicare	Total	Medicare	Total	Medicare
All beneficiaries	$1,904	$1,683	$2,058	$1,828	$2,267	$2,028
By MUA designation						
Not MUA	1,845	1,635	1,976	1,761	2,167	1,943
Whole-county MUA	1,944	1,715	2,166	1,922	2,411	2,156
Partial-county MUA	1,889	1,675	1,973	1,753	2,148	1,922
By HPSA designation						
Not HPSA	1,920	1,697	2,052	1,822	2,298	2,053
Whole-county HPSA	1,956	1,727	2,167	1,924	2,409	2,160
Partial-county HPSA	1,859	1,648	2,013	1,790	2,183	1,955

SOURCES: MEDPAR data for the 100 percent beneficiary population, Medicare Provider of Service Files, Medicare Provider Specific Files, Area Resource File.

ISSUES AND IMPLICATIONS

The information in this section covers a broad range of topics and issues regarding hospital inpatient services for Medicare beneficiaries in rural settings. Yet within the voluminous details, some key trends are identified that have implications for future Medicare payment policy for rural providers. These involve issues of both hospital supply and patterns of inpatient utilization by Medicare beneficiaries who reside in the less populated areas of our country.

Trends in Hospital Supply

From early in the decade of the 1990s, there was a gradual decline in the numbers of Medicare-certified hospitals serving counties outside MSAs. The declining trends varied, however, across geographic areas. Losses of non-metropolitan hospitals were greatest in the New York HHS region, and the Kansas City and Denver regions also had larger losses than other regions. The greatest losses also occurred in the most remote rural counties (those not adjacent to an MSA and without a town of at least 2,500 population), as well as in frontier counties (western counties with population densities equal to or less than six persons per square mile). As a result of these trends, there was in increase in the number of non-metropolitan counties that had no hospitals, as well as a decrease in the number of hospitals in counties with more than one hospital.

Despite the declining supply of non-metropolitan hospitals, the hospitals that continued to serve these areas showed signs of viability that are encouraging for the future. For example, increased staffing levels over time suggest that hospitals were operating at higher levels of operation than they were in the earlier years of the decade, although much of the increase could be for outpatient services rather than inpatient census. In addition, growing numbers of hospitals are offering home care and hospice services and have established organized psychiatric inpatient units, which should enhance access to these services for Medicare beneficiaries.

Geographic access to hospital services has been a chronic issue for beneficiaries living in the more remote areas of the country, and this issue is likely to continue into the future. Our analysis documented that the most sparse supplies of non-metropolitan hospital services, whether measured as certified beds per 1,000 population or certified beds per square mile, were in the most remote counties (per the UIC categories). Yet frontier counties had bed ratios similar to more urbanized counties. The richest supplies were in counties with a city of at least 10,000 population, especially counties adjacent to MSAs.

Of interest, the mix of hospital ownership shifted as the number of hospitals declined. Growing percentages of the non-metropolitan hospitals were owned by independent hospital districts or authorities, and ownership by local municipal governments decreased. This shift suggests that local governments were using hospital districts as a vehicle to protect them from financial risk and to offer greater flexibility for hospital management and financing. Trends in for-profit hospitals differed by county categories, with the percentage of hospitals that were for-profit ownership increasing in some categories of non-metropolitan counties but decreasing in others. The net effect across all non-metropolitan counties was little overall change in for-profit ownership. These location-specific changes may reflect strategic choices by the for-profit owners for rural locations that appeared to be most viable for hospital operation.

As the overall supply of hospitals changed during the 1990s, there also were changes in the mix of hospitals that obtained designations for Medicare special payment provisions or were reclassified for wage indexes for higher payments. The percentage of non-metropolitan hospitals with special payment designations decreased from 54.8 percent in 1992 to 38.2 percent in 1998. Most of this reduction occurred when the Medicare-dependent hospital designation was discontinued after 1993. At the same time, the percentage of hospitals reclassified for wage index declined from 25.8 percent to 12.7 percent, probably as a result of revisions made to the reclassification criteria. Hospitals designated as rural referral centers were much larger, on average, than other non-metropolitan hospitals, and they provided more diverse services. The rural referral centers also were more likely than the sole community hospitals to elect wage index reclassification. The sole community hospitals were more similar to hospitals that did not have a special designation, although they were in more isolated locations, as specified in the eligibility criteria.

This complex pattern of hospital characteristics and classifications reflects a number of policy changes made in the Medicare program during the 1990s. For example, the decrease in number of RRCs is partly attributable to the triennial review instituted in FY1994 to ensure that hospitals meet the RRC criteria. The BBA reinstated those that lost RRC status in this review, which explains the increase in RRCs in 1998. Others gave up their RRC status and instead requested geographic reclassification for the standardized amount. Similarly, the Medicare-dependent hospitals were discontinued in FY1994 and then reinstated by the BBA in 1998. Resource limitations precluded more in-depth analysis of the policies that might explain patterns observed in this research, and we expect that policymakers and other users of this information will track other policy effects that we have not been able to identify.

Medicare Inpatient Utilization and Spending

Given these trends in supplies of non-metropolitan hospitals, what changes occurred in utilization of these hospitals and in total usage of hospital inpatient services by Medicare beneficiaries residing in non-metropolitan counties? We looked at this question from two perspectives: inpatient services provided by non-metropolitan hospitals and inpatient services utilized by beneficiaries residing in non-metropolitan counties regardless of hospital location.

From 1992 to 1998, the total number of Medicare inpatient stays served by non-metropolitan hospitals increased by 12 percent, even as the number of hospitals declined. No apparent change was found in the distribution of total stays across county categories (degrees of rurality), but there were changes in the shares provided by hospitals with Medicare special payment designations. The percentages of total inpatient stays increased over time for sole community hospitals and for hospitals with no special payment designation, where as percentages decreased for rural referral centers.

In general, sole community hospitals had the largest shares of the Medicare inpatient stays provided by hospitals in the more remote counties (i.e., remote counties with a town of 2,500 population or without any town), whereas rural referral centers had the largest shares of stays among hospitals in counties with a city of 10,000 population or greater (either adjacent to an MSA or remote). Rural referral centers had much higher case mixes than other hospitals, as reflected in the average DRG weights for inpatient stays at these hospitals. By 1998, transfers from other hospitals were the sources for 53 percent of admissions to rural referral centers, which was much higher than for other non-metropolitan hospitals. Although coding errors may be inflating these estimates, high rates of referrals are consistent with the nature of rural referral centers.

These differences in utilization of different types of non-metropolitan hospitals are reflected in the average spending for their inpatient stays. The average Medicare payment per stay for rural referral centers was higher than payments for other hospitals with special payment designation (with the exception of Indian Health Service hospitals) or for hospitals with no special designation. When the payments per stay are standardized to payments for a DRG equal to 1.0, however, the average payments for rural referral centers and sole community hospitals become more similar. Average standardized payments for all groups of hospitals with special payment designations remain higher than those for hospitals with no special designation, reflecting the increased payments provided under these designations.

From a population perspective, inpatient services provided by non-metropolitan hospitals are an important component of inpatient care obtained by beneficiaries living in those non-metropolitan counties, but they are by no means the only sources of care. Throughout the decade, metropolitan hospitals served 31 percent of the inpatient stays utilized by beneficiaries in non-metropolitan counties, which represented more than 45 percent of total Medicare spending on inpatient care for these beneficiaries. The average payment per stay provided by metropolitan hospitals was much greater than payments for stays at non-metropolitan hospitals, likely reflecting higher acuity case mix as well as higher payment rates for metropolitan facilities.

Beneficiaries residing in the more remote counties tended to have higher utilization rates than those in more urbanized non-metropolitan counties, despite the generally longer distances to hospital locations. The average Medicare payment per inpatient stay, however, tended to be lower for beneficiaries in remote counties. As a result, the average Medicare payments per beneficiary were similar across the five categories of non-metropolitan counties.

Utilization and spending patterns for beneficiaries in frontier counties contrast sharply with those for other remote counties as defined by the UICs, suggesting that unique factors were influencing demand for inpatient care in these very sparsely populated counties. Beneficiaries in frontier counties had the lowest rates of inpatient utilization per 1,000 beneficiaries, yet the average Medicare spending per inpatient stay was higher than for any of the other remote counties. The resulting average payment per beneficiary for frontier counties was the lowest of all categories of non-metropolitan counties.

Inpatient Services in Underserved Areas

Our analyses of hospital supply and utilization for non-metropolitan MUAs and HPSAs allow us to focus on access issues for locations that have been identified as underserved based on provider supply and other criteria. The information from these analyses complements our findings regarding overall utilization and spending trends for inpatient care and offers some additional insights regarding implications for access to care. Not surprisingly, the most visible differences we find are between counties that are whole-county shortage areas (either MUA or HPSA) and other counties, either non-shortage areas or counties containing partial-county shortage areas. Pervasive provider shortages across an entire county would be more likely to affect access and utilization than would shortages in more localized areas or for specific population groups.

There were more hospitals in whole-county MUAs than in other counties, whereas there were fewer hospitals in whole-county HPSAs, which reflects the larger number of counties designated as MUAs. Beneficiaries living in whole-county MUAs utilized inpatient services at higher rates than did those in other counties; a similar but weaker difference was found for whole-county HPSAs. The average Medicare payment per inpatient stay tended to be lower for beneficiaries in whole-county MUAs than for those in other counties but higher for beneficiaries in whole-county HPSAs. Average per capita payments (i.e., per beneficiary) are a net effect of use rates and payment per stay. These per capita payments were higher for whole-county shortage areas than for other counties.

Discussion

Despite continuing concerns regarding the viability of the hospital infrastructure in rural areas, the findings of these descriptive analyses offer some evidence of stability in the supply of Medicare-certified hospitals during the 1990s. The hospitals with Medicare special payment designations appeared to play important roles in the delivery of services to beneficiaries in non-metropolitan counties, as shown by their shares of both inpatient stays and Medicare payments. An underlying policy issue, however, is the extent to which the special payments to these hospitals have contributed to their financial viability and retention as operating institutions. This issue could be assessed fully using hospital cost report data, but resource constraints prevented us from pursuing this analysis. However, estimates of the portions of total hospital payments attributable to the special payment provisions can shed some light on this issue.

Another general issue highlighted by the utilization analysis is that of the relationships between geographic access to hospital inpatient care, beneficiary health status, and observed utilization of inpatient services. Clearly, beneficiaries residing in the most remote rural counties, including the frontier counties, have to travel longer distances to hospitals, and access to hospitals with specialty capability may be even more difficult. This issue argues for the special payment provisions for rural referral centers to help ensure that such facilities remain available in rural areas. We found that beneficiaries in remote locations and in shortage areas (MUAs and HPSAs) had higher rates of inpatient stays than other rural beneficiaries, despite apparent access challenges. Could this utilization include some hospital stays or rehospitalizations that could have been avoided if they had better access to outpatient services? We also found lower average payments per beneficiary for these beneficiaries, suggesting that their hospital stays were for less intensive procedures, or that they were less likely to travel to urban hospitals for care.

5. TRENDS FOR RURAL HEALTH CLINICS AND FEDERALLY QUALIFIED HEALTH CENTERS

The research reported in this section examined trends in service use and payments for Rural Health Clinics and Federally Qualified Health Centers for the time period of 1991 through 1998. The analyses were designed to generate information regarding implications for access to care for beneficiaries in non-metropolitan counties and for cost impacts for Medicare. Our analyses address the following research questions:

- What were growth trends in the number and characteristics of facility-based RHCs, provider-based RHCs, and non-metropolitan FQHCs and how did they differ?

- In what types of geographic locations was this growth concentrated, as defined by categories of non-metropolitan counties, frontier counties, and HHS regions?

- How did utilization of RHCs and FQHCs by Medicare beneficiaries change over time as the supply of these facilities changed?

- What were trends in aggregate Medicare costs, per capita costs, and costs per unit of service for RHC and FQHC services to beneficiaries residing in non-metropolitan counties, and how do these costs vary across categories of counties?

SUPPLY OF RHCs AND FQHCs

This subsection provides information on the total numbers of Rural Health Clinics and Federally Qualified Health Centers during the 1990s. This information includes the number of facilities by type and calendar year and the ownership and staffing characteristics of the facilities. Generally, we do not report information separately for RHCs in metropolitan counties and those in non-metropolitan counties. However, we do report trends separately for FQHCs by metropolitan or non-metropolitan county location. Within the non-metropolitan counties, the distributions of RHCs and FQHCs are examined for the five categories of counties based on levels of "rurality" and status as a frontier county.

Numbers of Facilities

Table 5.1 shows the total number of provider-based and independent RHCs and the number of FQHCs located in non-metropolitan and metropolitan counties, for calendar years 1992 through 1998. For RHCs, the percentages by facility type also are presented. The total number of both provider-based and independent RHCs increased over the seven-year study period. The number of independent RHCs more than doubled over the study period and the increase in provider-based RHCs was much more dramatic. As a result, the provider-based RHCs increased from 23.1 percent of total RHCs in 1992 to 49.6 percent in 1998. The fastest growth in provider-based RHCs occurred through 1997, with some leveling off in growth in 1998.

Table 5.1
Number of Rural Health Clinics and Federally Qualified Health Centers, by Type, 1992–1998

Type of Clinic	1992	1993	1994	1995	1996	1997	1998
Total number of RHCs	1,072	1,419	2,145	2,596	3,361	3,688	3,749
Provider-based RHCs							
Number	248	454	827	1,136	1,590	1,783	1,860
Percentage of total RHCs	23.1%	32.0%	38.6%	43.8%	47.3%	48.3%	49.6%
Independent RHCs							
Number	824	965	1,318	1,460	1,771	1,905	1,889
Percentage of total RHCs	76.9%	68.0%	61.4%	56.2%	52.7%	51.6%	50.4%
Number of FQHCs							
Non-metropolitan	364	529	629	676	729	763	795
Metropolitan	469	683	803	877	982	1,042	1,079

SOURCE: Medicare Provider of Service files.

NOTES: Non-metropolitan counties are defined as counties not in Metropolitan Statistical Areas. Includes all certified RHCs irrespective of geographic location. The distribution of RHCs by metropolitan and non-metropolitan location is analyzed later in this section.

We obtained counts of the number of certified RHCs in years before 1992 from published CMS data (HRSA, 1991). There were 581 certified RHCs as of October 1990, an increase from 483 certified RHCs in July 1989. Thus, the number of RHCs increased by an average of 245 facilities per year between 1990 and 1992, which was slower than the growth occurring in 1993 through 1996 (see Table 5.1).

The non-metropolitan FQHCs doubled in number from 1992 to 1998, as shown in Table 5.2. There were 364 facilities in 1992, increasing to 795 facilities in 1998. (We report counts for all FQHCs, metropolitan FQHCs, and non-metropolitan FQHCs later in this section).

Table 5.2 shows the annual percentage changes in the volume of non-metropolitan FQHCs, provider-based RHCs, and independent RHCs, by calendar year, converting the counts of facilities in Table 5.1 to percentage changes from year to year. The largest growth in the number of facilities was for provider-based RHCs, which increased by 83.1 percent between 1992 and 1993 and by 82.2 percent between 1993 and 1994. There also was a substantial 45 percent increase in the number of FQHCs between 1992 and 1993, with similar rates of growth for those in metropolitan and non-metropolitan counties. Rates of increase in facilities dropped markedly by the end of 1996, although the number of provider-based RHCs grew by 12.1 percent during 1997.

Table 5.2
Annual Percentage Change in Number of FQHCs and RHCs, by Type,
1993–1998

Type of Clinic	% Change from Previous Year					
	1993	1994	1995	1996	1997	1998
Metropolitan FQHCs	45.8	18.1	8.8	11.9	6.2	3.5
Non-metropolitan FQHCs	45.3	18.9	7.5	7.8	4.7	4.2
Provider-based RHCs	83.1	82.2	37.4	40.0	12.1	4.3
Independent RHCs	17.1	36.6	10.8	21.3	7.6	−0.8
Total RHCs	32.4	51.2	21.0	29.5	9.7	1.6

SOURCE: Medicare Provider of Service files.

Clinic Characteristics

Nearly all the provider-based clinics that had a parent identified were found to have a hospital as the parent. The percentages of provider-based RHCs that had a short-term hospital as a parent are as follows: 91.2 percent in 1996, 93.0 percent in 1997, and 94.2 percent in 1998. We do not report percentages for earlier years because of high rates of missing data for this variable. A small number of RHCs (under 10 annually) had a SNF identified as the parent provider.

Table 5.3 shows the total number and percentage of non-metropolitan FQHCs and RHCs (including both metropolitan and non-metropolitan RHCs) by ownership status for 1992 through 1998. As discussed above, FQHCs must be private nonprofit organizations or governmental entities. The ownership status of non-metropolitan FQHCs was relatively stable across the study period, with a modest shift from public and private ownership to the "other" category. RHCs may have any type of ownership, including for-profit organizations. Ownership of provider-based RHCs also has been relatively stable over time, although there was a small shift from for-profit to nonprofit ownership. By contrast, the ownership mix for independent RHCs changed substantially from 1992 to 1998, resulting in a smaller percentage of nonprofit facilities and a larger percentage of for-profit facilities by 1998.

As discussed earlier, one objective of the legislation that created Rural Health Clinics was to permit Medicare reimbursement for non-physician practitioners to support rural clinics that relied on these professionals to serve beneficiaries. Table 5.4 shows the staffing characteristics of Rural Health Clinics during the 1990s, including the average number of physicians, nurse practitioners, and physician assistants by clinic type.[18] In 1992, the independent RHCs had greater average total staff FTEs than the provider-based RHCs, but the average FTEs for physicians, nurse practitioners, and physician assistants were similar for the two types of RHCs. Total staffing levels for both RHC types increased slightly from 1992 to 1998. Physician staffing remained stable over the decade for provider-based RHCs, but it increased for the

---

[18] Staffing data for FQHCs were not reported in the POS files. For any reported staffing values for the RHCs that were 100 or greater, the values were replaced with the 95th percentile value for that staffing variable, for that particular year. This applies to four variables: total physicians, total nurse practitioners, total physician assistants, and total salaried staff.

independent RHCs from 1.1 FTEs in 1992 to 1.5 FTEs in 1998. Throughout this time, average FTEs for nurse practitioners and physicians did not change. Despite the increase in physician FTEs for the independent RHCs, these three clinical staff categories remained at about the same percentage of total staff FTEs (58 percent in 1992 and 56 percent in 1998), indicating growth in other, non-clinical staff in these clinics.

Table 5.3
Ownership Status of RHCs, by Type, 1992–1998

Type of Clinic	Number of Clinics and % Distribution, by Type of Ownership						
	1992	1993	1994	1995	1996	1997	1998
Non-metropolitan FQHCs							
Number	364	529	629	676	729	763	795
Public	8.2%	7.6%	7.0%	6.5%	6.6%	6.7%	6.5%
Private	46.2	41.4	38.6	39.6	38.0	37.6	38.7
Other	45.6	51.0	54.4	53.8	55.4	55.7	54.7
Provider-based RHCs							
Number	248	454	827	1,136	1,590	1,783	1,860
Public	26.2%	25.3%	26.7%	25.9%	26.5%	25.9%	25.6%
Nonprofit	50.8	52.6	49.3	48.6	50.5	52.7	55.5
For-profit	23.0	22.0	23.9	25.5	23.0	21.4	18.9
Independent RHCs							
Number	824	965	1,318	1,460	1,771	1,905	1,889
Public	10.9%	9.8%	8.9%	7.9%	6.7%	6.9%	6.2%
Nonprofit	43.7	37.1	33.5	31.2	29.9	29.4	28.5
For-profit	45.4	53.1	57.7	60.9	63.4	63.7	65.3
All RHCs							
Number	1,072	1,419	2,145	2,596	3,361	3,688	3,749
Public	14.4%	14.8%	15.8%	15.8%	16.1%	16.1%	15.8%
Nonprofit	38.9	42.1	39.6	38.8	39.7	40.6	41.9
For-profit	46.6	43.1	44.7	45.4	44.3	43.2	42.2

SOURCE: Medicare Provider of Service files.

NOTES: Collapsed categories for FQHCs are defined as follows: public (POS codes for state/county government, combined government, or voluntary); private (POS codes for proprietary, religious affiliated, or private); and other (POS code for other). Collapsed categories for RHCs are defined as follows: public (POS codes for state, local, or federal); nonprofit (POS codes for nonprofit individual, corporation, or partnership); and for-profit (POS codes for-profit individual, corporation, or partnership).

Table 5.4
Staffing Mix of RHCs, 1992–1998

Type of RHC and FTEs	1992	1993	1994	1995	1996	1997	1998
Provider-based RHCs							
Physicians	0.9	1.0	1.0	1.0	1.0	1.0	1.0
Nurse practitioners	0.4	0.4	0.5	0.5	0.5	0.5	0.5
Physician assistants	0.6	0.5	0.6	0.4	0.4	0.5	0.5
Total staff FTE	4.8	4.6	5.0	5.0	4.9	4.9	5.1
Clinical as percentage of all FTEs	46%	48%	47%	47%	48%	48%	49%
Independent RHCs							
Physicians	1.1	1.1	1.2	1.3	1.4	1.5	1.5
Nurse practitioners	0.5	0.4	0.4	0.4	0.5	0.5	0.5
Physician assistants	0.6	0.6	0.5	0.5	0.5	0.6	0.6
Total staff FTE	5.8	5.2	5.3	5.5	5.9	6.2	6.2
Clinical as percentage of all FTEs	58%	58%	57%	57%	56%	55%	56%
Total RHCs							
Physicians	1.0	1.1	1.1	1.2	1.4	1.3	1.3
Nurse practitioners	0.5	0.5	0.4	0.4	0.5	0.5	0.5
Physician assistants	0.6	0.6	0.5	0.5	0.5	0.5	0.5
Total staff FTE	4.8	5.0	5.2	5.3	5.4	5.6	5.6
Clinical as percentage of all FTEs	55%	54%	53%	52%	52%	52%	53%

SOURCE: Medicare Provider of Service files.

NOTE: Staffing is reported in FTEs; a few facilities (e.g., 4 in 1992) with zero values for all staffing values are excluded.

Proximity of RHCs to Other Clinics

A key item for understanding trends in the distribution of RHCs is the extent to which RHCs are close to other similar facilities. Several reports and studies have suggested that some RHCs are in areas with multiple facilities (e.g., US GAO, 1996) and that consequently they may not be appropriately distributed with respect to access needs of Medicare beneficiaries. With a county-level analysis, we determined the proportion of counties having any FQHCs or RHCs that had more than one health clinic. The measures that we report include the proportion of counties that have any RHC or FQHC, at least one RHC, at least one FQHC, and at least one RHC and one FQHC. We note the limitation that these measures cannot capture the proximity of facilities within county boundaries. In addition, these measures do not necessarily indicate that beneficiaries residing in a county with multiple clinics are served by more than one of these clinics. Also, many FQHCs have multiple delivery sites, some of which may be in counties other than the location of the main clinic, which cannot be captured from the POS data available to us. As well, some FQHCs serve only special populations, such as migrant workers or homeless persons.

Table 5.5 provides county-level figures on facility collocation in non-metropolitan RHCs and non-metropolitan FQHCs. For each year, the total number of counties refers to those identified as non-metropolitan that have at least one FQHC or RHC. The number of non-metropolitan counties with at least one clinic doubled from 1992 to 1998, so that 1,533 of the 2,292 non-metropolitan counties have at least one clinic in 1998. Counties with at least one provider-based RHC increased most rapidly, in both absolute numbers and percentages of counties that contained any clinics. The number of counties with at least one of the other types of clinics also increased, but the percentage of counties that included each of these types did not increase.

Another approach to understanding the proximity of these health clinics is determining the proportion of each type of facility that is located within the same county as at least one other RHC or FQHC. As noted earlier, we determined for each RHC the number of other clinics in the same county each year. We did this by generating aggregate counts of facility types per county per calendar year and then assigning these aggregate counts to each facility record.

Table 5.5
Total Non-Metropolitan Counties with RHCs and FQHCs, Selected Years

Non-Metropolitan Counties with Clinics	1992	1994	1996	1998
Number of counties with any clinics	737	1,206	1,483	1,533
With 1or more FQHCs				
Number of counties with this type	261	444	491	518
Percentage of counties with any clinics	35.4%	36.8%	33.1%	33.8%
Maximum number of FQHCs	6	9	9	10
With 1 or more provider-based RHCs				
Number of counties with this type	177	506	796	894
Percentage of counties with any clinics	24.0%	42.0%	53.7%	58.3%
Maximum number of this RHC type	4	6	10	12
With 1 or more independent RHCs				
Number of counties with this type	429	654	815	819
Percentage of counties with any clinics	58.2%	54.2%	55.0%	53.4%
Maximum number of this RHC type	9	13	11	12

SOURCE: Medicare Provider of Service files.
NOTE: Percentages do not add to 100 percent because more than one category may be relevant.

Table 5.6 shows the distributions of rural FQHCs and RHCs by the total number of clinics in a county. For all types of clinics, the percentage of facilities that were the only facility in a county decreased steadily from 1992 to 1998. For example, 40.4 percent of FQHCs were the only facility in their county in 1992, and only 18.1 percent of FQHCs had that status by 1998. As expected given the significant growth in provider-based RHCs, the number (and percentage) of FQHCs and independent RHCs in counties that also had RHCs grew most significantly over the 1990s. For example, in 1992, 12.9 percent of non-metropolitan FQHCs were in a county with one or more RHCs. By 1998, this figure had grown to 26.3 percent. In contrast, the number of FQHCs in a non-metropolitan county with only FQHCs declined slightly from 26.7 percent to 21.4 percent.

It is important to note that the figures in Table 5.6 are based on individual facilities that are identified by unique Medicare provider numbers. Review of the clinic characteristics in the POS data shows that some distinct facilities with similar names are present in the same county. Some of these facilities have a common parent provider, but others do not.

Table 5.6
Number of RHCs and Non-Metropolitan FQHCs in the Same County
as One or More Other Clinics, 1992–1998

Type of Clinic and Colocation[b]	Number of Clinics[a] and Percentage Distribution, by Types of Other Clinics in County						
	1992	1993	1994	1995	1996	1997	1998
FQHC							
Number	364	529	629	676	729	763	795
No other clinics	40.4%	37.2%	28.1%	24.0%	21.4%	19.5%	18.1%
1+ FQHCs only	26.7	26.5	22.9	22.6	21.4	20.8	21.4
1+ RHCs only	12.9	16.3	23.5	26.3	26.6	26.6	26.3
1+ RHCs and FQHCs	20.2	20.0	25.4	27.1	30.6	33.0	34.2
Provider-based RHC							
Number	248	454	827	1,136	1,590	1,783	1,860
No other clinics	41.5%	32.3%	26.1%	20.7%	16.4%	15.1%	15.3%
1+ FQHCs only	2.8	7.3	6.5	5.9	4.0	3.5	4.1
1+ RHCs only	51.6	50.4	53.3	57.0	59.8	60.1	58.8
1+ RHCs and FQHCs	4.0	9.5	14.0	16.4	19.8	21.3	21.8
Independent RHC							
Number	824	965	1,318	1,460	1,771	1,905	1,889
No other clinics	33.1%	29.4%	20.6%	18.6%	15.5%	13.2%	12.3%
1+ FQHCs only	8.7	9.0	7.3	6.8	5.8	5.2	5.0
1+ RHCs only	43.9	44.5	48.6	49.8	52.9	53.8	53.8
1+ RHCs and FQHCs	14.2	17.1	23.4	24.9	25.8	27.8	28.8

SOURCE: Medicare Provider of Service files.

NOTES: Includes all RHCs (including those in metropolitan counties) and only non-metropolitan FQHCs.

[a]Clinics with a shared parent provider are counted as separate clinics (i.e., by unique provider number).

[b]Refers to number of clinics other than the referent clinic, when counting colocated clinics of the same type.

Information reported in the POS file allowed us to examine the extent to which facilities changed status between RHC and FQHC designations. We evaluated this for RHCs using the "former provider number" variable reported in the POS file, as reported in Table 5.7. Of the 248 provider-based RHCs in the 1992 POS, for example, none had a former Medicare provider number for a provider-based RHC, 12 had a former number for an independent RHC, and one had a former Medicare number for a short-term general hospital. Of the 1,860 provider-based RHCs in the 1998 POS, eight had a former Medicare provider number for a provider-based RHC, 176 had a former number for an independent RHC, two had a former number for indicated a SNF, eight had a former Medicare number for a short-term general hospital, and one had a former number for another type of facility. We note that these are not annual transition counts but are the cumulative number of facilities with former provider numbers. This means that former provider status recorded for facilities in the 1998 POS file could have occurred earlier than 1992 or sometime during the 1990s. We take this issue into consideration in interpreting these results.

Several interesting patterns are observed from the information in Table 5.7. First, the only RHCs that appear to have converted from previous status as FQHCs are independent RHCs, and only small percentages of them did so. Second, the highest rates of conversion were between provider-based and independent RHCs, with more RHCs converting from independent to provider-based than vice versa. Third, few RHCs had a change in provider number each year without changing facility type, which we measure as RHCs that only changed ownership.

Table 5.7
Former Provider Type Among RHCs, by Type, 1992–1998

Current Type and Year	Number of RHCs, by Former Provider Type and % of Total RHCs, by Type			
	FQHC	Provider-Based RHC[a]	Independent RHC[a]	Other[b]
Provider-based RHCs				
1992	0 (0.0%)	0 (0.0%)	12 (4.8%)	1 (0.4%)
1993	0 (0.0%)	0 (0.0%)	26 (5.7%)	0 (0.0%)
1994	0 (0.0%)	1 (0.1%)	67 (8.1%)	5 (0.6%)
1995	0 (0.0%)	0 (0.0%)	73 (6.4%)	5 (0.4%)
1996	0 (0.0%)	1 (0.1%)	111 (7.0%)	9 (0.6%)
1997	0 (0.0%)	7 (0.4%)	151 (8.5%)	9 (0.5%)
1998	0 (0.0%)	8 (0.4%)	176 (9.5%)	11 (0.5%)
Independent RHCs				
1992	31 (3.8%)	13 (1.6%)	5 (0.6%)	6 (0.7%)
1993	16 (1.7%)	22 (2.3%)	2 (0.2%)	0 (0.0%)
1994	7 (0.5%)	56 (4.2%)	4 (0.3%)	0 (0.0%)
1995	3 (0.2%)	27 (1.8%)	3 (0.2%)	0 (0.0%)
1996	10 (0.6%)	57 (3.2%)	4 (0.2%)	0 (0.0%)
1997	10 (0.5%)	85 (4.5%)	4 (0.2%)	0 (0.0%)
1998	3 (0.2%)	83 (4.4%)	4 (0.2%)	1 (0.1%)

SOURCE: Medicare Provider of Service files.

[a]Clinics with a former provider number of the same type have had a change in ownership. Those that switched from one type to another may also have had a change in ownership or may have retained the same ownership.

[b]"Other" includes short-term hospital, skilled nursing facility, or other facility.

Several reports have discussed the fact that some RHCs converted to FQHC status after the FQHC option became available in 1990. FQHCs that previously had been certified RHCs are identified by an indicator in the POS file. Judging by counts of the non-metropolitan FQHCs that had converted from previous RHC status, provided in Table 5.8, an estimated 20 percent of FQHCs formerly were RHCs. These numbers are not annual transition counts but are the cumulative number of facilities with former provider numbers.

Table 5.8
Non-Metropolitan FQHCs That Previously Were
Medicare-Certified as RHCs, 1992–1998

Year	Number That Were RHCs	% of Total FQHCs
1992	76	20.9%
1993	117	22.1
1994	134	21.3
1995	145	21.4
1996	152	20.8
1997	164	21.5
1998	160	20.1

SOURCE: Medicare Provider of Service files.
NOTE: POS data indicate whether an FQHC was formerly an RHC but do not identify the RHC type.

Distribution of FQHCs and RHCs by Type of Rural Areas

In this subsection, we examine the distributions of RHCs and FQHCs relative to the extent of rurality of their county locations, HHS regions, and designation of counties as medically underserved areas, including locations in MUAs and HPSAs. This analysis combines POS data about the RHCs and FQHCs with information extracted from the ARF county-level file to assess the extent to which RHCs and FQHCs are serving medically underserved areas and more remote areas, as intended by the enabling legislation.

Table 5.9 shows FQHC and RHC locations during the 1990s by the set of rural designations we derived using the Urban Influence Code (see the methods in Section 2). For RHCs, we provide counts for those in metropolitan and non-metropolitan counties, along with percentage distributions of non-metropolitan clinics by five categories of rurality defined by the UICs. We also show counts of clinics in frontier counties. For FQHCs, we limited the analysis to those centers that were in non-metropolitan counties, providing counts and percentage distributions by rurality category.

As the numbers of RHCs and FQHCs grew during the 1990s, their distributions across types of non-metropolitan counties also shifted moderately. Both provider-based and independent RHCs were more heavily represented in counties that lacked significant urbanized centers. Greater than 40 percent of each type of RHC was located in remote counties with no town or with towns of fewer than 10,000 residents, and another large percentage was in counties adjacent to metropolitan areas that did not have a city of 10,000 or greater population. However, the distributions for provider-based and independent RHCs changed in different directions over time.

With substantial growth in the number of provider-based RHCs, increasing percentages of these RHCs were in counties adjacent to metropolitan areas and remote counties with a city, whereas the two categories of more remote counties had declining shares (although we note that the absolute numbers of facilities did increase for these counties). Shifts in the distributions of independent RHCs were smaller. The counties adjacent to metropolitan areas with no city and remote counties with a city gained in shares of these facilities relative to other non-metropolitan counties. The most remote counties, without a town, had a smaller share that declined from 20.3 percent to 15.2 percent of independent RHCs in non-metropolitan counties.

Table 5.9
Geographic Location of RHCs and Non-Metropolitan FQHCs, 1992–1998

Type of Clinic and Location	% of Rural Counties	Number of Clinics and % Distributions						
		1992	1993	1994	1995	1996	1997	1998
Provider-based RHCs								
Number metropolitan		30	47	92	159	249	293	296
Number non-metropolitan		218	407	735	977	1,341	1,490	1,564
Percentage distribution								
Adjacent, city 10,000+	10.9	7.8%	8.6%	8.2%	9.6%	11.6%	11.9%	11.7%
Adjacent, no city 10,000+	32.6	31.5	37.1	35.1	36.0	34.8	34.0	34.2
Remote, city 10,000+	10.2	5.2	6.6	7.6	9.2	10.1	10.5	10.3
Remote, town 2,500–10,000	24.0	27.5	23.8	25.6	24.8	24.1	24.2	24.6
Remote, no town 2,500+	22.3	27.5	23.8	23.5	20.4	19.5	19.3	19.2
Number frontier		45	66	107	119	147	164	174
Independent RHCs								
Number metropolitan		184	191	250	280	353	387	392
Number non-metropolitan		640	774	1,068	1,180	1,418	1,518	1,497
Percentage distribution								
Adjacent, city 10,000+	10.9	12.1%	13.2%	12.2%	12.8%	12.2%	12.2%	12.3%
Adjacent, no city 10,000+	32.6	31.9	30.2	31.8	33.3	35.0	36.0	35.1
Remote, city 10,000+	10.2	9.2	11.0	12.1	11.0	10.9	10.6	10.3
Remote, town 2,500–10,000	24.0	27.3	27.0	27.0	26.3	25.4	25.4	27.1
Remote, no town 2,500+	22.3	20.3	18.6	16.8	16.6	16.4	15.7	15.2
Number frontier		120	119	133	133	150	139	133
Non-metropolitan FQHCs								
Number of clinics		364	529	629	676	729	763	795
Percentage distribution								
Adjacent, city 10,000+	10.9	9.6%	12.7%	11.8%	12.3%	12.8%	12.7%	13.1%
Adjacent, no city 10,000+	32.6	43.1	39.3	37.8	36.5	35.4	35.8	35.1
Remote, city 10,000+	10.2	8.8	11.0	12.6	12.9	13.4	13.1	13.2
Remote, town 2,500–10,000	24.0	17.6	19.5	20.7	21.2	21.4	21.5	22.1
Remote, no town 2,500+	22.3	20.9	17.6	17.2	17.2	17.0	16.9	16.5
Number frontier		32	62	72	75	78	81	87

SOURCES: Medicare Provider of Service files; analysis file based on 1998 Area Resource File.

NOTE: Percentages within the non-metropolitan classification refer to total clinics in the particular rural classification, as a percentage of total clinics in non-metropolitan areas.

Similar distributions and trends are found for the FQHCs in non-metropolitan counties. The shares of FQHCs grew from 1992 to 1998 for counties adjacent to metropolitan areas with a city and in remote counties with a town or city (two categories). Shares of FQHCs declined for counties adjacent to metropolitan areas with no city and for the most remote counties with no town. Again, the numbers of FQHCs in these areas grew but at a smaller rate than in the areas with increasing shares. The FQHCs in the frontier counties may include many of the tribal clinics and migrant farm worker clinics. We are not able to test this possibility, however, because of missing data for federal program funding in the POS.

The rates of growth of RHCs and FQHCs in frontier counties differ strongly relative to the overall growth rates of each type of facility. The rates of increase in both provider-based and independent RHCs in frontier counties, although substantial, were much smaller than their overall rates of growth. The provider-based RHCs had an overall growth rate of 617 percent from 1992 to 1998, whereas the growth rate for frontier counties was only 287 percent. The independent RHCs increased overall by 134 percent during this time, whereas they increased by only 11 percent in the frontier counties. By contrast, growth rates were higher for FQHCs in frontier counties (172 percent increase) than the overall growth rate for all non-metropolitan FQHCs (118 percent increase).

Distributions of RHCs and FQHCs by HHS regions, shown in Table 5.10, reveal some clear geographic clustering in the locations of the different types of facilities as well as regional differences in their growth in numbers. In 1992, the non-metropolitan FQHCs were concentrated in the Atlanta, Philadelphia, and Chicago regions. By 1998, the largest numbers of these facilities were in the Atlanta, Philadelphia, and Dallas regions, with moderate growth in other regions. For the RHCs in 1992, the largest numbers of provider-based RHCs were in the Dallas and Kansas City regions, and the largest numbers of independent RHCs were in the Atlanta region (185 clinics) in 1992. Dallas, Kansas City, Denver, and San Francisco also had close to 100 independent RHCs. By 1998, there were substantial numbers of RHCs of both types in all the regions except Boston, New York, and Seattle. In 1998, the Dallas region had the largest number of provider-based RHCs and the Atlanta region had the most independent RHCs.

Locations of RHCs and non-metropolitan FQHCs by MSA areas, HPSA designations, and MUA designations for 1993 and 1997, presented in Table 5.11, reflect requirements that these facilities be located in underserved areas. In 1993, 89.0 percent of non-metropolitan FQHCs were in primary care HPSAs, and this percentage decreased slightly to 86.5 percent in 1997. Larger percentages of FQHCs were in MUAs in both years (95.8 percent in 1993 and 91.9 percent in 1997). These findings indicate that FQHCs are clustered in counties with both HPSA and MUA designations. When considering HPSAs and MUAs together, the percentages of FQHCs in counties without either type of area were 2 percent in 1992 and 3 percent in 1993. The FQHCs outside MUAs probably are those that have qualified for certification by serving a medically underserved population.

Table 5.10
Number of RHCs and Non-Metropolitan FQHCs, by HHS Region and Type of Clinic,
1992 and 1998

HHS Region	Non-Metropolitan FQHCs		Provider-Based RHCs		Independent RHCs	
	1992	1998	1992	1998	1992	1998
All regions	364	795	248	1,860	824	1,889
1. Boston	0	38	0	27	26	69
2. New York	0	15	0	0	23	10
3. Philadelphia	69	116	0	79	65	115
4. Atlanta	151	240	37	391	185	524
5. Chicago	50	75	15	213	64	344
6. Dallas	0	127	97	564	105	247
7. Kansas City	16	25	54	332	98	257
8. Denver	33	50	31	115	96	107
9. San Francisco	17	56	12	98	93	136
10. Seattle	28	53	2	41	69	80

SOURCES: Medicare Provider of Service files; analysis file based on 1998 Area Resource File.

We find smaller percentages of RHCs than FQHCs in primary care HPSAs (see Table 5.11). In 1993, 70.0 percent of provider-based RHCs and 76.9 percent of independent RHCs were in HPSAs, and the percentages declined slightly in 1997 for both types of RHCs. On the other hand, substantially larger percentages of RHCs were in MUAs, with percentages similar to those for the FQHCs. Small percentages of RHCs were in counties without either a HPSA or MUA, although slightly larger percentages were outside these designated areas than was the case for non-metropolitan FQHCs. These probably were facilities in governor-designated shortage areas, which we could not identify with available data. This information would have to be verified for each area by HRSA or the states in question.

The percentages of facilities located in MSAs, according to the 1998 MSA designations, reflected the differences in the rules applicable to each type of facility. The very small percentages for the non-metropolitan FQHCs reflect the measurement error introduced by discrepancies between the 1993 UIC codes and the 1998 MSA boundaries. By contrast, RHCs may be designated in non-urbanized areas within metropolitan counties, which is reflected in the counts in Table 5.9. Approximately one-fifth of the independent RHCs were in MSAs in 1993 and 1998, and somewhat smaller percentages of provider-based RHCs were in MSAs.

Table 5.11
**Total Non-Metropolitan FQHCs and RHCs, by Location
in Underserved Areas and Type of Clinic, 1993 and 1997**

Clinic Location	Non-Metropolitan FQHCs		Provider-Based RHCs		Independent RHCs	
	1993	1997	1993	1997	1993	1997
Total number of clinics	529	763	454	1,783	965	1,905
In MSAs (1998 designations)						
Number of clinics	6	11	47	299	191	397
Percentage of total clinics	1.1%	1.4%	10.4%	16.8%	19.8%	20.8%
In primary care HPSAs[a]						
Number of clinics	471	660	318	1,211	742	1,428
Percentage of total clinics	89.0%	86.5%	70.0%	67.9%	76.9%	75.0%
Number in partial-county HPSAs	216	246	183	576	300	549
Number in whole-county HPSAs	255	414	135	635	442	879
In MUAs						
Number of clinics	507	701	414	1,591	870	1,681
Percentage of total clinics	95.8%	91.9%	91.2%	89.2%	90.2%	88.2%
Number in partial-county MUAs	384	512	326	1,115	534	1,031
Number in whole-county MUAs	123	189	88	476	336	650
In either a HPSA or MUA						
Number of clinics	523	743	448	1,722	933	1,841
Percentage of total clinics	98.7%	97.0%	98.7%	96.6%	96.7%	96.6%

SOURCES: Medicare Provider of Service files; analysis file based on 1998 Area Resource File.

NOTE: Excludes facilities in Alaska.

[a]Uses 1993 HPSA designations for the 1993 counts and 1997 HPSA designations for the 1997 counts.

TRENDS IN CLINIC UTILIZATION AND COSTS

Utilization and cost trends for RHC and FQHC services during the 1990s are presented here, using provider claims for the 5 percent sample of rural Medicare beneficiaries for the years 1992, 1994, 1996, and 1998. This analysis is a population-based analysis of trends in utilization and costs based on beneficiary county of residence, which provides insights into who is using the services of RHCs and FQHCs by degree of "rurality" and how that translates into patterns and trends in payments to the facilities that serve them and in Medicare spending on its share of those payments.

It is useful to consider this work in the context of previous studies that have examined RHC costs. The GAO used 1993 claims data to estimate the mean payment for a medical care visit based on the Medicare fee schedule, using procedure codes "that CMS officials said would most closely approximate an RHC visit" for independent RHCs (where RHC services included primary medical care and laboratory tests) (US GAO, 1997). These estimates were based exclusively on claims and did not account for year-end cost settlements for the RHCs. The GAO reported that intermediaries indicated that cost-report settlements usually increased the total payments to RHCs. The mean payment for independent RHCs (the claimed cost) computed from a sample of cost reports, from the four-state sample, was compared to the fee schedule.

The report concluded that "Medicare paid at least 43 percent more for cost-based reimbursement to RHCs than it paid to other providers who were paid under the fee schedule."[19]

To document trends in utilization, we measured the percentage of beneficiaries who use each of the types of RHCs and FQHCs, which we compared for beneficiaries residing in categories of metropolitan and non-metropolitan counties. This analysis was performed separately for each type of facility, to observe the roles of each facility type in different areas. Thus, beneficiaries who obtained services at more than one type of facility are included in the percentages for each type they used, and the percentages cannot be summed across facility types.

The results of this analysis, presented in Table 5.12, indicate that only a small fraction of Medicare beneficiaries residing in metropolitan counties use RHCs or FQHCs; beneficiaries in the more remote rural counties are heavier users of each type of facility. In particular, RHCs are used by much larger percentages of beneficiaries in the most remote counties—those with no town of at least 2,500 population—than by residents of any other location. The percentages of FQHC users in these remote areas also are substantial but somewhat smaller.

The percentages of clinic users increased slowly for FQHCs and at much more rapid rates for RHCs. The percentages using FQHCs increased most for beneficiaries residing in counties adjacent to metropolitan areas with a city of 10,000 population, and all the growth had occurred by 1996. By comparison, the percentage of beneficiaries using both provider-based and independent RHCs more than doubled between 1991 and 1998 for all non-metropolitan county categories except the most remote. Percentages increased yet faster for those in remote counties with either a city of 10,000 or a town of 2,500 to 10,000. For the most remote counties, there was little growth in the percentage of users of independent RHCs; users of provider-based RHCs increased from 12.7 percent to 18.6 percent of beneficiaries in those counties.

---

[19] Our analysis also works with payment amounts that precede the year-end reconciliations. Therefore, as discussed in the GAO report, these amounts should be conservative estimates of Medicare costs for RHC and FQHC services.

Table 5.12
Percentage of Beneficiaries Using an FQHC or RHC, by County Category, Selected Years

Clinic Type and County Category	1991	1992	1994	1996	1998
FQHCs					
Metropolitan residents	0.5%	0.5%	0.8%	0.9%	1.0%
Non-metropolitan residents					
Adjacent, city 10,000+	1.6	1.5	2.2	2.4	2.4
Adjacent, no city 10,000+	4.6	3.4	4.4	4.5	4.6
Remote, city 10,000+	2.2	2.3	2.3	2.6	2.8
Remote, town 2,500–10,000	3.4	3.3	4.9	5.2	4.6
Remote, no town 2,500+	8.5	7.8	10.6	10.7	10.1
Provider-based RHCs					
Metropolitan residents	0.1	0.1	0.2	0.3	0.4
Non-metropolitan residents					
Adjacent, city 10,000+	1.2	1.5	2.4	3.1	3.2
Adjacent, no city 10,000+	4.1	6.1	8.0	9.4	9.5
Remote, city 10,000+	0.7	1.0	2.2	4.4	5.2
Remote, town 2,500–10,000	3.6	4.6	6.4	8.3	10.2
Remote, no town 2,500+	12.7	10.9	15.2	16.7	18.6
Independent RHCs					
Metropolitan residents	0.3	0.3	0.4	0.5	0.6
Non-metropolitan residents					
Adjacent, city 10,000+	2.1	3.0	4.6	5.5	6.3
Adjacent, no city 10,000+	4.7	5.7	6.6	8.7	10.1
Remote, city 10,000+	1.9	2.7	4.2	4.7	5.8
Remote, town 2,500–10,000	4.3	6.5	9.6	11.1	12.1
Remote, no town 2,500+	16.4	14.4	15.2	16.7	15.8

SOURCES: Medicare Provider of Service files; analysis file based on 1998 Area Resource File; Medicare institutional outpatient claims for 5 percent beneficiary sample.

NOTES: Figures are based on claims for the 5 percent beneficiary sample aggregated by county of residence, multiplied by 20 to represent total volume for each year. Percentages are based on all beneficiaries obtaining services at a given type of facility; those who used more than one type are counted in the percentages for each type used.

Total Medicare spending for RHC and FQHC services increased substantially between 1991 and 1996 and then declined somewhat by 1998, as shown in Table 5.13. Medicare spent an estimated $54.5 million on these services in 1991. Spending increased to $415.1 million in 1996, followed by lower spending of $390.3 million in 1998. These amounts include all payments made to RHCs and FQHCs, including the cost reimbursement for core services and payments for other services provided that are covered by Medicare fee schedules. During this time, the distribution of spending shifted so that increasing shares of spending were for services to rural beneficiaries. An estimated 47.1 percent of the spending in 1991 was for services to beneficiaries residing in metropolitan counties, which dropped to 29.2 percent in 1998.

Table 5.13
Estimated Medicare Spending for FQHC and RHC Services,
by County Category and Type of Clinic, Selected Years

County Category	1991	1992	1994	1996	1998
Estimated total payments ($1,000)	$54,524	$75,537	$175,796	$415,102	$390,307
Percentage by county location					
Metropolitan residents	47.1%	40.3%	34.6%	31.4%	29.2%
Non-metropolitan residents					
Adjacent, city 10,000+	7.7	7.7	9.0	9.3	9.0
Adjacent, no city 10,000+	19.1	21.4	21.2	22.8	23.8
Remote, city 10,000+	4.8	5.9	7.4	7.8	7.9
Remote, town 2,500–10,000	10.5	12.9	15.7	17.1	18.5
Remote, no town 2,500+	10.9	11.8	12.2	11.6	11.7
Percentage by type of clinic					
FQHC	46.7	40.8	42.7	37.6	33.9
Provider-based RHC	6.2	8.5	16.4	23.7	28.8
Independent RHC	47.1	50.7	40.9	38.7	37.3

SOURCES: Medicare Provider of Service files; analysis file based on 1998 Area Resource File; Medicare institutional outpatient claims for 5 percent beneficiary sample.

NOTES: Payments are the amounts paid by Medicare based on claims for the 5 percent sample of beneficiaries and multiplied by 20 to estimate total payments. The amounts include the cost-based reimbursements for the core services as well as payments for services covered under other Medicare fee schedules. Includes claims with zero and negative paid amounts, which reflect application of deductibles and any payments by primary payers.

Within the non-metropolitan counties, the largest share of Medicare spending for RHC and FQHC services was for beneficiaries residing in counties adjacent to metropolitan areas with no city of at least 10,000, and that share increased slightly from 19.1 percent in 1991 to 23.8 percent in 1998 (see Table 5.13). Spending for beneficiaries in the two most remote county categories was an estimated 21.4 percent (sum of the percentages for the two categories) of the total 1991 Medicare spending, rising to 30.2 percent in 1998. Only 4.8 percent of Medicare spending on RHC and FQHC services in 1991 went for beneficiaries in remote counties with a city of at least 10,000, but this share increased by 54 percent by 1994, to 7.4 percent of total spending on these services, and then grew at a slower rate to 7.9 percent in 1998.

Looking at the distribution of Medicare spending by type of facility, spending for provider-based RHC services grew substantially from 6.2 percent of total spending in 1991 to 28.8 percent in 1998. This growth was taken from the shares for FQHCs and independent RHCs, both of which declined during this seven-year period.

Although the payment limits for independent RHCs and freestanding FQHCs increased over time, as did provider costs, the average Medicare spending per encounter remained virtually the same through 1994 and then increased in subsequent years. As reported in Table 5.14, we estimated that Medicare paid approximately $40 per encounter in 1991, 1992, and 1994 for all types of RHCs and FQHCs; these amounts rose to $42 in 1996 and $46 in 1998. The average payment for beneficiaries residing in metropolitan areas was $45 per encounter in 1991, $47 in 1994, and $54 in 1998. These amounts compared to lower average payments of $35 to $42 per encounter for residents in non-metropolitan areas in 1991, and remained steady through 1994 and reached $41 to $44 in 1998.

Table 5.14
Average Medicare Spending per Encounter for FQHC and RHC Services,
by County Category and Type of Clinic, Selected Years

County Category	1991	1992	1994	1996	1998
Average spending per encounter	$40	$39	$40	$42	$46
By county location					
Metropolitan residents	45	44	47	52	54
Non-metropolitan residents					
Adjacent, city 10,000+	39	38	38	40	43
Adjacent, no city 10,000+	35	35	36	38	44
Remote, city 10,000+	42	41	39	38	41
Remote, town 2,500–10,000	38	36	37	37	42
Remote, no town 2,500+	36	36	39	40	43
By type of clinic					
FQHC	47	46	50	59	62
Provider-based RHC	35	29	31	33	42
Independent RHC	37	37	37	38	39

SOURCES: Medicare Provider of Service files; analysis file based on 1998 Area Resource File; Medicare institutional outpatient claims for 5 percent beneficiary sample.

NOTES: Payments are the amounts paid by Medicare based on claims for the 5 percent sample of beneficiaries and multiplied by 20 to estimate total payments. Includes claims with zero and negative paid amounts, which reflect application of deductibles and any payments by primary payers.

Some clear differences are found for trends in average Medicare payments for the services of FQHCs and the two types of RHCs (see Table 5.14). Medicare payments for FQHC services were an average $47 per encounter in 1991 and increased to $62 in 1998. Average payments for provider-based RHC services declined from $35 per encounter in 1991 to $31 in 1994, and then increased to $42 in 1998. Average payments for independent RHCs remained the fairly constant at $37 to $39 per encounter. Increases in Medicare spending per FQHC encounter appear to be offset by the simultaneous reduction in per encounter spending for the provider-based RHCs, suggesting that clinics newly certified in the mid-1990s may have had lower average costs per encounter than their predecessors, or that changes in core services affected costs.

The next four tables present estimated average payment amounts per beneficiary, normalized to two different measures of beneficiary populations. The payments are the amounts paid by Medicare and the total allowed payment amounts, which include the Medicare payment plus any payments by other primary payers and by beneficiaries for deductibles and coinsurance. Tables 5.15 and 5.16 report these payment amounts measured on a per capita basis for which the denominator is the number of beneficiaries residing in counties from which each type of FQHC or RHC received patients (measured by having a claim for a beneficiary residing in a county). Tables 5.17 and 5.18 report the payments on the basis of counts of beneficiaries residing in all the counties included in each metropolitan or non-metropolitan category, whether or not a payment claim was made for beneficiaries in the county.

Table 5.15
Average Medicare per Capita Payments for Beneficiaries in Counties Served by a Clinic, by County Category and Type of Clinic, 1991, 1994, and 1998

Year and County Category	FQHC	Provider-Based RHC	Independent RHC
1991			
Metropolitan residents	$1.17	$0.03	$0.42
Non-metropolitan residents			
Adjacent, city 10,000+	2.88	1.72	3.58
Adjacent, no city 10,000+	8.34	4.92	7.10
Remote, city 10,000+	4.67	0.71	3.00
Remote, town 2,500–10,000	5.43	4.15	6.84
Remote, no town 2,500+	15.75	18.56	25.61
1994			
Metropolitan residents	1.86	.21	.59
Non-metropolitan residents			
Adjacent, city 10,000+	4.73	2.55	6.86
Adjacent, no city 10,000+	8.99	9.86	10.61
Remote, city 10,000+	4.58	2.92	6.80
Remote, town 2,500–10,000	9.84	6.68	15.24
Remote, no town 2,500+	21.53	24.68	24.64
1998			
Metropolitan residents	2.94	.60	1.07
Non-metropolitan residents			
Adjacent, city 10,000+	6.59	5.27	11.27
Adjacent, no city 10,000+	12.33	19.58	18.97
Remote, city 10,000+	7.40	8.50	10.44
Remote, town 2,500–10,000	12.38	19.86	23.35
Remote, no town 2,500+	27.02	39.71	34.40

SOURCES: Medicare Provider of Service files; analysis file based on 1998 Area Resource File; Medicare institutional outpatient claims for 5 percent beneficiary sample.

NOTES: Payments are the amounts that Medicare paid the providers as reported on the claims. The beneficiaries included in the denominator for each per capita payment were those residing in counties in which each type of clinic had provided at least one service to a beneficiary in the county.

The patterns of Medicare payments per beneficiary in served counties, shown in Table 5.15, are quite similar to the utilization patterns reported in Table 5.12. Per capita payments for all three types of providers are highest in the most remote non-metropolitan counties and, relative to other geographic categories, payments also are higher in counties adjacent to metropolitan areas with no city. Per capita payments for residents in all locations increased from 1991 to 1994. Geographic patterns are similar for the total allowed amounts per beneficiary in served counties, reported in Table 5.16.

Table 5.16
Average Total Allowed per Capita Amounts for Beneficiaries in Counties Served by a Clinic, by County Category and Type of Clinic, 1991, 1994, and 1998

Year and County Category	FQHC	Provider-Based RHC	Independent RHC
1991			
Metropolitan residents	$1.65	$0.04	$0.61
Non-metropolitan residents			
Adjacent, city 10,000+	4.24	2.45	5.05
Adjacent, no city 10,000+	12.03	7.42	10.13
Remote, city 10,000+	6.62	1.00	4.13
Remote, town 2,500–10,000	7.86	6.00	9.74
Remote, no town 2,500+	22.56	26.11	36.41
1994			
Metropolitan residents	2.29	.33	.85
Non-metropolitan residents			
Adjacent, city 10,000+	5.66	3.77	9.79
Adjacent, no city 10,000+	10.88	14.60	14.96
Remote, city 10,000+	5.60	4.15	9.55
Remote, town 2,500–10,000	11.84	9.80	21.25
Remote, no town 2,500+	25.79	34.86	33.76
1998			
Metropolitan residents	3.63	.88	1.55
Non-metropolitan residents			
Adjacent, city 10,000+	8.05	7.63	16.21
Adjacent, no city 10,000+	14.95	26.94	27.53
Remote, city 10,000+	8.90	12.56	15.37
Remote, town 2,500–10,000	15.12	27.64	33.60
Remote, no town 2,500+	32.61	55.91	49.23

SOURCES: Medicare Provider of Service files; analysis file based on 1998 Area Resource File; Medicare institutional outpatient claims for 5 percent beneficiary sample.

NOTES: Allowed payments are the total amounts the provider received, as approved by Medicare, which include the amounts paid by Medicare, other primary payers, and beneficiary deductibles and coinsurance. The beneficiaries included in the denominator for each per capita payment were those residing in counties in which each type of clinic had provided at least one service to a beneficiary in the county.

When the two types of payment amounts are normalized to the total number of beneficiaries residing in the counties in each geographic category, the resulting per capita payments are based on constant population sizes within each category. Thus, it is possible to obtain a sum of the per capita payments for services provided by the three types of facilities to assess the aggregate financial impacts for geographic areas of differing degrees of "rurality." Despite the differences in denominators, we find the same general patterns of spending by category of counties in 1991, as shown in Table 5.17. The highest rates are in the most remote counties, followed by remote counties with a town of 2,500–10,000 and counties adjacent to metropolitan counties with no city of 10,000.

Table 5.17
Medicare per Capita Payments for All Beneficiaries in Each County,
by County Category and Type of Clinic, 1991, 1994, and 1998

Year and County Category	FQHC	Provider-Based RHC	Independent RHC	Annual per Capita Total
1991				
All beneficiaries	$0.72	$0.10	$0.72	$1.54
Metropolitan residents	0.68	0.01	0.27	0.96
Non-metropolitan residents				
Adjacent, city 10,000+	0.46	0.07	1.42	1.95
Adjacent, no city 10,000+	1.07	0.40	2.61	4.07
Remote, city 10,000+	0.70	0.06	0.95	1.71
Remote, town 2,500–10,000	0.70	0.37	2.23	3.30
Remote, no town 2,500+	1.80	2.07	5.24	9.11
1994				
All beneficiaries	2.05	.79	1.96	4.80
Metropolitan residents	1.59	0.11	0.49	2.19
Non-metropolitan residents				
Adjacent, city 10,000+	2.36	0.76	4.01	7.12
Adjacent, no city 10,000+	4.00	3.56	6.40	13.96
Remote, city 10,000+	2.34	1.33	4.62	8.28
Remote, town 2,500–10,000	3.67	3.09	9.04	15.80
Remote, no town 2,500+	7.54	10.62	14.11	32.28
1998				
All beneficiaries	3.44	2.93	3.79	10.16
Metropolitan residents	2.64	0.46	0.95	4.05
Non-metropolitan residents				
Adjacent, city 10,000+	3.88	3.54	7.48	14.90
Adjacent, no city 10,000+	6.62	12.47	14.00	33.10
Remote, city 10,000+	4.48	5.62	7.81	17.91
Remote, town 2,500–10,000	6.56	14.74	17.23	38.53
Remote, no town 2,500+	11.86	28.80	24.69	65.35

SOURCES: Medicare Provider of Service files; analysis file based on 1998 Area Resource File; Medicare institutional outpatient claims for 5 percent beneficiary sample.

NOTES: Payments are the amounts that Medicare paid the providers, as reported on the claims. The beneficiaries included in the denominators to calculate payments per beneficiary consist of all beneficiaries residing in all counties included each geographic category.

Table 5.18
Total Allowed per Capita Payments for All Beneficiaries in Each County,
by County Category and Type of Clinic, 1991, 1994, and 1998

Year and County Category	FQHC	Provider-Based RHC	Independent RHC	Annual per Capita Total
1991				
All beneficiaries	$1.02	$0.14	$1.03	$2.19
Metropolitan residents	0.96	0.01	0.39	1.35
Non-metropolitan residents				
Adjacent, city 10,000+	0.68	0.11	2.00	2.78
Adjacent, no city 10,000+	1.54	0.60	3.72	5.86
Remote, city 10,000+	1.00	0.08	1.30	2.38
Remote, town 2,500–10,000	1.01	0.54	3.18	4.73
Remote, no town 2,500+	2.57	2.91	7.45	12.94
1994				
All beneficiaries	2.50	1.15	2.76	6.41
Metropolitan residents	1.96	0.17	0.69	2.82
Non-metropolitan residents				
Adjacent, city 10,000+	2.82	1.12	5.72	9.66
Adjacent, no city 10,000+	4.84	5.27	9.03	19.14
Remote, city 10,000+	2.86	1.88	6.49	11.23
Remote, town 2,500–10,000	4.41	4.53	12.61	21.56
Remote, no town 2,500+	9.04	15.00	19.34	43.38
1998				
All beneficiaries	4.22	4.13	5.48	13.83
Metropolitan residents	3.27	0.68	1.38	5.32
Non-metropolitan residents				
Adjacent, city 10,000+	4.74	5.12	10.76	20.63
Adjacent, no city 10,000+	8.03	17.16	20.32	45.51
Remote, city 10,000+	5.39	8.30	11.50	25.19
Remote, town 2,500–10,000	8.01	20.51	24.80	53.32
Remote, no town 2,500+	14.31	40.56	35.33	90.20

SOURCES: Medicare Provider of Service files; analysis file based on 1998 Area Resource File; Medicare institutional outpatient claims for 5 percent beneficiary sample.

NOTES: Allowed payments are the total amounts the provider received, as approved by Medicare, which include the amounts paid by Medicare, other primary payers, and beneficiary deductibles and coinsurance. The beneficiaries included in the denominators used to calculate payments per beneficiary are all beneficiaries residing in all counties included each geographic category.

A substantial increase in Medicare spending on RHC/FQHC services occurred between 1991 and 1994, which continued through 1998 (see Table 5.17). Large increases in spending rates per beneficiary occurred for beneficiaries in several of the non-metropolitan categories, which are especially visible in the total spending rates that are the sums of the amounts for the three types of clinics. These increases are larger than those obtained for rates based on beneficiaries in served counties because the base population is more stable. The number of beneficiaries in "served counties" in a category increased over time due to both growth in the counties served by RHCs and FQHCs and underlying growth in the Medicare population. The

- 115 -

beneficiaries in "all counties" in a category increased only because of Medicare population growth. The greatest growth in total payments per beneficiary (summed for the three provider types) occurred in the most remote counties. The other categories of remote counties also had substantial increases in Medicare payments. As shown in Table 5.18, patterns are similar for total allowed payments per beneficiary, for both geographic differences in a year and rates of increase from 1991 to 1998.

ISSUES AND IMPLICATIONS

Although RHCs and FQHCs differ in the scope of services they provide and, in many cases, the populations they serve, they both have grown to become important health care resources for rural populations across the country. This growth is seen not only in the basic numbers of facilities, which have increased substantially during the 1990s, but also in shifts in the locations of the facilities across HHS regions and across counties with differing degrees of "rurality." The combination of provider-level data in the Provider of Service files and claims for RHC and FQHC services to Medicare beneficiaries has offered rich information to better understand the history, distribution, and activities of these providers in rural areas.

The growth in the number of RHCs was fairly slow during the 1980s after they were authorized by Congress. The major expansion of RHCs began in the early 1990s, reportedly in response to legislative changes that improved payments and other operating requirements. The number of FQHCs, on the other hand, began to grow almost immediately after the passage of OBRA-89 and OBRA-90, which created the FQHC program. As a result, although the starting points differed by a decade, the rapid growth in the two programs coincided in the first half of the 1990s.

The trend analyses we present in this report certainly reflect those growth patterns. We observe somewhat different growth trends for each of the three types of facilities examined in this study: non-metropolitan FQHCs, provider-based RHCs, and independent RHCs. In general, the greatest growth in FQHCs tended to occur in counties adjacent to metropolitan areas and in remote counties with a city of at least 10,000 population. This trend may reflect the role of FQHCs of serving vulnerable populations that tend to reside in more urbanized areas. The independent RHCs also increased faster in the more urbanized non-metropolitan counties, whereas growth in the provider-based RHCs tended to be in more remote counties with smaller towns.

The most remote counties are of special policy interest with respect to access to care for rural beneficiaries. We defined these counties as remote counties with no town of at least 2,500 population. Although these counties had a declining share of the total number of providers for FQHCs and both types of RHCs, the number of facilities in the counties did indeed increase. As of 1991, the most remote counties already were the heaviest users of FQHCs and RHCs, and with growing numbers of facilities, the percentage of beneficiaries in the counties who used each type of facility also increased. Similar increases were found for remote counties with small towns, which also are quite sparsely populated.

The expanding supply of FQHCs and RHCs led to growth in the number of facilities serving within individual counties. This trend must be interpreted with caution, however, because geographically large counties could contain multiple provider sites without significant overlap in their service area boundaries. A more detailed analysis at the service area level would be required to assess the extent to which a balance is maintained between a goal of improving access to care and the risk of duplicating services.

With greater numbers of FQHCs and RHCs delivering primary care services to Medicare beneficiaries across rural areas, Medicare costs escalated accordingly. Judging by data from provider claims for the 5 percent beneficiary sample, Medicare spending for all FQHC and RHC services (for rural and urban beneficiaries) was an estimated $54.5 million in 1991. Spending more than tripled to $175.8 million in 1994 and then more than doubled again to $415.1 million in 1996, followed by lower spending of $390.3 million in 1998. The average Medicare spending per beneficiary also tripled from $1.54 in 1991 to $4.80 in 1994 and then doubled again to $10.16 in 1998. This trend indicates that all but a small portion of the increase was due to growth in the amount of services per beneficiary rather than to the size of the beneficiary population. Despite this rapid growth, the Medicare per capita costs remain small, with the 1998 amount of $10.16 representing less than one dollar per capita on a monthly basis (which is the basis for the AAPCC rates).

With such a substantial growth rate in Medicare spending for this primary care program, two obvious questions should be examined. First, what associated changes, if any, are occurring in utilization and spending for other ambulatory care services, i.e., is there a substitution effect in reductions of other services? Second, what effect is the larger supply of FQHCs and RHCs having on timely access to care for rural beneficiaries? Answers to the first question will help inform analyses addressing the second question.

A related issue has been raised in the health policy community regarding the extent to which existing physician practices are converting to RHCs to improve their revenues from cost-based reimbursement, even though they could continue to be viable as they are. To the extent this behavior is occurring, conversion to an RHC should not change the volume of services being provided by a practice, unless better payments encourage the practice to work to attract new patients. Such initiative is in fact the behavior being encouraged through cost reimbursement. This issue could be informed by profiling trends in the number of beneficiaries served by each provider, number of encounters billed, and associated Medicare spending.

The analysis performed of the locations of FQHCs and RHCs in HPSAs and MUAs has confirmed that the facility locations are consistent with the rules governing the programs. Several questions merit further attention. First, how are Medicare spending and total allowed payments distributed across HPSAs and MUAs? We would expect to see a concentration of spending increases in these areas because that is where the clinics are located. Second, how densely are the facilities populating the HPSAs and MUAs, and what are the implications for excess capacity in some of these areas?

The trend of decreasing Medicare payment per encounter merits further attention because we would expect these payment amounts to increase with inflation rather than decrease. Changes in service mix could yield lower amounts, where the core services may be accompanied by fewer other services paid by fee schedules. Alternatively, the newer RHCs and FQHCs may be more efficient and able to keep their average cost (and all-inclusive rate) lower than those of already existing facilities.

6. UTILIZATION AND SPENDING FOR PHYSICIAN SERVICES

The analyses presented in this section describe trends during the 1990s in the distribution and characteristics of both basic payments and bonus payments made to physicians on behalf of rural Medicare beneficiaries in non-metropolitan counties and in counties with a HPSA designation. The analyses were designed to address the following basic questions:

- How have total payments and bonus payments for physician services provided to rural Medicare beneficiaries changed during the decade of the 1990s? What proportion of these payments is for beneficiaries residing in rural HPSAs and those residing outside HPSAs?

- How has the distribution of bonus payments across primary and specialty care physicians changed over time?

- What are the trends in the mix of primary care and other services that have a bonus payment attached?

The perspective taken for the analyses presented in this section is that of the Medicare beneficiary. As described in Section 2, the sample was selected based on the state and county of residence for beneficiaries in non-metropolitan counties. This population-based approach is intended to gain a better understanding of the extent to which non-metropolitan beneficiaries utilize physician services, particularly in underserved areas, and related bonus payment costs.

DISTRIBUTION OF TOTAL AND BONUS PAYMENTS

We begin by reporting basic Medicare spending for physician services and for bonus payment amounts, by county category as defined by UICs. As shown in Table 6.1, Medicare spent more than $5 billion on physician services for non-metropolitan beneficiaries in 1992, which increased to $7.4 billion by 1998. Although total payments for physician services increased during the 1990s, the distribution of these payments across county categories remained virtually the same over time. Physicians serving beneficiaries residing in counties adjacent to an MSA received more than half the total Medicare payments in each year studied.

Bonus payments to physicians increased through 1996, followed by a decline by 1998 (see Table 6.1). In 1992, physicians received $25 million through the bonus payment program, and amounts reached $42 million in 1996. Bonus payments declined by 13 percent over the next two years to $36 million in 1998.

Similar to Medicare spending for physician services, the distribution of bonus payments across county categories varied little over time (see Table 6.1). The majority of bonus payments were for services provided to beneficiaries residing in counties without a city of 10,000 or more population, including those in counties adjacent to an MSA and those that are not. Physicians providing services to beneficiaries residing in counties adjacent to an MSA but without a large city received over one-third of all bonus payments made in each year studied. This pattern reflects the fact that more than one-third of the whole-county HPSAs in non-metropolitan counties are in counties adjacent to an MSA without a large city.

Looking at bonus payments as a percentage of Medicare payments, we find that, overall, bonus payments grew from 0.5 percent to 0.7 percent of Medicare payments from 1992, and then declined to 0.5 percent of payments by 1998 (see Table 6.1). The highest levels of bonus payments, expressed as percentages of service payments, were found for services to beneficiaries living in the more remote counties, including frontier counties. The lowest percentages of bonus payments were for beneficiaries in counties that had a city of 10,000 or more population.

Table 6.1
Distribution of Basic Medicare Payments to Physicians and Bonus Payments
for Services to Non-Metropolitan Beneficiaries, by County Category, Selected Years

County Category	1992	1994	1996	1998
Total basic payments ($1,000)	$5,025,344	$5,926,700	$6,739,377	$7,389,105
Percentage by county category				
Adjacent, city 10,000+	26.4%	26.3%	26.1%	26.0%
Adjacent, no city 10,000+	30.2	30.3	30.4	30.2
Remote, city 10,000+	17.7	17.7	17.7	17.8
Remote, town 2,500–10,000	19.1	18.8	18.9	19.0
Remote, no town	6.7	6.8	6.9	6.9
Frontier counties	3.7	3.8	3.8	3.7
Total bonus payments ($1,000)	$25,401	$38,532	$42,019	$36,420
Percentage by county category				
Adjacent, city 10,000+	18.3%	19.0%	17.0%	16.0%
Adjacent, no city 10,000+	36.1	35.1	36.4	37.6
Remote, city 10,000+	11.2	12.4	12.9	11.5
Remote, town 2,500–10,000	22.4	23.2	23.3	24.6
Remote, no town	11.9	10.3	10.4	10.3
Frontier counties	5.1	4.6	4.5	5.1
Bonus payments as a percentage of basic physician payments				
All non-metropolitan counties	0.5%	0.7%	0.6%	0.5%
By county category				
Adjacent, city 10,000+	0.4	0.5	0.4	0.3
Adjacent, no city 10,000+	0.6	0.8	0.7	0.6
Remote, city 10,000+	0.3	0.5	0.5	0.3
Remote, town 2,500–10,000	0.6	0.8	0.8	0.6
Remote, no town	0.9	1.0	0.9	0.7
Frontier counties	0.7	0.8	0.7	0.7

SOURCE: Physician/supplier claims for the 5 percent sample of beneficiaries.

NOTES: Total payment amounts are estimated by multiplying the payment amounts for the 5 percent sample by 20. Bonus payments are estimated by multiplying the payment amounts for the 5 percent sample by (0.1 x 20).

The total bonus payment amounts reported in Table 6.1 are 10 to 13 percent lower than those reported for rural HPSAs (see Table 1.5). The payments presented in Table 1.5 represent all bonus payments made to physicians, by rural or urban HPSA location, whereas the bonus payments presented in Table 6.1 are only those for physician services provided to beneficiaries residing in non-metropolitan counties. These amounts do not include bonus payments for services provided to urban county residents who received services in rural HPSAs. On the other hand, they do include bonus payments for services provided to non-metropolitan county residents who received care in urban HPSAs (Medicare paid almost $3 million in bonus payments to physicians for services provided to non-metropolitan beneficiaries in an urban HPSA).

From Table 6.2, we find that the distribution of basic Medicare payments for physician services by HPSA designation changed somewhat over time. Between 1994 and 1996, the percentage of total Medicare spending on physician services for beneficiaries residing in partial county HPSAs increased by 6.6 percent whereas the overall percentage of spending for care provided to beneficiaries in non-HPSA counties declined. This was a result of the addition of new partial-county HPSA designations in 1996 in counties that did not have them in 1994. Medicare spending for services to beneficiaries in whole-county HPSAs did not change during this time frame.

Table 6.2
Distribution of Basic Medicare Payments to Physicians and Bonus Payments for Services to Non-Metropolitan Beneficiaries, by Health Professional Shortage Area, Selected Years

Type of Shortage Area	1992	1994	1996	1998
Total basic payments ($1,000)	$5,025,344	$5,926,700	$6,739,377	$7,389,105
Percentage by HPSA designation				
Whole-county HPSA	19.4%	19.6%	20.1%	18.1%
Partial-county HPSA	37.8	38.0	44.6	44.4
Not HPSA	42.9	42.5	35.3	37.5
Total bonus payments ($1,000)	$25,401	$38,532	$42,019	$36,420
Percentage by HPSA designation				
Whole-county HPSA	56.7%	58.5%	58.0%	60.9%
Partial-county HPSA	28.2	29.6	32.9	30.3
Not HPSA	15.0	11.9	9.1	8.8
Bonus payments as a percentage of basic physician payments				
All non-metropolitan counties	0.5%	0.7%	0.6%	0.5%
By HPSA designation				
Whole-county HPSA	1.5	2.0	1.8	1.7
Partial-county HPSA	0.4	0.5	0.5	0.3
Not HPSA	0.2	0.2	0.2	0.1

SOURCE: Physician/supplier claims for the 5 percent sample of beneficiaries.

NOTES: Total payment amounts are estimated by multiplying the payment amounts for the 5 percent sample by 20. Bonus payments are estimated by multiplying the payment amounts for the 5 percent sample by (0.1 x 20).

As expected, the largest share of bonus payments was made to physicians for services provided to beneficiaries residing in a whole-county HPSA. The share of bonus payments going for beneficiaries in whole-county HPSAs increased by 4.2 percent (from 56.7 percent in 1992 to

60.9 percent in 1998), and the share for those in partial-county HPSAs increased by 2.1 percentage points, whereas bonus payments for beneficiaries in non-HPSA counties declined.

Table 6.3 summarizes the distribution of basic Medicare payments and bonus payments to physicians for services provided to beneficiaries in non-metropolitan areas by Medically Underserved Area designations. MUA designation is based on primary care physician supplies as well as community income levels and other factors in a county or region. Many counties qualified as both HPSAs and MUAs. In each year, between 71 and 81 percent of all whole-county HPSAs were also designated as whole-county MUAs. Therefore, it is not surprising that counties designated as whole-county MUAs received the largest proportion of bonus payments.

Table 6.3
Distribution of Basic Medicare Payments to Physicians and Bonus Payments for Services to Non-Metropolitan Beneficiaries, by Medically Underserved Area, Selected Years

Type of Underserved Area	1992	1994	1996	1998
Total basic payments ($1,000)	$5,025,344	$5,926,700	$6,739,377	$7,389,105
By MUA designation				
Whole-county MUA	43.8%	43.7%	44.1%	44.2%
Partial-county MUA	35.5	35.6	35.1	34.8
Not MUA	20.7	20.7	20.9	21.0
Total bonus payments ($1,000)	$25,401	$38,532	$42,019	$36,420
By MUA designation				
Whole-county MUA	69.2%	69.4%	68.2%	69.2%
Partial-county MUA	22.4	22.3	22.7	20.7
Not MUA	8.5	8.3	9.1	10.1

SOURCE: Physician/supplier claims for the 5 percent sample of beneficiaries.

NOTES: Total payment amounts are estimated by multiplying the payment amounts for the 5 percent sample by 20. Bonus payments are estimated by multiplying the payment amounts for the 5 percent sample by (0.1 x 20).

PER CAPITA SPENDING FOR NON-METROPOLITAN BENEFICIARIES

In Table 6.4, we report estimated Medicare per capita spending on physician services and bonus payments for beneficiaries residing in non-metropolitan counties. Overall, Medicare per capita spending increased 36 percent between 1992 and 1998, rising from an estimated $574 per beneficiary to $783 per beneficiary. Bonus payment spending increased from an estimated $3 per beneficiary in 1992 to $5 per beneficiary in 1996 but declined in 1998 to $4 per beneficiary.

For each year, we find lower Medicare per capita spending on physician services for beneficiaries residing in the more remote non-metropolitan counties, with the lowest rates of per capita spending in frontier counties (see Table 6.4). The difference in spending on beneficiaries in counties with a large city adjacent to an urban county and beneficiaries in frontier counties is an estimated $114 (19 percent) per beneficiary for 1992 (= $606 – $492) and $150 (18 percent) per beneficiary in 1998.

In contrast to basic Medicare per capita spending patterns, the highest average per capita bonus payment in each year was for beneficiaries in remote counties with no large town (see

Table 6.4). The smallest per capita bonus payments were for beneficiaries in counties with a city of 10,000 or more, including counties adjacent to an MSA and those that are not.

Table 6.4
Distribution of Medicare per Capita Spending and Bonus Payments to Physicians
for Services to Non-Metropolitan Beneficiaries, by County Category, Selected Years

County Category	1992	1994	1996	1998
Basic payments				
All beneficiaries	$574	$656	$726	$783
By non-metropolitan county category				
Adjacent, city 10,000+	606	690	758	815
Adjacent, no city 10,000+	584	667	738.	788
Remote, city 10,000+	570	652	720	784
Remote, town 2,500–10,000	547	620	691	753
Remote, no town	511	601	671	727
Frontier counties	492	573	621	665
Bonus payments				
All beneficiaries	3	4	5	4
By non-metropolitan county category				
Adjacent, city 10,000+	2	3	3	3
Adjacent, no city 10,000+	4	5	6	5
Remote, city 10,000+	2	3	3	3
Remote, town 2,500–10,000	3	5	5	5
Remote, no town	5	6	7	6
Frontier counties	4	5	5	5

SOURCE: Physician/supplier claims for the 5 percent sample of beneficiaries.

NOTES: Total payment amounts are estimated by multiplying the payment amounts for the 5 percent sample by 20. Bonus payments are estimated by multiplying the payment amounts for the 5 percent sample by (0.1 x 20). Per capita payments are measured as total or bonus payments divided by the number of Medicare beneficiaries residing in each category of non-metropolitan county.

In Table 6.5, we present per capita Medicare basic spending and bonus payments by HPSA county designation. Medicare spending on beneficiaries residing in counties with no HPSA designation received the highest per capita spending for physician services, and per capita spending for beneficiaries in either whole- or partial-county HPSAs was moderately lower.[20]

Per capita bonus payments (see Table 6.5) follow a pattern similar to that for aggregate bonus payment amounts (see Table 6.2). Just as the highest proportion of bonus dollars was spent on beneficiaries residing in HPSA counties, per capita bonus payments are also highest in these counties, especially the whole-county HPSAs. Although per capita bonus payment spending declined between 1996 and 1998, the difference in spending between beneficiaries in

---

[20] We used all beneficiaries residing in a non-metropolitan county as the denominator for per capita cost estimates. This denominator slightly underestimated per capita costs, as discussed under hospital use rates in Section 2, but the effect on estimates was small.

whole-county HPSAs and those in non-HPSA counties increased over time from $8 (= $9 – $1) in 1992 to $12 in 1998.

Table 6.5
Distribution of Basic Medicare per Capita Spending and Bonus Payments to Physicians for Services to Beneficiaries, by Health Professional Shortage Area, Selected Years

Type of Shortage Area	1992	1994	1996	1998
Basic payments				
All beneficiaries	$574	$656	$726	$783
By HPSA designation				
Whole-county HPSA	572	660	721	779
Partial-county HPSA	564	646	724	774
Not HPSA	585	664	732	796
Bonus payments				
All non-metropolitan beneficiaries	3	4	5	4
By HPSA designation				
Whole-county HPSA	9	13	13	13
Partial-county HPSA	2	3	3	3
Not HPSA	1	1	1	1

SOURCE: Physician/supplier claims for the 5 percent sample of beneficiaries.

NOTES: Total payment amounts are estimated by multiplying the payment amounts for the 5 percent sample by 20. Bonus payments are estimated by multiplying the payment amounts for the 5 percent sample by (0.1 x 20). Per capita payments are measured as total or bonus payments divided by the number of Medicare beneficiaries residing in each category of non-metropolitan county.

Trends by HHS regions in per capita spending for basic Medicare payments and bonus payments for physician services, shown in Table 6.6, document steady increases in per capita payments from 1992 to 1998, as well as wide regional variations in spending for these services within each year. In 1992, for example, the Dallas region had the highest average level of basic Medicare spending ($618 per beneficiary), whereas the lowest average level was in the Denver region ($462 per beneficiary). By 1998, the Atlanta region had the highest level of $853 per beneficiary (the Dallas region was second highest) and the Seattle region had the lowest level of $622 per beneficiary.

By contrast, there do not appear to be consistent trends in per capita spending on physician bonus payments by HHS region. The highest bonus payment rates in 1992 were $4 per beneficiary for the New York, Atlanta, Dallas, and San Francisco regions. Bonus payment trends for individual regions fluctuated during the intervening years, ultimately resulting in a wider range in per capita payments. In 1998, Medicare paid an average of $6 per beneficiary in bonus payments for non-metropolitan beneficiaries in the Atlanta, Dallas, and San Francisco regions, and spending for all other regions except New York was at $3 per beneficiary or less.

Table 6.6
Distribution of Medicare per Capita Spending and Bonus Payments to Physicians
for Services to Non-Metropolitan Beneficiaries, by HHS Region, Selected Years

HHS Region	1992	1994	1996	1998
Basic payments				
All beneficiaries	$574	$656	$726	$783
By CMS region				
1. Boston	549	639	702	740
2. New York	582	685	772	783
3. Philadelphia	599	688	719	754
4. Atlanta	604	692	795	853
5. Chicago	541	632	707	771
6. Dallas	618	693	752	826
7. Kansas City	550	621	691	769
8. Denver	462	526	584	640
9. San Francisco	607	687	704	752
10. Seattle	532	578	606	622
Bonus payments				
All beneficiaries	3	4	5	4
By CMS region				
1. Boston	<1	1	1	1
2. New York	4	6	8	4
3. Philadelphia	2	3	4	3
4. Atlanta	4	6	7	6
5. Chicago	2	4	3	3
6. Dallas	4	7	6	6
7. Kansas City	2	3	3	3
8. Denver	3	3	3	3
9. San Francisco	4	4	5	6
10. Seattle	1	1	1	1

SOURCE: Physician/supplier claims for the 5 percent sample of beneficiaries.

NOTES: Total payment amounts are estimated by multiplying the payment amounts for the 5 percent sample by 20. Bonus payments are estimated by multiplying the payment amounts for the 5 percent sample by (0.1 x 20). Per capita payments are measured as total or bonus payments divided by the number of Medicare beneficiaries residing in each category of non-metropolitan counties.

BONUS PAYMENTS ATTRIBUTABLE TO PRIMARY CARE

The following set of tables examines the extent to which bonus payments are being made for services provided by primary care physicians or for primary care services. Because access to primary care is a priority for underserved areas, we focus on how the bonus payment program may enhance access to such services. The measures used for this analysis were the percentage of total bonus payments that are spent on (1) primary care physicians as a compared to other physician specialties and (2) on primary care services versus other services. These tables extend some of the analyses performed by the Physician Payment Review Commission (PPRC) on the early progress of the bonus payment program, the results of which were published in its report to Congress (PPRC, 1994a). (Refer to Section 1 for a summary of these results.) A word of caution: We cannot directly compare our results to the PPRC numbers primarily because our analyses were limited to bonus payments for services to beneficiaries residing in non-metropolitan counties rather than the entire bonus payment program. Therefore, we cannot account for all bonus payments because our analyses do not include payments for beneficiaries in metropolitan counties.

Bonus Payments for Primary Care Physicians

As described in Section 2, we defined physician services as services by providers with the Medicare specialty codes listed in Table 2.2, and primary care physicians were defined as those in general practice, family practice, and internal medicine. As shown in Table 6.7, slightly more than half of all Medicare bonus payments for services to beneficiaries in non-metropolitan counties were made to primary care physicians, and the percentages paid to these physicians declined gradually from 1992 through 1998. This decline was due to reductions over time in bonus payments to both general practice and family practice physicians, whereas payments to internal medicine physicians increased slightly.

Table 6.7
Distribution of Medicare Bonus Payments to Physicians for Services to Non-Metropolitan Beneficiaries, by Physician Specialty, Selected Years

Physician Specialty	1992	1994	1996	1998
Total bonus payments	$25,401,126	$38,531,638	$42,019,470	$36,420,069
Primary care	55.9%	52.4%	50.3%	49.7%
General practice	11.8	9.9	8.0	7.7
Family practice	27.6	24.5	22.7	23.3
Internal medicine	16.6	17.9	19.7	19.3
Other specialties	44.1	47.6	49.7	50.3
General surgery	10.4	10.3	9.8	9.0
Cardiology	2.1	3.3	3.1	3.1
Gynecology	<1.0	<1.0	<1.0	<1.0
All other	31.6	34.1	36.8	37.6

SOURCE: Physician/supplier claims for the 5 percent sample of beneficiaries.

NOTES: Total payment amounts are estimated by multiplying the payment amounts for the 5 percent sample by 20. Bonus payments are estimated by multiplying the payment amounts for the 5 percent sample by (0.1 x 20).

Table 6.8 summarizes the distribution of bonus payments by physician specialty and HPSA county designation for 1994 and 1998. In both years, primary care physicians providing care to beneficiaries in whole-county HPSAs received the largest share of bonus payment dollars, although their share declined slightly during the four-year period. The percentage of bonus payments to primary care physicians serving beneficiaries in partial-county HPSAs declined more sharply (5 percentage points) between 1994 and 1998, whereas the payment shares increased for those serving beneficiaries in non-HPSA counties.

Table 6.8
Distribution of Medicare Bonus Payments to Physicians for Services to Non-Metropolitan Beneficiaries in Health Professional Shortage Areas, by Physician Specialty, 1994 and 1998

Year and Physician Specialty	Whole-County HPSA	Partial-County HPSA	Not HPSA
1994			
Primary care	54.8%	49.7%	46.7%
General practice	10.8	8.7	8.5
Family practice	25.9	22.8	22.2
Internal medicine	18.1	18.2	16.0
Other specialties	45.2	50.3	53.3
General surgery	10.9	9.2	10.4
Cardiology	3.1	3.6	3.1
Gynecology	0.3	0.4	0.3
All other	30.9	37.1	39.5
1998			
Primary care	52.9	44.9	51.0
General practice	8.1	7.0	8.3
Family practice	24.5	20.2	25.9
Internal medicine	20.4	17.8	16.7
Other specialties	47.1	55.1	49.0
General surgery	9.5	8.1	7.9
Cardiology	3.2	3.2	1.9
Gynecology	0.3	0.5	0.5
All other	34.1	43.3	38.8

SOURCE: Physician/supplier claims for the 5 percent sample of beneficiaries.

NOTE: Bonus payments are estimated by multiplying the payment amounts for the 5 percent sample by (0.1 x 20), and percentages are calculated based on total amounts.

Bonus Payments for Primary Care Services

The percentage of Medicare bonus payments spent on primary care services for non-metropolitan beneficiaries rose steadily during the 1990s, as summarized in Table 6.9. Between 1992 and 1998, bonus payments paid for primary care services increased from 29.7 percent to 37.0 percent of total bonus payments for services to non-metropolitan beneficiaries. Despite this trend, the majority of bonus payments (70.3 percent in 1992 and 63.0 percent in 1998) went to other services that were not included in the definition of primary care services.

Similar trends of increased bonus payments for primary care services occurred for whole-county HPSAs, partial-county HPSAs, and non-HPSA counties, as also shown in Table 6.9. Between 1996 and 1998, the largest increase in the share of bonus payments occurred for services provided to beneficiaries residing in a non-HPSA county (a spending increase of 7.9 percentage points).

Table 6.9
Distribution of Medicare Bonus Payments to Physicians for Services to Non-Metropolitan Beneficiaries in Health Professional Shortage Areas, by Type of Service, Selected Years

Year and Type of Service	All Non-Metropolitan Counties	Whole-County HPSA	Partial-County HPSA	Not HPSA
1992				
Primary care	29.7%	29.5%	31.2%	27.6%
Other	70.3	70.5	68.8	72.4
1994				
Primary care	30.8	31.4	30.2	29.4
Other	69.2	68.6	69.8	70.6
1996				
Primary care	31.9	32.8	30.5	31.0
Other	68.1	67.2	69.5	69.0
1998				
Primary care	37.0	37.2	36.0	38.9
Other	63.0	62.8	64.0	61.1

SOURCE: Physician/supplier claims for the 5 percent sample of beneficiaries.

NOTES: Bonus payments are estimated by multiplying the payment amounts for the 5 percent sample by (0.1 x 20), and percentages are calculated based on total amounts. Primary care services defined by OBRA-87 as "physicians' services" by HCPCS codes: office medical services, home medical services, emergency room services, skilled nursing, intermediate care, and long-term care medical services (nursing home and custodial care). Defined to be compatible with definitions used in PPRC (1994b).

In Tables 6.10 and 6.11, we examine the extent to which bonus payments for primary care services to beneficiaries residing in non-metropolitan counties were paid to primary care physicians. An estimated 79.9 percent of bonus payments paid for primary care services were paid to primary care physicians in 1992, declining to 70.7 percent in 1998. Within the primary care physician category, most of the decline in shares of bonus payments for primary care services was experienced by general practice physicians, although family practice shares also decreased at a slower rate. Payment shares increased for internal medicine physicians. With this decline in payment shares for primary care physicians during the 1990s, the role of specialty physicians in providing primary care services increased, as reflected in payment shares that rose from 20.1 percent of all primary care bonus payments in 1992 to 29.3 percent of the total in 1998.

Table 6.10
Distribution of Medicare Bonus Payments to Physicians for Primary Care Services
to Non-Metropolitan Beneficiaries, by Physician Specialty, Selected Years

Type of Care and Specialty	1992	1994	1996	1998
Bonus payments for primary care services	$7,523,404	$11,876,060	$13,401,411	$13,466,950
Primary care	79.9%	76.6%	73.9%	70.7%
General practice	20.0	17.5	14.6	12.8
Family practice	40.9	37.9	36.1	35.1
Internal medicine	19.0	21.2	23.3	22.8
Other specialties	20.1	23.4	26.1	29.3

SOURCE: Physician/supplier claims for the 5 percent sample of beneficiaries.

NOTES: Bonus payments are estimated by multiplying the payment amounts for the 5 percent sample by (0.1 x 20), and percentages are calculated based on total amounts. Primary care services defined by OBRA-87 as "physicians' services" by HCPCS codes: office medical services, home medical services, emergency room services, skilled nursing, intermediate care, and long-term care medical services (nursing home and custodial care). Defined to be compatible with definitions used in PPRC (1994b).

Primary care physicians providing services to beneficiaries in whole-county HPSAs received a slightly larger share of bonus payments for primary care services than those serving beneficiaries in other county designations (see Table 6.11). Between 1994 and 1998, there was an increase of almost 9 percent in the share of bonus payments for primary care services provided by specialists to beneficiaries in partial-county HPSAs.

The definition of the primary care physician excludes certain specialties that do perform primary care services as a routine part of their practice (e.g., gynecologists—see below). Of note, in Table 6.11, a larger share of primary care services for partial-county HPSA residents was provided by specialists. During this same time period (between 1994 and 1998), the number of counties with a partial-county HPSA designation increased slightly (from 1,083 counties to 1,197 counties), reflecting a growing number of areas that meet the criteria for a health professional shortage area. In essence, this trend may reflect the growing role that specialists are playing in providing primary care services because of an undersupply of primary care physicians.

Table 6.11
**Distribution of Medicare Bonus Payments to Physicians for Primary Care Services
in Health Professional Shortage Areas and Other Areas, by Physician Specialty, 1994 and 1998**

Year and Physician Specialty	Whole-County HPSA	Partial-County HPSA	Not HPSA
1994			
Total bonus payments for primary care services	$7,052,834	$3,432,223	$1,339,116
Primary care	77.4%	76.1%	74.0%
General practice	18.0	16.3	17.9
Family practice	38.6	37.0	37.0
Internal medicine	20.9	22.7	19.1
Other specialties	22.6	23.9	26.0
1998			
Total bonus payments for primary care services	$8,171,592	$3,931,189	$1,238,472
Primary care	72.1%	67.2%	72.2%
General practice	13.3	11.7	13.2
Family practice	35.2	33.2	40.1
Internal medicine	23.5	22.4	18.9
Other specialties	27.9	32.8	27.8

SOURCE: Physician/supplier claims for the 5 percent sample of beneficiaries.

NOTES: Total payment amounts are estimated by multiplying the payment amounts for the 5 percent sample by 20. Bonus payments are estimated by multiplying the payment amounts for the 5 percent sample by (0.1 x 20). Primary care services are defined by OBRA-87 as "physicians' services" by HCPCS codes: office medical services, home medical services, emergency room services, skilled nursing, intermediate care, and long-term care medical services (nursing home and custodial care). Defined to be compatible with definitions used in PPRC (1994b).

Trends in Bonus Payments for Primary Care by Specialty

The previous tables report the proportion of bonus payments made to physicians by specialty and bonus payments made for primary care and other services. By definition, those tables reflect only the services for which a bonus payment was claimed. However, physicians may have provided primary care services in underserved areas without claiming a bonus payment. Therefore, we now examine basic Medicare payments to physicians for primary care services to assess the percentage of these payments that were paid to primary care and specialty physicians, as summarized in Table 6.12. We include gynecologists and urologists as other specialty physicians who are known to provide primary care services to Medicare beneficiaries.

Payments for primary care services as a share of aggregate basic Medicare payments for physician services increased by 4.6 percentage points between 1992 and 1994. This trend was evident across all specialties, indicating that rural beneficiaries received relatively more primary care services over time regardless of the specialty of the provider. Primary care services constituted a much larger share of Medicare payments to primary care physicians than payments to specialty physicians, and this share increased from 34 percent of Medicare payments in 1992 to about 40 percent in 1998. An estimated one-quarter of Medicare payments to gynecologists were for primary care services, although they were not included as primary care physicians. However, this was not reflected in the claims by gynecologists for bonus payments.[21]

Table 6.12
Distribution of Medicare Payments to Physicians for Primary Care Services to Non-Metropolitan Beneficiaries as a Share of Total Physician Payments, by Physician Specialty, Selected Years

Physician Specialty	1992	1994	1996	1998
Primary care payments ($1,000)	$703,514	$954,199	$1,149,814	$1,375,631
% of total basic payments	14.0%	16.1%	17.1%	18.6%
Primary care	34.0	37.1	38.4	40.1
General practice	48.8	51.4	52.3	53.2
Family practice	40.5	42.8	44.5	47.5
Internal medicine	25.1	28.9	30.8	32.4
Other specialties	7.2	9.1	10.3	11.7
General surgery	7.8	8.3	8.4	9.4
Cardiology	6.1	7.1	8.6	9.3
Gynecology	20.5	24.5	25.6	28.2
Urology	8.9	9.9	9.5	10.4
All other	7.0	9.3	10.6	12.2

SOURCE: Physician/supplier claims for the 5 percent sample of beneficiaries.

NOTES: Total payment amounts are estimated by multiplying the payment amounts for the 5 percent sample by 20. Bonus payments are estimated by multiplying the payment amounts for the 5 percent sample by (0.1 x 20). Primary care services defined by OBRA-87 as "physicians' services" by HCPCS codes: office medical services, home medical services, emergency room services, skilled nursing, intermediate care, and long-term care medical services (nursing home and custodial care). Defined to be compatible with definitions used in PPRC (1994b). Proportion of payments for primary care services was calculated as the total line payments made for primary care services by specialty divided by total line payments for all services by specialty.

We also analyzed bonus payments for primary care services, by physician specialty, for each category of HPSA designation (whole-county HPSA, partial-county HPSA, and non-HPSA counties). We found that trends in the percentage of bonus payments for primary care services paid to primary care physicians by HPSA designation did not differ significantly from the overall trends reported in Table 6.12.

PAYMENTS TO NON-PHYSICIAN PRACTITIONERS

In this final analysis, we explored the role of NPPs in providing services to Medicare beneficiaries in non-metropolitan counties, as reflected in Medicare payments. According to federal legislation, non-physician practitioners in independent practice may bill Medicare independently, and through 1998, they were reimbursed at 75 percent of the Physician Fee Schedule amount (payments were increased to 85 percent by the BBA). Physicians may bill for NPP services when the NPP works directly under a physician's supervision and the physician is

---

[21] Gynecologists claimed less than 1 percent of all bonus payments overall and for primary care services specifically in each year studied (data not shown).

actively involved in the course of treatment. NPPs are not currently eligible for bonus payments for independently billed services, although policymakers have considered this option (PPRC, 1994b).

As described in Section 2, NPPs were defined for this analysis to include physician assistants, nurse practitioners, certified nurse midwives, certified clinical nurse specialists, and certified nurse anesthetists. Table 6.13 presents estimates of the percentage of Medicare spending for services that NPPs billed directly as a fraction of all dollars spent on NPP and physicians' services (as previously defined), overall and by county category. Total payments to NPPs for independently billed services increased from $80.5 million in 1992 to $133.6 million in 1998, reflecting a 66 percent increase over time (see Table 6.13). These payments, however, represent a small fraction of the total Medicare payments to physician and non-physician practitioners. The largest share of Medicare dollars spent on NPP services was for services provided to beneficiaries residing in the most remote counties. Additionally, the largest share of NPP services was provided to residents of whole-county HPSAs.

Table 6.13
Distribution of Medicare Payments to NPPs for Services to Non-Metropolitan Beneficiaries, by County Category and HPSA Designation, Selected Years

County Category	1992	1994	1996	1998
Medicare payments to NPPs	$80,481,296	$86,671,169	$101,077,418	$133,583,606
Percentage of total Medicare payments to physicians and NPPs				
All non-metropolitan counties	1.6%	1.4%	1.5%	1.8%
By county category				
Adjacent, city 10,000+	1.3	1.2	1.2	1.5
Adjacent, no city 10,000+	1.5	1.4	1.4	1.7
Remote, city 10,000+	1.6	1.5	1.5	1.8
Remote, town 2,500–10,000	1.9	1.7	1.8	2.2
Remote, no town	2.0	1.9	1.9	2.2
Frontier counties	2.0	1.9	2.0	2.4
By HPSA designation				
Whole-county HPSA	1.8	1.6	1.5	1.8
Partial-county HPSA	1.5	1.4	1.4	1.7
Not HPSA designation	1.6	1.4	1.5	1.8

SOURCE: Physician/supplier claims for the 5 percent sample of beneficiaries.

NOTES: Total payment amounts are estimated by multiplying the payment amounts for the 5 percent sample by 20. NPPs include Nurse Practitioners, Physician's Assistants, Certified Nurse Midwives, Certified Nurse Anesthetists, and Certified Clinical Nurse Specialists. The numerator for each percentage is the sum of Medicare payments for NPP services only and the denominator is the sum of Medicare payments for services by physicians or NPPs.

ISSUES AND IMPLICATIONS

The analytic results contained in this report provide a descriptive framework regarding Medicare payments for physician services for Medicare beneficiaries in non-metropolitan areas, with a focus on the special payment policy offering 10 percent bonus payments for services provided in HPSAs. These analyses have identified some trends with implications for future

Medicare payment policy for rural providers. In this subsection, we synthesize our findings and consider some of the issues they pose regarding access to physician services for rural beneficiaries that might be addressed in further analyses in this project.

Medicare Spending for Physician Bonus Payments

While Medicare spending for physician services to non-metropolitan beneficiaries increased steadily during the 1990s, this trend did not translate into the same growth pattern for bonus payments. After substantial increases during the first half of the decade, total bonus payments began to level off between 1994 and 1996 and then declined by 13.3 percent between 1996 and 1998. This trend also is reflected in bonus payments measured as a percentage of basic Medicare payments, which were 0.5 percent of basic payments in 1992, 0.7 percent in 1994, 0.6 percent in 1996, and 0.5 percent in 1998. Of note, these percentages of less than 1 percent highlight that bonus payments represent an extremely small share of total Medicare costs for physician services to non-metropolitan beneficiaries.

As expected, the majority of bonus payments for non-metropolitan beneficiaries were for those residing in HPSAs, but substantial shares also were paid for those in non-HPSA locations. For each of the four years studied, close to an estimated 60 percent of bonus payments were made for physician services to beneficiaries residing in whole-county HPSAs, and 30 percent were for beneficiaries in partial-county HPSAs, including those not living within the HPSA boundaries. A relatively substantial balance of 10 percent of bonus payments was attributable to services for beneficiaries residing in non-HPSA counties. An unknown percentage would be added to this portion for beneficiaries in partial-county HPSAs but not in the HPSA portion of the county (which would be subtracted from the percentage for partial-county HPSAs). These findings suggest that bonus payments may have contributed to access on a broader geographical scale than the strict limits of the HPSA boundaries, possibly reflecting the distances that rural beneficiaries often travel for care.

Looking at bonus payment trends by HPSA designation, we find a decrease in bonus payments for non-HPSA counties between 1992 and 1998. For example, the share of total bonus payments for non-metropolitan beneficiaries that were paid for those residing in non-HPSA counties declined from 15.0 percent in 1992 to 8.8 percent in 1998 (a 41 percent decrease). Expressed differently, bonus payments for non-HPSA counties were halved from 0.2 percent of basic Medicare payments for physician services in 1992 to 0.1 percent in 1998. This decrease in bonus payments might diminish some of the possible improvements in access for beneficiaries residing in these counties, unless the increase in number of available RHCs and FQHCs contributed to ensuring availability of primary care services.

To examine regional variations in bonus payments for non-metropolitan beneficiaries, we calculated average per capita payments by HHS region for both basic Medicare physician payments and bonus payments. The overall steady growth in basic physician payments over time also was found within each region, although there was substantial variation across regions for each year in the average per capita payments. For per capita bonus payments, the regions varied substantially in both the average levels of payments and trends over time. The New York, Philadelphia, Atlanta, Chicago, and Dallas regions reflected the overall pattern of increased per capita bonus payments from 1992 to the mid-1990s followed by a decline through 1998. The average per capita bonus payment increased over time in the San Francisco region and remained fairly constant in the other four regions. The Boston and Seattle regions had the lowest average bonus payments of $1 per beneficiary or less. These findings suggest there may be systematic regional differences in how providers or carriers have approached use of the bonus payments, but additional analysis would be needed to identify underlying behavioral mechanisms.

Bonus Payments for Primary Care Services

Two distinct aspects of bonus payments for primary care were considered in our analysis: payments to primary care physicians and payments for primary care services. In both cases, we found that bonus payments had targeted primary care, which were encouraging findings with respect to the goals of policymakers when this program was introduced at the start of the decade. For example, 55.9 percent of total bonus payments in 1992 were paid to primary care providers, although their shares decreased steadily over time to reach 49.7 percent in 1998. Ricketts et al. (2000) observed a decline in shares for family practice physicians, one of the three physician specialties defined as primary care, which supports this trend in declining shares for primary care physicians.

In 1992, payments for primary care services represented 14.0 percent of total basic Medicare payments for physician services and 29.7 percent of total Medicare bonus payments for beneficiaries residing in non-metropolitan counties. By 1998, these shares had grown to 18.6 percent of total Medicare payments and 37.0 percent of total bonus payments. Thus, both the levels and growth trends were higher for bonus payments made for primary care services, compared to overall physician payments.

Our findings regarding primary care services by specialists are consistent with PPRC findings (1994a). The authors of that report suggested that two distinct factors may contribute to these results: (1) the broad definition of primary care services that encompasses some services provided by specialty physicians and (2) an inadequate supply of primary care physicians in underserved areas that results in specialists providing some primary care services they would not provide in more urban areas. Anecdotal information suggests that the increase in the share of primary care services provided by specialists may also reflect insufficient specialty business and that specialists are providing primary care services to build up their practices. According to one study, however, obstetricians-gynecologists and general surgeons were the only specialists in rural areas found to provide services outside their specialty areas (Baldwin et al., 1998). Thus, we have more to learn about the services provided by rural specialty physicians.

Role of Non-Physician Practitioners

The analysis of payments to non-physician practitioners indicates that NPP services that have been billed directly to Medicare have been a very small fraction of Medicare payments for physician/NPPs services (sum of physician and NPP services) to Medicare beneficiaries in non-metropolitan areas. NPP payments were very small shares of total combined payments for physicians and NPPs in both 1992 (1.6 percent) and 1998 (1.8 percent). By county category, NPP payments were only 1.5 percent of physician/NPP payments in counties adjacent to an MSA with a city of 10,000 population (most urbanized) and were 2.2 percent in the most remote counties with no town and 2.4 percent in frontier counties. We did not find much variation in the share of NPP payments based on the HPSA designation of counties, which would be expected to the extent that NPPs were more important providers of care in the underserved areas represented by HPSAs. Although slight differences in shares between whole-county HPSAs and non-HPSA counties existed in the early years, they disappeared by 1998.

An important limitation to our analyses of Medicare payments for NPP services was identified in discussions with CMS staff. Physicians and NPPs had a financial incentive to bill Medicare for NPP services through physicians' practices rather than independent billing by the NPPs, to obtain payment at the full fee schedule rates rather than at 75 percent. Anecdotal information indicates that physicians have been submitting Medicare claims and paying NPPs from the payments received. The extent of these billing practices is not known. Medicare regulations allow for such arrangements if the NPP is practicing under the active supervision of the physician. As a result, the Medicare claims for services directly billed by NPPs appear to represent a small fraction of Medicare spending for NPP services, especially when considering services by NPPs employed in clinics or group practices, RHCs, FQHCs, or community or mental health centers, for which the clinics bill Medicare.

Discussion

The trends in physician bonus payments during the 1990s raise issues regarding the ongoing effectiveness of the bonus payment program. Some evidence was found that this program has been successful in supporting primary care providers and services and, possibly, has enhanced services for beneficiaries residing in the more remote parts of our country, especially those in HPSAs. On the other hand, low levels of bonus payments in general, coupled with declines in those amounts since 1994, bode ill for its future potential to support physicians practicing in rural areas and, thus, to protect access for rural Medicare beneficiaries. For these goals to be achieved, physicians must use the bonus payments, yet they clearly are not taking advantage of the extra payment amounts available to them. If bonus payments continue to decline in the face of steady increases in basic Medicare payments for physician services, their effects will be further diluted.

Factors that could be contributing to these trends in bonus payments include, for example, the extent to which physicians are knowledgeable about bonus payments, the perceived value of the payments to physicians, and effects of administrative procedures on the ease of receiving the payments. Because the bonus payments are administered by the Medicare carriers, policies and procedures for informing physicians, administering payment requests, and auditing appropriateness of payments may vary widely across carriers, which could explain some of the observed regional variation. With the data used for our analyses, we are limited in our ability to explore the relative contributions of such factors to the declining trends in bonus payments.

When considering the policy option of extending bonus payments to NPP services, the small share of Medicare payments for NPP services makes it clear that such a policy would have limited short-term financial impact for Medicare, even if NPPs submitted claims for all eligible services. One might speculate, however, that NPP bonus payments would grow over time because these payments might be a stronger financial incentive for these practitioners than for physicians.

7. 1990–1997 TRENDS IN AAPCC CAPITATION RATES

The AAPCC rates that CMS published each year through 1997 were set at 95 percent of the adjusted average per capita costs for Medicare fee-for-service beneficiaries. These rates were the basis for capitation payments to Medicare health plans, which were risk-adjusted using demographic factors. Medicare AAPCCs were calculated for more than 3,100 counties and similar geographic areas within the continental United States.[22] The AAPCC rates were replaced in 1998 by the new capitation rates established by the BBA of 1997. The 1997 AAPCCs were the baseline capitation rates for calculation of these new capitation rates. The BBA also mandated an improved risk-adjustment methodology, which began being used in 2000.

The research reported here is designed to document trends in Medicare base capitation rates from 1990 through 1997 for rural and urban counties and to examine factors that may have contributed to observed payment trends. Relationships between AAPCCs and managed care participation also are examined. The analysis includes consideration of AAPCCs for urban areas to provide a reference point for assessing the levels and volatility of the rural AAPCC rates. These analyses address the following specific research questions:

- How do the levels and volatility of Medicare AAPCC rates differ among rural underserved areas, other rural counties, and urban counties?

- How do these differences change over time?

- What are the relationships between capitation rates and Medicare health plan enrollments in rural areas, with comparisons to urban area relationships?

Our analyses of the AAPCC rates provide a historical summary of trends in the rates that were in use before the current capitation policy was put in place. Furthermore, by anchoring the analyses on the 1997 AAPCC rates, we will be able to contribute to a more detailed understanding of the factors that influenced the baseline rates that will drive Medicare capitation rates for some time to come.

DISTRIBUTIONS OF AAPCC RATES

Trends in AAPCC rates were compared across the defined county categories for each of our three AAPCC measures: average AAPCC rates, the Part A share of the AAPCCs, and the volatility of the AAPCCs over time. Relationships between AAPCC rates and several measures of county demographics and provider supply were examined, estimating multivariate models of determinants of AAPCCs. We also examined 1997 enrollment rates for Medicare health plans, with comparisons to 1993 enrollments, to assess the extent to which Medicare managed care had a presence in non-metropolitan locations. We present the results of this research below.

---

[22] AAPCC rates also are calculated for geographic areas outside the United States, including Guam, Puerto Rico, the Virgin Islands, and several other areas. These areas are not included in our analyses.

Levels of AAPCCs over Time

In the first step of our analysis of trends in AAPCC capitation rates, we compare levels of AAPCCs over time for several groupings of counties. First, we compare average AAPCCs for metropolitan, non-metropolitan, and frontier counties. Then we perform similar comparisons by region. Finally, we compare AAPCCs for HPSA and MUA counties, also categorized by metropolitan, non-metropolitan, and frontier categories.

The well-known differences in AAPCC rates for metropolitan and non-metropolitan counties are documented in Table 7.1, which presents average AAPCC rates for 1990, 1994, and 1997. These averages are weighted by the number of Medicare beneficiaries residing in each county. For each year, the overall average AAPCC rates for metropolitan counties were $100 higher than those for non-metropolitan counties. The large metropolitan counties had the highest AAPCC rates, averaging $349 in 1990 and increasing to $535 in 1997. Within the non-metropolitan counties, differences in AAPCC rates for counties adjacent to MSAs and remote counties became larger over time. In 1990, rates were similar for all five categories of non-metropolitan counties, ranging from $243 to $232 (a difference of 4.7 percent).

Table 7.1
Average AAPCC Capitation Rates, by Metropolitan, Non-Metropolitan, and Frontier Counties, 1990, 1994 and 1997

County Category	Average AAPCC Rates ($) (weighted by Medicare population)			Annual % Change
	1990	1994	1997	1990–1997
Metropolitan	320	407	493	6.4
Large counties	349	446	535	6.3
Small counties	275	351	432	6.7
Non-metropolitan	238	306	386	7.2
Adjacent, city 10,000+	243	317	399	7.3
Adjacent, no city 10,000+	239	308	391	7.3
Remote, city 10,000+	235	299	374	6.9
Remote, town 2,500–10,000	233	297	376	7.0
Remote, no town	232	295	374	7.0
Frontier county status				
Frontier counties	244	296	356	5.5
Other non-metropolitan counties	237	306	387	7.3

SOURCE: Area Resource File for 1999 with relevant Medicare data added.

NOTE: Change in average AAPCC rates is measured as average compounded annual percentage change from 1990 to 1997.

By 1997, AAPCC rates ranged from $399 for adjacent counties with a city of at least 10,000 to $374 for the more remote counties (a difference of 6.7 percent) (see Table 7.1). The average AAPCC rate of $244 for frontier counties in 1990 was as high as the average AAPCC for non-metropolitan counties adjacent to an MSA with a city, but by 1997, the $356 average AAPCC rate for frontier counties was the lowest of all county groups.

The differences in the 1990 and 1997 AAPCC rates are the result of differing rates of increase in AAPCCs for metropolitan and non-metropolitan counties during this time period (see

Table 7.1). Overall, AAPCCs for non-metropolitan counties increased at a compounded rate of 7.2 percent annually, compared with an average 6.4 percent increase for metropolitan counties. The AAPCCs for non-metropolitan counties adjacent to MSAs grew fastest at 7.3 percent annually. The lowest rate of growth was an average 5.5 percent annually for the frontier counties.

One measure of the variation in AAPCC rates for metropolitan and non-metropolitan counties is the range of AAPCCs across counties within each category. In 1997, the AAPCCs for metropolitan counties ranged from $256 to $767, and the AAPCCs for the large metropolitan counties tended to be higher within that range, but varying substantially from $283 to $767 (data not shown). For non-metropolitan counties, the AAPCCs ranged from $221 to $693, with similarly wide ranges within each of the five categories of counties.

In Table 7.2, we find variation among regions in the average levels of AAPCC rates and the rates at which they increased over time. The San Francisco region had the highest rates in 1990 for both metropolitan and non-metropolitan counties. The New York and Philadelphia regions also had high metropolitan AAPCC rates, and non-metropolitan rates were high in the Philadelphia region. Annual increases in the metropolitan AAPCC rates ranged from a high of 7.5 percent for the Dallas region to a low of 4.3 percent for the Seattle region. Increases for non-metropolitan counties ranged from 8.7 percent for the Atlanta region to 4.7 percent for the Seattle region. These variations in AAPCC rate increases yielded a different regional distribution of rates by 1997. The New York region had the highest average AAPCC rate for metropolitan counties in 1997, followed closely by the San Francisco and Philadelphia regions. At the same time, regional average AAPCC rates for non-metropolitan counties changed noticeably between 1990 and 1997, resulting in the Philadelphia region having the highest average rate in 1997, followed by the Atlanta region.

Table 7.2
Average AAPCCs for Metropolitan, Non-Metropolitan, and Frontier Counties
by HHS Region, 1990 and 1997

HHS Region	Metropolitan Counties			Non-Metropolitan Counties (not Frontier)			Frontier Counties		
	1990	1997	Change	1990	1997	Change	1990	1997	Change
1. Boston	$305	$495	7.2%	$237	$372	6.7%	0	0	—
2. New York	332	543	7.3	231	367	6.8	0	0	—
3. Philadelphia	333	510	6.3	262	423	7.1	0	0	—
4. Atlanta	297	487	7.3	232	416	8.7	0	0	—
5. Chicago	318	472	5.8	233	361	6.5	0	0	—
6. Dallas	291	483	7.5	240	401	7.6	243	360	5.8
7. Kansas City	301	436	5.4	220	343	6.5	228	353	6.4
8. Denver	276	409	5.8	232	343	5.7	248	352	5.1
9. San Francisco	365	522	5.2	266	403	6.1	257	386	6.0
10. Seattle	288	387	4.3	258	355	4.7	236	337	5.6

SOURCE: Area Resource File for 1999 with relevant Medicare data added.

NOTES: Averages are weighted by the Medicare population in each county. There are no frontier counties in the eastern regions. Change in average AAPCC rates is measured as average compounded annual percentage change from 1990 to 1997.

Some regional differences in AAPCC rates were found for frontier counties. The San Francisco region had the highest average rate in both 1990 and 1997. The frontier counties in the Denver region also had high AAPCC rates during the 1990s, but with the lowest rate of increase over time (5.1 percent annualized), frontier counties in this region had the lowest AAPCC rates by 1997. This finding is notable given the large percentage (61.0 percent) of counties in the region that qualify as frontier counties (see Table 3.3).

Average AAPCC rates for counties designated as HPSAs or MUAs are presented in Table 7.3 for 1990, 1994, and 1997. These rates are grouped by metropolitan, non-metropolitan, and frontier categories, and comparisons are provided for counties within each category that were not designated as a HPSA (or MUA) or were whole-county or partial-county designations. We observe some similar patterns in AAPCC rates for the HPSA and MUA counties. Among the metropolitan counties, the counties designated as partial-county HPSAs or MUAs had the highest average AAPCC rates for all three years reported. The whole-county HPSAs or MUAs had the lowest rates (with the exception of the metropolitan MUA counties in 1997 which had the same rates as non-MUA counties).

Among the non-metropolitan counties, the average 1990 AAPCC rates were similar for whole-county, partial-county, and non-designated counties, but the rates diverged between 1990 and 1997 (see Table 7.3). For HPSA designations in non-metropolitan counties, the 1997 average AAPCC rate was highest for counties designated as partial-county HPSAs and lowest for non-HPSA counties. For MUA designations in non-metropolitan counties, the counties designated as whole-county MUAs had the highest average AAPCC rate in 1997, and the partial-county MUAs and non-designated counties had similar rates. Finally, among the frontier counties, the average AAPCC rates also were similar in 1990, diverging over time such that the non-designated frontier counties had the highest AAPCC rates for both the HPSA and MUA designations.

Part A Share of AAPCC Capitation Rates

The second aspect of the AAPCC rates that we examined was variations across counties in the shares of the rates that are attributable to Part A and Part B per capita spending in fee-for-service Medicare. We also wanted to assess the extent to which these shares may have changed over time, as the outpatient and inpatient service mix changed across the country. The measure we used for this analysis was the Part A AAPCC expressed as a percentage of the total AAPCC (the sum of Part A and Part B amounts). As shown in Tables 7.4 and 7.5, there are few differences across metropolitan, non-metropolitan, and frontier counties in the average Part A share of the AAPCC rates.

Table 7.3
Average AAPCC Capitation Rates, by Metropolitan and Non-Metropolitan
Health Professional Shortage Areas, 1990, 1994, and 1997

Type of Shortage Area	Average AAPCC Rates (weighted by Medicare population)			Annual % Change
	1990	1994	1997	1990–1997
Health professional shortage areas	(1991 HPSA)	(1993 HPSA)	(1997 HPSA)	
Metropolitan				
Whole-county	$283	$365	$437	6.4%
Partial-county	330	417	505	6.3
Not HPSA	296	384	457	6.4
Non-metropolitan				
Whole-county	235	310	396	7.7
Partial-county	241	305	385	6.9
Not HPSA	236	305	381	7.1
Frontier				
Whole-county	250	294	349	4.9
Partial-county	241	294	354	5.6
Not HPSA	246	302	368	5.9
Medically underserved areas				
Metropolitan				
Whole-county	278	365	458	7.4
Partial-county	327	415	502	6.3
Not MUA	294	377	458	6.5
Non-metropolitan				
Whole-county	237	310	400	7.8
Partial-county	238	303	376	6.8
Not MUA	238	301	373	6.6
Frontier				
Whole-county	242	287	346	5.2
Partial-county	247	297	362	5.6
Not MUA	246	309	367	5.9

SOURCE: Area Resource File for 1999 with relevant Medicare data added.

NOTE: Change in average AAPCC rates is measured as average compounded annual percentage change from 1990 to 1997.

Table 7.4
Part A Percentage Share of AAPCC Capitation Rates, by Metropolitan, Non-Metropolitan, and Frontier Counties, 1990, 1994, and 1997

County Category	1990	1994	1997
Metropolitan			
Large counties	59.0%	64.0%	65.4%
Small counties	60.9	63.5	64.9
Non-metropolitan			
Adjacent, city 10,000+	60.9	64.1	65.8
Adjacent, no city 10,000+	62.7	64.5	65.7
Remote, city 10,000+	61.7	64.0	65.6
Remote, town 2,500–10,000	62.6	64.0	65.7
Remote, no town	64.1	65.1	65.9
Frontier county status			
Frontier counties	62.8	64.2	65.5
Other non-metropolitan counties	62.1	64.3	65.7

SOURCE: Area Resource File for 1999 with relevant Medicare data added.

NOTE: Averages are weighted by the Medicare population in each county.

The Part A share increased slightly from 1990 to 1997 for all categories of counties, and shares also converged over that time period. In 1990, the average Part A shares ranged from a low of 59.0 percent of total AAPCCs for large metropolitan counties to a high of 64.1 percent for remote non-metropolitan counties with no town (a difference of 5.2 percent). In 1997, the shares ranged from an average 65.4 percent of total AAPCCs for large metropolitan counties to 65.9 percent for remote counties with no town (narrowing to only 0.8 percent difference). The 1997 Part A shares for individual counties varied moderately from those averages, ranging from 51.5 percent to 77.5 percent for metropolitan counties and from 48.9 percent to 80.5 percent for non-metropolitan counties (data not shown). We found an increase in the Part A shares, which suggests that any declines in hospital inpatient admissions were more than offset by increased utilization of other Part A services. The increase in use of skilled nursing and home health services during this decade could be the source of such an offset.

Looking at counties that are designated as HPSAs or MUAs, few differences in the Part A share of the AAPCCs were found, as shown in Table 7.5. The only consistent pattern was the slightly higher Part A shares for counties designated as whole-county HPSAs or whole-county MUAs. Yet most differences were too small to be important from a policy perspective. The Part A shares increased slightly (1.0 percent or less) for designated and non-designated counties between 1990 and 1997. For the frontier counties, however, we observe that counties designated as either whole- or partial-county HPSAs or MUAs had lower rates of increases in the Part A share, compared to frontier counties without a designation of HPSA or MUA.

Table 7.5
Part A Percentage Share of AAPCC Capitation Rates, by Metropolitan and Non-Metropolitan Health Professional Shortage Areas, 1990, 1994, and 1997

Type of Shortage Area	Average Part A Share of AAPCC Rates			Annual % Change
	1990	1994	1997	1990–1997
Health professional shortage areas	(1991 HPSA)	(1993 HPSA)	(1997 HPSA)	
Metropolitan				
Not HPSA	60.5%	64.0%	65.4%	1.1
Whole-county	63.2	64.6	67.0	0.8
Partial-county	59.4	63.7	65.1	1.3
Non-metropolitan				
Not HPSA	62.4	64.4	66.0	0.8
Whole-county	63.4	64.8	66.3	0.6
Partial-county	61.2	63.8	65.2	0.9
Frontier				
Not HPSA	62.5	64.3	66.1	0.8
Whole-county	63.8	64.3	65.5	0.4
Partial-county	62.5	64.1	65.1	0.6
Medically underserved areas				
Metropolitan				
Not MUA	60.7	64.1	64.9	1.0
Whole-county	60.5	62.8	64.5	0.9
Partial-county	59.6	63.8	65.3	1.3
Non-metropolitan				
Not MUA	61.7	63.4	65.5	0.9
Whole-county	62.9	62.7	66.1	0.7
Partial-county	61.5	63.6	65.3	0.9
Frontier				
Not MUA	62.0	64.6	66.3	1.0
Whole-county	63.6	64.6	65.5	0.4
Partial-county	61.9	62.8	64.4	0.6

SOURCE: Area Resource File for 1999 with relevant Medicare data added.

NOTES: Averages are weighted by the Medicare population in each county. Change in average Part A share of AAPCC rates is measured as average compounded annual percentage change from 1990 to 1997.

Volatility of AAPCC Rates

Conceptually, we would expect to see greater volatility in AAPCCs for counties with smaller Medicare populations because a few unpredictable health care events during a year are more likely to affect the average costs estimated for smaller populations. Thus, we are interested in examining the magnitude of year-to-year differences in AAPCCs within each county, as well as the variation in these differences across counties within each category of metropolitan, non-metropolitan, and frontier counties.

As described in the Section 2, we calculated five-year average measures of volatility in AAPCC rates for each of the years 1990 through 1995. For example, the volatility measure for 1990 was calculated using AAPCCs for 1988 through 1992. The numerator for the measure was the sum of the absolute deviations of the 1988, 1989, 1991, and 1992 AAPCCs from the five-year average AAPCC for 1988 through 1992 (i.e., centered on 1990). The denominator was the five-year average AAPCC. These standardized measures of relative volatility control for increases in the AAPCC levels over time, thus isolating the volatility effect.

We report in Table 7.6 the means and standard deviations for the relative volatility of AAPCCs, as well as changes in the means from 1990 to 1995. The 1995 AAPCCs for non-metropolitan counties were more volatile than those for metropolitan counties, as shown by the means for the relative volatility measures. Although the differences in means appear small, there was an 11.6 percent difference between the largest non-metropolitan mean (12.1) and the smallest metropolitan mean (10.7) in 1990, and a 15.9 percent difference between the same measures for 1995. Thus, the metropolitan/non-metropolitan differences in AAPCC rate volatility increased between 1990 and 1995.

Table 7.6
Volatility of AAPCC Capitation Rates, by Metropolitan, Non-Metropolitan,
and Frontier Counties, 1990 and 1995

County Category	1990 AAPCC Rates		1995 AAPCC Rates		Annual % Change in Mean 1990–1995
	Mean	Std. Dev.	Mean	Std. Dev.	
Metropolitan					
Large counties	10.7	2.1	9.5	2.2	−2.4
Small counties	10.7	2.9	10.1	2.4	−1.1
Non-metropolitan					
Adjacent, city 10,000+	12.1	3.3	10.9	2.9	−2.1
Adjacent, no city 10,000+	11.5	3.4	11.3	3.2	−0.4
Remote, city 10,000+	11.1	3.0	10.7	3.2	−0.7
Remote, town 2,500–10,000	11.3	3.6	11.1	3.5	−0.4
Remote, no town	11.0	4.4	11.2	3.8	0.4
Frontier county status					
Frontier counties	10.5	4.4	9.1	3.7	−2.8
Other non-metropolitan counties	11.5	3.4	11.2	3.2	−0.5

SOURCE: Area Resource File for 1999 with relevant Medicare data added.

NOTES: Averages are weighted by the Medicare population in each county. Change in average volatility of AAPCC rates is measured as average compounded annual percentage change from 1990 to 1997.

The standard deviations of the volatility measures also were larger for non-metropolitan counties than for metropolitan counties for both 1990 and 1995, indicating a wider variation across non-metropolitan counties in AAPCC rate volatility. This variation in relative volatility also was seen for the 1995 AAPCCs for individual counties, which ranged from 1.9 percent to 22.1 percent across metropolitan counties and from 0.5 percent to 28.7 percent across non-metropolitan (data not shown). Changes in hospital reclassifications that occurred during the study period might have contributed to the volatility of AAPCCs for non-metropolitan counties.

Most of this effect would have been in counties adjacent to an MSA, so if these reclassification changes had not occurred, there would be greater differences in average volatility between adjacent and remote counties.

The 1990 AAPCCs for the frontier counties are 8.7 percent (= 10.5/11.5 – 1) less volatile than the non-frontier non-metropolitan county AAPCCs, and the 1995 AAPCCs are 18.7 percent less volatile (see Table 7.6). Yet the standard deviations of the frontier county volatility measures are 30 percent larger than those for non-frontier non-metropolitan counties. These findings are the opposite of what we would expect for counties with very small populations.

Examining this issue with the information in Table 7.7, we found heterogeneity in the sizes of Medicare populations in frontier counties, although all had small numbers of beneficiaries. In addition, we found that the AAPCCs for frontier counties with 300 beneficiaries or fewer were more volatile than those for other frontier counties, and AAPCCs for counties with 1,200 beneficiaries or more were the least volatile. Furthermore, variation in AAPCC volatility across frontier counties declines with increases in the beneficiary populations, as reflected in the standard deviations for the volatility measures by size category. Thus, although the average AAPCC volatility for frontier counties indeed is lower than those for other non-metropolitan counties, we do find the expected higher volatility related to the "small numbers" within the group of frontier counties.

Table 7.7
Volatility of 1995 AAPCC Capitation Rates for Frontier Counties,
by Size of Medicare Population

Size of Medicare Population	Frontier Counties		Relative Volatility of the 1995 AAPCCs	
	Number	%	Mean	Std. Dev.
All frontier counties	377	100.0	9.1	3.7
Medicare population				
300 or fewer	56	14.9	9.8	5.4
301 to 600	75	19.9	9.5	4.5
601 to 900	86	22.8	9.9	4.4
901 to 1,200	57	15.1	9.6	4.1
1,201 or more	103	27.3	8.5	3.1

SOURCE: Area Resource File for 1999 with relevant Medicare data added.

NOTE: Averages are weighted by the Medicare population in each county.

Relationships between AAPCC volatility and HPSA or MUA counties are summarized in Table 7.8, including comparisons by metropolitan, non-metropolitan, and frontier county categories for 1990, 1993, and 1995. Within each category, means and standard deviations for the volatility measure are presented for whole-county and partial-county HPSAs (or MUAs) and for other counties not designated as a HPSA or MUA.

We highlight three findings from Table 7.8. First, for both metropolitan and non-metropolitan counties, the AAPCCs for counties designated as partial-county HPSAs or MUAs were more volatile than those for counties with whole-county designations. Second, the reverse pattern was found for frontier counties in 1990, but these differences fade over time. Finally, we find contrasting trends between metropolitan and non-metropolitan counties in the rates and directions of change in AAPCC volatility between 1990 to 1995. Average AAPCC volatility decreased for metropolitan counties over time, whether or not they were designated as HPSAs or MUAs, but the strongest decreases were for metropolitan counties designated as whole-county HPSAs or whole-county MUAs. Volatility declined less for non-metropolitan counties regardless of HPSA or MUA designation. Frontier counties had the largest declines in AAPCC volatility from 1990 to 1995, including those for counties designated as whole-county HPSAs (3.7 percent), whole-county MUAs (5.1 percent), or not designated as a HPSA (4.0 percent).

Table 7.8
Volatility of AAPCC Capitation Rates, by Metropolitan
and Non-Metropolitan Underserved Areas, 1990, 1993, and 1995

| | Volatility of AAPCC Rates (mean and standard deviation) | | | Annual % Change |
Underserved Area	1990	1993	1995	1990–1995
Health professional shortage areas	(1991 HPSAs)	(1993 HPSAs)	(1995 HPSAs)	
Metropolitan				
Whole-county	10.5 (2.5)	11.6 (2.9)	9.9 (2.3)	−1.2
Partial-county	13.9 (3.6)	12.6 (3.2)	11.9 (2.8)	−3.1
Not HPSA	10.7 (2.3)	11.4 (2.8)	9.6 (2.3)	−2.1
Non-metropolitan				
Whole-county	11.5 (3.3)	11.3 (3.1)	10.9 (3.0)	−1.1
Partial-county	12.4 (3.8)	11.9 (3.4)	12.3 (3.7)	−0.2
Not HPSA	11.0 (3.3)	10.5 (3.3)	10.7 (3.1)	−0.6
Frontier				
Whole-county	11.0 (3.6)	8.4 (3.8)	9.1 (3.9)	−3.7
Partial-county	9.4 (4.5)	8.6 (3.8)	9.2 (4.0)	−0.4
Not HPSA	10.8 (4.7)	8.6 (3.6)	8.8 (3.4)	−4.0
Medically underserved areas				
Metropolitan				
Whole-county	10.4 (3.0)	11.4 (3.2)	9.8 (2.7)	−1.2
Partial-county	13.0 (3.4)	12.9 (3.1)	11.5 (3.1)	−2.4
Not MUA	10.6 (2.9)	11.5 (2.9)	10.0 (2.5)	−1.2
Non-metropolitan				
Whole-county	11.0 (3.7)	10.0 (3.5)	10.2 (3.5)	−1.5
Partial-county	11.7 (4.0)	11.4 (3.8)	11.8 (4.0)	0.2
Not MUA	10.4 (3.5)	10.2 (3.4)	10.3 (3.1)	−0.2
Frontier				
Whole-county	12.5 (4.5)	8.9 (4.1)	9.6 (5.1)	−5.1
Partial-county	9.7 (4.5)	9.0 (4.3)	9.6 (4.5)	−0.2
Not MUA	9.3 (3.7)	7.6 (3.3)	9.2 (3.6)	−0.2

SOURCE: Area Resource File for 1999 with relevant Medicare data added.

NOTE: Averages are weighted by the Medicare population in each county.

DETERMINANTS OF AAPCC LEVELS

In this multivariate analysis, we build upon results of the bivariate analyses to estimate the independent contributions of various factors to levels of AAPCC rates in metropolitan, non-metropolitan, and frontier counties. Because the AAPCCs are derived from historical Medicare health care spending for fee-for-service beneficiaries, this analysis allows us to estimate the relative importance of various factors on these spending patterns. These analyses provide useful information in their own right, and they also will provide a foundation for subsequent work to estimate the relative contributions of Medicare special payments to non-metropolitan providers to overall levels of the 1997 AAPCC rates.

Using weighted least squares regression methods, we estimated three separate models with the 1997 AAPCC rates as the dependent variables and an array of county-level geographic, demographic, and provider supply variables as the predictors. The first model includes all counties in our analysis, which allows us to make direct comparisons of effects on Medicare fee-for-service spending across all metropolitan and non-metropolitan counties. The second and third models are estimated separately for metropolitan and non-metropolitan counties. This approach allows us to "free" all the coefficients on predictor variables to test the extent to which the effects of predictors differ within metropolitan and non-metropolitan county groups.[23]

The results of the three regression models, presented in Table 7.9, reveal some clear contrasts between metropolitan and non-metropolitan counties in the factors associated with variations in AAPCC rates. Differences in the predictive power of the models highlight these differences, where both the all-county and metropolitan models explain more than 40 percent of the variation in AAPCCs across counties, but the non-metropolitan model explains only 13.6 percent of the variation. These results indicate there are other important determinants of Medicare costs for non-metropolitan fee-for-service beneficiaries that remain unmeasured, which may include health care preferences of the beneficiaries, access issues, and possibly the contributions of Medicare special payments for non-metropolitan providers.

Differences that the bivariate analyses identified in AAPCC rates across county categories were present in the regression estimates for all three regression models. The reference (omitted) county category variable for the all-county and metropolitan models was the small metropolitan county; for the non-metropolitan model it was the remote county with no town. We found higher AAPCC rates for large metropolitan counties and smaller rates for all categories of non-metropolitan counties, when compared with the small metropolitan county rates, although the coefficients for the non-metropolitan counties adjacent to MSAs were not statistically significant. Frontier county status did not have a significant effect on AAPCC rates. Effects found in the separate metropolitan and non-metropolitan models were consistent with these all-county model results.

In the model for all counties, designations as HPSAs or MUAs had large positive effects on AAPCC levels, as shown by their large coefficients and strong statistical significance. Other factors that were positively associated with AAPCC rates included the percentage of Medicare

---

[23] In specifying the models, we tested for collinearity among the predictor variables. Although we found some correlations among individual variables, few were correlated so strongly to cause problems for model viability. We selected variables to include in the models from among the identified groups of similar variables (e.g. hospitals versus hospital beds).

beneficiaries and provider-to-population ratios for physicians, hospitals, and home health agencies. In addition, we found a positive interaction effect between physician-to-population ratios and large metropolitan county, yielding a coefficient on the physician ratio variable equal to 0.178 (= 0.050 + 0.128) for large metropolitan counties and equal to 0.050 for all other counties. We found significant negative effects for SNF and nursing home supply ratios.

Although statistically significant, the estimated effects of provider ratios tended to be small in size, as reflected in the small coefficients generated. For example, according to estimates for the all-county model, an increase of 10 physicians per 100,000 population would be associated with $1.78 (= 10 x 0.178) increase in the AAPCC for a large metropolitan county and an increase of $0.50 (= 10 x 0.05) for all other counties. One additional hospital per 100,000 population would be associated with only a $1.57 increase in the AAPCC.

Table 7.9
Estimation of Factors Associated with Levels of AAPCC Capitation Rates, 1997

Variable	All Counties		Metropolitan Counties		Non-Metro Counties	
	Coefficient	t-Value	Coefficient	t-Value	Coefficient	t-Value
Per capita income	−0.001*	−2.06	−0.001	−1.60	0.007	1.32
Percentage Medicare	2.841***	7.30	4.319***	5.30	0.301	0.82
Physician ratio	0.050**	2.69	0.043	1.27	0.031	1.46
Hospital facility ratio	1.574*	1.94	−0.206	−0.05	0.910**	2.40
SNF facility ratio	−5.552***	−11.52	−10.519***	−7.31	−2.566***	−9.48
Nursing home ratio	−3.794***	−8.58	−7.846***	−4.01	−2.306***	−10.33
Home health agency ratio	1.459**	3.07	3.553*	2.26	0.945***	3.75
Rural health clinic ratio	0.274	0.60	−2.636	−0.75	0.228	1.10
Whole-county MUA	29.093***	5.27	25.841*	1.94	29.717***	7.54
Partial-county MUA	29.153***	7.32	33.306***	4.02	5.028	1.41
Whole-county HPSA	21.617**	2.95	31.767	1.40	6.976	1.68
Partial-county HPSA	18.128***	5.56	20.345***	3.05	−4.112	−1.40
Large metro county	72.399***	12.44	69.412***	6.51		
Adjacent, city 10,000+	−0.250	−0.02			21.297***	3.31
Adjacent, no city 10,000+	−16.644	−1.87			12.441*	2.10
Remote, city 10,000+	−38.771**	−2.79			−5.704	−0.86
Remote, town 2,500+	−35.889**	−2.54			−3.648	−0.61
Remote, no town	−29.377	−1.52			(ref)	
Frontier county	−16.772	−1.12			−21.930***	−3.24
Large metro x physician ratio	0.128***	5.52	0.129**	3.09		
Intercept	375.472***	37.34	383.479***	18.14	364.015***	29.10
Number of observations	3,078		816		2,262	
Adjusted R-squared	0.488		0.425		0.136	

SOURCE: Area Resource File for 1999 with relevant Medicare data added.

NOTES: * $p < 0.05$; ** $p < 0.01$; *** $p < 0.001$.

Weighted least squares regression models with the 1997 AAPCC rates as the dependent variable. Full interaction terms for physician ratios with each county category were tested, but only the statistically significant interactions are reported in the table.

The unexpected absence of effects for some variables provides useful insights. Neither rural health clinic ratios nor status as a frontier county were significantly associated with AAPCC rates. One might expect to see a positive effect on AAPCCs for rural health clinics—at least in the non-metropolitan model—to the extent they improve access to care and, therefore, utilization rates. On the other hand, residents of frontier counties would be expected to use less health care because of access barriers, which would yield lower AAPCC rates than other non-metropolitan counties.

We also found that some variables were significant in only one of the separate metropolitan or non-metropolitan models, although they were significant in the all-county model. For example, the percentage of Medicare beneficiaries and physician-to-population ratios were significant predictors only in the metropolitan model, as were designation as partial-county HPSA or partial-county MUA. The hospital-to-population ratio was significant only for the non-metropolitan model, and the home health agency ratio and designation as a whole-county MUA were more strongly significant for the non-metropolitan model than the metropolitan model.

These multivariate results offer useful perspectives on the diversity of factors that influence Medicare AAPCC rates in counties across the country. Yet caution should be used in interpreting these results, especially when attempting to identify direct or indirect "drivers" of Medicare fee-for-service spending for its beneficiaries. Many of the predictor variables in the model must be viewed as proxies for underlying causative factors, the most obvious examples being the county category variables and designations as HPSAs or MUAs. For example, variation in the average age or health status of beneficiaries residing in counties can be expected to influence per capita costs of care, and we were not able to measure these factors here.

MEDICARE MANAGED CARE ENROLLMENTS

When considering the levels and distributions of Medicare AAPCC capitation rates across the counties in the country, an important policy implication is the extent to which variations in the AAPCC rates influenced access to health plans and enrollments by Medicare beneficiaries. We use enrollment data for 1993 and 1997 to examine this issue here, which allows us to compare 1997 enrollments across counties and also to assess how managed care changed in the four years between 1993 and 1997. The data used for the analysis are the quarterly plan enrollment files published by CMS on its website. We used the files containing year-end enrollments for each of the years of interest.

In Table 7.10 we present Medicare health plan enrollment profiles for 1993 and 1997 for metropolitan, non-metropolitan, and frontier counties, according to the same format used in earlier tables. Two basic enrollment measures are provided for each year: the percentage of counties served by at least one health plan during the year and the percentage of beneficiaries residing in the county who were enrolled in a Medicare health plan. For enrollment rates, we provide an average enrollment across all counties in each category as well as an average across only those counties that had at least one health plan.

The essentially urban nature of Medicare managed care is shown in the enrollment information in Table 7.10. For both years, the percentages of counties with at least one Medicare health plan were much higher for metropolitan counties than for non-metropolitan counties, and the metropolitan/non-metropolitan contrast is yet greater for enrollment rates. Overall enrollment rates in 1997 were 18.9 percent for metropolitan county residents and only 3.5

percent for non-metropolitan county residents. Although enrollment rates were lower in 1993, the pattern of enrollments was the same as for 1997. As might be expected, managed care penetration was low in frontier counties, yet health plans were not totally absent from these counties. In 1993, 15.5 percent of frontier counties had at least one health plan, and the percentage rose to 20.1 percent of frontier counties by 1997. Enrollment rates for these counties were similar to those for the remote non-metropolitan counties.

Table 7.10
Medicare Health Plan Enrollments for Metropolitan, Non-Metropolitan,
and Frontier Counties, 1993 and 1997

| County Category | 1993 Medicare Health Plans | | | 1997 Medicare Health Plans | | |
| | % of Counties with a Plan | % Enrollment | | % of Counties with a Plan | % Enrollment | |
		All Counties	Counties w/1+ Plan		All Counties	Counties w/1+ Plan
Metropolitan	66.6	9.2	10.5	84.1	18.9	19.9
Large counties	82.9	12.6	13.2	94.5	24.0	24.2
Small counties	57.0	4.1	5.5	77.9	11.5	13.0
Non-metropolitan	25.7	1.6	4.3	36.7	3.5	6.5
Adjacent, city 10,000+	48.6	1.7	3.0	65.3	5.2	7.1
Adjacent, no city 10K+	27.5	1.5	4.1	42.9	3.9	7.2
Remote, city 10,000+	34.3	2.2	5.8	48.9	3.0	5.4
Remote, town 2,500–10,000	23.3	1.6	5.5	30.6	2.2	5.7
Remote, no town	10.6	1.0	6.1	14.3	1.1	5.1
Frontier county status						
Frontier counties	15.5	1.3	4.1	20.1	2.8	7.5
Other non-metro counties	27.9	1.7	4.3	40.1	3.6	6.6

SOURCES: Area Resource File for 1999 with relevant Medicare data added; quarterly enrollment reports for Medicare managed care plans.

Medicare health plan enrollment rates tended to be higher in counties with higher AAPCC rates, as shown in Table 7.11, and this effect was found within each category of metropolitan, non-metropolitan, and frontier counties. For example, the average AAPCC rate was $418 for large metropolitan counties with no health plans in 1997, and it was $536 for large metropolitan counties that had at least one health plan. These averages are weighted by the number of Medicare beneficiaries residing in each county who could enroll in a health plan if one were available. We also estimated AAPCC rates for counties with at least one plan, weighting by the number of plan enrollees, to examine the enrollee distributions by level of AAPCC. To continue the example of large metropolitan counties, we obtain a higher average AAPCC rate of $542 when weighting by the number of plan enrollees, indicating that enrollments are skewed toward counties with higher AAPCCs.

Finally, we look specifically at the health plans that served Medicare beneficiaries residing in non-metropolitan counties. As of the end of 1997, there were 398 Medicare health plans (not shown), of which 229 had enrollees living in non-metropolitan counties. This compares to 204 health plans in 1993 (not shown), of which 103 served non-metropolitan enrollees. In Table 7.12, we present the distributions of the health plans that served non-metropolitan beneficiaries during 1993 and 1997, based on the percentage of urban enrollees in each plan's Medicare membership. In both years, beneficiaries in metropolitan counties were the dominant portion of plan enrollees for all but a small fraction of these health plans. Although more plans served non-metropolitan areas in 1997, their mix of metropolitan and non-metropolitan enrollees was similar to the mix in health plans in 1993. In 1997, Medicare enrollments for 63.8 percent of the plans included 90 percent or more metropolitan beneficiaries, compared to 65.1 percent for plans in 1993.

Table 7.11
Average 1997 AAPCC Rates for Metropolitan, Non-Metropolitan,
and Frontier Counties, by the Presence or Absence of a Medicare Health Plan

County Category	No Plan in the County Beneficiary Weighted	One or More Plans in County Beneficiary Weighted	One or More Plans in County Plan-Enrollee Weighted
Metropolitan			
Large counties	$418	$536	$542
Small counties	400	436	453
Non-metropolitan			
Adjacent, city 10,000+	388	403	409
Adjacent, no city 10K+	379	402	418
Remote, city 10,000+	370	377	375
Remote, town 2,500–10,000	368	387	417
Remote, no town	368	394	419
Frontier county status			
Frontier counties	354	363	384
Other non-metro counties	376	396	409

SOURCES: Area Resource File for 1999 with relevant Medicare data added; quarterly enrollment reports for Medicare managed care plans.

Despite the predominance of metropolitan enrollees in health plans serving non-metropolitan areas, a small percentage of health plans were drawing most of their enrollees from residents of non-metropolitan counties (see Table 7.12). These plans may be viewed as true rural health plans, unlike their counterparts that reached into fringe non-metropolitan counties from a metropolitan enrollment base. In 1997, metropolitan enrollees were less than half the total enrollments for 19 health plans (8.3 percent). Although there were only eight such plans in 1993, they were 7.8 percent of the plans serving non-metropolitan areas—similar to the 1997 share.

Of the 35 health plans with at least 30 percent non-metropolitan enrollees in 1997, only 11 plans were contracting with CMS under risk contracts, under which they receive capitation payments based on the AAPCC rates and they bear full financial risk for the health care costs for their Medicare enrollees (data not shown). The remainder of the plans had cost contracts (11 plans) or Health Care Prepayment Plans (HCPP) contracts (13 plans), where they managed enrollees' health care but did not bear the same financial risk as risk-contracting health plans. Given the financial risk involved in covering health benefits for small populations, the health plans appear to have made good use of cost and HCPP contracts to mitigate their risk while serving non-metropolitan populations.

Table 7.12
Distribution of Medicare Health Plans Serving Non-Metropolitan Counties,
by Percentage of Non-Metropolitan Plan Enrollees, 1993 and 1997

% of Non-Metropolitan Enrollees	1993 Health Plans		1997 Health Plans	
	Number	Percent	Number	Percent
Greater than 60	7	6.8	14	6.1
51–60	1	1.0	5	2.2
41–50	4	3.9	7	3.1
31–40	4	3.9	9	3.9
21–30	6	5.8	14	6.1
16–20	6	5.8	16	7.0
11–15	8	7.8	18	7.9
6–10	4	3.9	26	11.4
5 or less	63	61.2	120	52.4
Total	103	100.0	229	100.0

SOURCES: Area Resource File for 1999 with relevant Medicare data added; quarterly enrollment reports for Medicare managed care plans.

ISSUES AND IMPLICATIONS

The analyses presented in this section are the only ones in this project that make direct comparisons between non-metropolitan and metropolitan areas. We have found these comparisons to be quite useful in reinforcing the clear differences in profiles of metropolitan and non-metropolitan counties both with respect to provider supply and mix and in Medicare spending levels for its fee-for-service beneficiaries. These differences have persisted over the past decade, although there has been some convergence in the AAPCC rates for metropolitan counties and counties adjacent to metropolitan counties.

The results of our regression models highlight these contrasts. The models for all counties and for metropolitan counties explained a large percentage of the variation in AAPCC rates across counties, but the model for non-metropolitan counties explained much less. In addition, many factors for the models for all counties and for metropolitan counties had significant effects on AAPCC rates, but far fewer factors were significant in the model for non-metropolitan counties. These results could be interpreted in two ways. There is a reasonable probability that other factors exist that we did not measure but are predictors of AAPCC rates in non-metropolitan areas. For example, the addition of beneficiary characteristics, such as case mix or average health status, could improve the explanatory power of the models. On the other hand, the county-level AAPCC rates in non-metropolitan areas may be the net result of such a diversity of local service use patterns that it may not be possible to explain much more of the variation in county rates than our models capture. For example, some remote counties may have many small urbanized locations (communities or cities) within them, each of which has enough providers to support the demand for primary health care, but others may have only one or two urbanized locations that make access more difficult for beneficiaries living outside those locations. In this example of diversity, two counties could have similar county-level averages of provider supply, but the rates of utilization (and resulting AAPCC rates) would be different.

We also have identified a measurement issue related to the limited clustering of non-metropolitan counties for different types of classification such as categories of non-metropolitan counties, designations as HPSAs and MUAs, and frontier counties. Conceptually, we would expect these counties to converge into a reasonably consistent set of groups based on factors such as proximity to urban health care or status as underserved areas. We did not find it in this phase of our research. Consistent with this issue, there also were few clear patterns of provider supply among non-metropolitan counties, although numbers of providers clearly are smaller in the remote counties and the counties with no city of at least 10,000 population.

Positive associations were found between physician and hospital supply and AAPCC rates but negative associations were found for SNFs, nursing homes and home health agencies. Although effects on AAPCCs were small, they do suggest that the mix of acute care and post-acute care services in non-metropolitan counties may be an important factor in access to care for Medicare beneficiaries and resulting service utilization and costs. The local mix in these services also would be likely to affect beneficiaries' choices to obtain acute care services locally or from more distant providers.

HPSAs and MUAs are, by definition, underserved areas. Therefore, there should be lower utilization rates by Medicare beneficiaries in these areas, which would be observable in lower AAPCC rates. The absence of negative relationships between AAPCC rates and either MUAs or HPSAs may reflect flaws in the criteria for these designation. For example, the designated areas may not be the most underserved areas, or there may be enough other underserved areas that were not designated to dilute observed differences in AAPCC rates between the two groups. Alternatively, we could hypothesize that these designations indeed had accomplished what was intended—increasing access to care for residents of the designated areas.

Another surprising finding was the weak evidence for both undersupply of providers and low utilization and costs for residents of frontier counties. We pursued examination of frontier counties far enough to confirm that the Medicare populations in these counties are indeed quite small. Yet most of the provider supply measures were similar to those of other non-metropolitan counties. Frontier county AAPCCs in 1990 were, on average, similar to AAPCCs for other non-metropolitan counties, but they increased at a slower rate from 1990 to 1997, indicating some differences in trends of access or utilization for their Medicare beneficiaries. One hypothesis that might explain some of these findings is that residents of frontier counties tend to settle in concentrated communities that are surrounded by large areas of unoccupied land. These communities could offer them an infrastructure that might include a level of health care services that a more dispersed population would not be able to sustain.

This set of findings regarding the characteristics of non-metropolitan counties and trends in AAPCC rates for these counties highlights the continuing challenges to be faced in identifying and measuring the factors that contribute to lower service utilization in rural areas compared with urban areas. We used county boundaries for the analysis of historical trends in AAPCC rates because these rates were set at the county level. As we have discussed in this report, however, it is well understood that county boundaries are a poor choice for defining groups of homogeneous rural areas, especially given the large land areas included in rural counties in many of the states. With each of those land areas there are diverse local communities surrounded by remote areas, each with their unique supply of health care providers and service networks.

8. SPECIAL HOSPITAL PAYMENTS AND PART A PER CAPITA COSTS

The analysis reported in this section examines the effects of special payment provisions for qualified rural hospitals on Medicare spending for beneficiaries residing in non-metropolitan counties. The analyses addressed the following research questions:

- To what extent have Medicare special payment policies for rural hospitals increased total Medicare payments made to hospitals serving beneficiaries in non-metropolitan areas?

- How were the extra payments created by these special payment policies distributed across counties of differing degrees of rurality, as measured by the UIC categories?

- How much additional Medicare payments have rural hospitals with special designations received due to these provisions, above what they would have been paid under the standard Medicare Prospective Payment System?

- What was the contribution of Medicare special payments for rural hospitals to the total Part A cost per capita for Medicare (and therefore to the AAPCCs)?

SIMULATION OF THE SPECIAL PAYMENT CONTRIBUTION

The first step in estimating effects of special payment provisions on Medicare spending was to estimate the share of payments for hospital inpatient services attributable to the special payment provisions. Then we estimated the contribution of the special payment amounts to total Part A per capita spending, which serves as the basis for the Part A AAPCC. We examined overall effects on Medicare spending for inpatient care for non-metropolitan beneficiaries as well as effects on payments to rural hospitals qualified for the special payments. The relevant payment amounts were defined as follows:

Total payment	= DRG price + pass-through costs	(8.1)
Medicare payment	= Medicare amount + pass-through costs	(8.2)
where DRG price	= operating DRG price + capital DRG price	
	= Medicare amount + primary payer amount + beneficiary liability	

We simulated the operating DRG price that would be paid in the absence of the provisions, and then we recalculated the total payment amount for each claim as well as the amount paid by Medicare. We refer to the original payments as "actual payments" and to the simulated payments as "adjusted payments." Details of the simulation method and formulas are presented in Section 2.

The claims for which adjusted payments were simulated were those for hospital inpatient stays for all beneficiaries residing in non-metropolitan counties provided by (1) sole community hospitals, (2) rural referral centers, (3) hospitals qualified as both a sole community hospital and rural referral center, and (4) Medicare-dependent small hospitals. We excluded any claims for which Medicare was not primary payer, the patient had only a one-day inpatient stay (which included transfers to other hospitals), or payment was not made under PPS. We used MEDPAR claims for 1996, 1997, and 1998, calculating three-year average amounts centered on 1997. This was done to smooth any volatility in spending from year to year because of the small beneficiary populations residing in many of the rural counties. Adjusted payments were not simulated for

EACH/RPCH/CAHs because there were few of these facilities during the study period and they represented an extremely small share of total inpatient stays, many of which were only one or two days in length (so would have been excluded from adjusted payments).

The results of this analysis can be viewed from two policy perspectives. On the one hand, the difference in spending with and without the special payment provisions represents the amount by which payments for inpatient services for rural Medicare beneficiaries have been increased by these provisions. Alternatively, the difference shows the amount by which spending would decline in the absence of these provisions. We present the results from the second perspective, estimating the percentage reductions in revenue that hospitals would experience (which would be cost reductions for Medicare) if the special payment provisions were eliminated. We first report differences in overall spending with and without the special payment provisions in effect, followed by examination of patterns of spending by non-metropolitan county categories and by hospitals eligible for the provisions. For these analyses, we measure spending for inpatient care per beneficiary as well as per inpatient stay, each of which offers distinct information on the costs of care. Finally, we examine effects on total Medicare Part A costs per beneficiary, consisting of costs for hospital inpatient services, skilled nursing care, home health care, and hospice services.

As shown in Table 8.1, the overall three-year average actual per beneficiary payments for inpatient care were $2,293 for total payments and $2,048 for Medicare payments. The Medicare payment was 89.3 percent of the total payment. The total payments ranged from $2,250 to $2,328 across the three years included in the average, whereas the Medicare payments ranged from $2,010 to $2,083. Within each year, variation across counties was greater for Medicare payment amounts than for total payments, as shown by the county-weighted coefficients of variation. County-weighted variation decreased slightly when payments for the three years were averaged.

The simulation results show that the average total payment per capita without the special payment provisions (the adjusted amount) was an estimated 2.3 percent smaller than the average actual payment. The difference was slightly greater for Medicare payments, for which the average adjusted per capita amount was 2.6 percent smaller than the actual amount.

In the next three tables, we provide descriptive information on variations in the extent to which non-metropolitan counties are influenced by the Medicare special payment provisions for rural hospitals. These include distributions of counties based on the percentage of hospital stays for county residents provided by special payment hospitals, the average payment per stay, and the percentage reduction in payment per stay when the portion attributable to the special payment provisions is removed.

Table 8.2 shows that the non-metropolitan counties varied widely in the percentage of inpatient stays provided by special payment hospitals to beneficiaries residing in the county. An estimated 40.4 percent of counties had 20 percent or fewer special payment inpatient stays, and another 23.6 percent had greater than 60 percent of these stays. This distribution reflects the relative number of special payment hospitals present in the counties.

Table 8.1
Average Total and Medicare Inpatient Payments per Non-Metropolitan Beneficiary, Actual and Adjusted Amounts and Coefficients of Variation, Three-Year Average and 1996–1998

Type of Payment	Three-Year Average	1996	1997	1998
Total payments per beneficiary				
Actual	$2,293	$2,250	$2,328	$2,302
Adjusted (without special payment)	2,242	2,202	2,278	2,241
Percentage difference	–2.3%	–2.1%	–2.1%	–2.7%
Coefficients of variation				
(Case weighted)				
Actual	18.2%	18.2%	18.1%	18.0%
Adjusted (without special payment)	18.2	18.4	18.2	18.0
(County weighted)				
Actual	19.2	20.8	20.8	20.3
Adjusted (without special payment)	19.2	20.9	20.8	20.1
Medicare payment per beneficiary				
Actual	$2,048	$2,010	$2,083	$2,051
Adjusted (without special payment)	1,996	1,963	2,034	1,990
Percentage difference	–2.6%	–2.3%	–2.4%	–3.0%
Coefficients of variation				
(Case weighted)				
Actual	18.5%	18.5%	18.5%	18.3%
Adjusted (without special payment)	18.2	18.7	18.5	18.3
(County weighted)				
Actual	19.6	21.1	21.3	20.8
Adjusted (without special payment)	19.5	21.1	21.2	20.6

SOURCES: MEDPAR data for the 100 percent beneficiary population, Medicare Impact Files, Medicare 100 percent Denominator Files, Area Resource File.

NOTES: Spending is measured as total spending or Medicare spending per beneficiary for beneficiaries in non-metropolitan counties. Adjusted payments are simulated payments excluding special payment amounts. Averages are weighted by the number of beneficiaries in each county. Coefficient of variation is the standard deviation as a percentage of the average payment amount.

Table 8.2
Distribution of Non-Metropolitan Counties, by the Percentage of Medicare Inpatient Stays at Hospitals with Special Payments, Three-Year Average 1996–1998

Special Payment Stays as a % of All Stays	Number of Counties	%
20 percent or fewer	929	40.4%
21 to 40 percent	423	18.4
41 to 60 percent	405	17.6
61 to 80 percent	425	18.5
Greater than 80 percent	118	5.1

SOURCES: MEDPAR data for the 100 percent beneficiary population, Medicare Impact Files, Medicare 100 percent Denominator Files, Area Resource File.

Table 8.3 shows the variation in average payment amounts per inpatient stay across counties. Only 1.4 percent of non-metropolitan counties had average total payments of less than $5,000, and 8.3 percent had average payments of $7,000 or greater. The county distribution shifts downward for average Medicare payments per stay, with 15.5 percent of counties having Medicare payments of less than $5,000 per stay and only 3.2 percent having Medicare payments of $7,000 or greater.

Table 8.3
Distribution of Non-Metropolitan Counties, by Average Actual Payment
per Medicare Inpatient Stay for Total and Medicare Payments, Three-Year Average 1996–1998

Average Payment Amount per Inpatient Stay	Total Payment		Medicare Payment	
	Number of Counties	%	Number of Counties	%
Less than $5,000	32	1.4%	356	15.5%
$5,000 to $5,499	189	8.2	639	27.8
$5,500 to $5,999	535	23.3	617	26.8
$6,000 to $6,499	636	27.7	377	16.4
$6,500 to $6,999	718	31.2	238	10.4
$7,000 or greater	190	8.3	73	3.2

SOURCES: MEDPAR data for the 100 percent beneficiary population, Medicare Impact Files, Medicare 100 percent Denominator Files, Area Resource File.

NOTE: Spending is measured as total spending or spending by Medicare per inpatient stay by county of residence for beneficiaries residing in non-metropolitan counties.

The special payment provisions affected payments for inpatient hospital stays for beneficiaries residing in virtually all non-metropolitan counties, as shown in Table 8.4. The effects were small for almost half the counties when the special payment component was removed from the actual payment. Specifically, we estimated less than a 1.0 percent decrease for 49.2 percent of counties for total payment per stay and 46.9 percent of counties for Medicare payment per stay. An estimated 5 percent or greater reduction occurred for 14.4 percent of counties for total payment per stay and 16.9 percent of counties for Medicare payment per stay.

Table 8.4
Distribution of Non-Metropolitan Counties, by Reduction in Payment per Medicare Inpatient Stay
with Special Payments Removed, Three-Year Average 1996–1998

% Reduction in Payment per Stay	Total Payment		Medicare Payment	
	Number of Counties	%	Number of Counties	%
5 percent or greater	331	14.4%	388	16.9%
3.0 to 4.9 percent	307	13.4	304	13.2
2.0 to 2.9 percent	220	9.6	217	9.4
1.0 to 1.9 percent	310	13.5	311	13.5
Less than 1.0 percent	1,132	49.2	1,080	46.9

SOURCES: MEDPAR data for the 100 percent beneficiary population, Medicare Impact Files, Medicare 100 percent Denominator Files, Area Resource File.

NOTES: Spending is measured as total spending or spending by Medicare per inpatient stay by county of residence for beneficiaries in non-metropolitan counties. Adjusted payments are simulated payments excluding special payment amounts.

SPECIAL PAYMENT EFFECTS BY COUNTY LOCATION

Effects of the special payment provisions on payments per inpatient stay varied noticeably across categories of non-metropolitan counties and frontier counties. As shown in Table 8.5, when the special payment portion is removed, the reductions in total payments ranged from 1.4 percent for beneficiaries in counties adjacent to an MSA with no city of 10,000 to 3.8 percent for remote counties with a city of 10,000. These effects reflect differences across county categories in the presence of sole community hospitals, rural referral centers, or Medicare-dependent hospitals. The largest reduction of 4.0 percent occurred for beneficiaries residing in frontier counties, reflecting relatively greater use of these hospitals compared to other beneficiaries in non-metropolitan counties. Reductions in Medicare payments were larger than those for total payments and they followed the same pattern across county categories.

Table 8.5
Average Medicare Payments per Medicare Inpatient Stay, Before and After Removing Special Payment Amounts, by Non-Metropolitan County Category, Three-Year Average 1996–1998

County Category	Total Payment per Stay			Medicare Payment per Stay		
	Actual	Adjusted	Change	Actual	Adjusted	Change
All non-metropolitan counties	$6,406	$6,258	–2.3%	$5,721	$5,574	–2.6%
Rural county category						
Adjacent, city 10,000+	6,645	6,514	–2.0	5,947	5,817	–2.2
Adjacent, no city 10,000+	6,507	6,418	–1.4	5,826	5,736	–1.5
Remote, city 10,000+	6,404	6,160	–3.8	5,700	5,458	–4.2
Remote, town 2,500–10,000	6,125	5,969	–2.5	5,454	5,299	–2.8
Remote, no town	6,032	5,850	–3.0	5,379	5,198	–3.4
Frontier county status						
Frontier counties	6,468	6,210	–4.0	5,798	5,541	–4.4
Other non-metro counties	6,403	6,261	–2.2	5,718	5,576	–2.5

SOURCES: MEDPAR data for the 100 percent beneficiary population, Medicare Impact Files, Medicare 100 percent Denominator Files, Area Resource File.

NOTES: Spending is measured as spending by Medicare per inpatient stay by county of residence for beneficiaries in non-metropolitan counties. Adjusted payments are simulated payments excluding special payment amounts. Averages are weighted by the number of beneficiaries in each county.

The percentage reductions in average payments per beneficiary are shown in Table 8.6. The percentages are the same as those for payments per inpatient stay, reflecting the fact that, in each case, the same denominator was used to calculate both actual and adjusted payments.

Table 8.7 shows the average actual and adjusted Medicare payments per beneficiary for different levels of actual Medicare payments per inpatient stay. Counties generally had similar average costs per beneficiary, regardless of the size of the average payment per stay. Removal of the special payment component tended to equalize further the per beneficiary payment across categories, with larger reductions for counties with more costly stays.

Table 8.6
Average Medicare Payments per Medicare Beneficiary, Before and After Removing Special Payment Amounts, by Non-Metropolitan County Category, Three-Year Average 1996–1998

County Category	Total Payment per Beneficiary			Medicare Payment per Beneficiary		
	Actual	Adjusted	Change	Actual	Adjusted	Change
All non-metropolitan counties	$2,222	$2,171	–2.3%	$1,986	$1,934	–2.6%
Non-metro category						
Adjacent, city 10,000+	2,229	2,185	–2.0	1,995	1,951	–2.2
Adjacent, no city 10,000+	2,249	2,218	–1.4	2,013	1,982	–1.5
Remote, city 10,000+	2,165	2,082	–3.8	1,927	1,845	–4.2
Remote, town 2,500–10,000	2,217	2,161	–2.5	1,974	1,919	–2.8
Remote, no town	2,247	2,179	–3.0	2,003	1,936	–3.4
Frontier county status						
Frontier counties	2,044	1,964	–3.9	1,831	1,752	–4.3
Other non-metro counties	2,230	2,181	–2.2	1,992	1,942	–2.5

SOURCES: MEDPAR data for the 100 percent beneficiary population, Medicare Impact Files, Medicare 100 percent Denominator Files, Area Resource File.

NOTES: Spending is measured as spending by Medicare per inpatient stay by county of residence for Medicare beneficiaries in non-metropolitan counties. Adjusted payments are simulated payments excluding special payment amounts. Averages are weighted by the number of beneficiaries in each county.

Table 8.7
Difference Between Actual and Adjusted Medicare Payments per Non-Metropolitan Beneficiary, by Actual Payment Category, Three-Year Average 1996–1998

Category of Average Actual Payment per Stay	Number of Counties	Actual Payment per Beneficiary	Adjusted Payment per Beneficiary	% Reduction
Less than $5,000	356	$2,122	$2,089	–1.6%
$5,000 to $5,499	639	1,981	1,947	–1.7
$5,500 to $5,999	617	2,020	1,969	–2.5
$6,000 to $6,499	377	2,084	2,023	–2.9
$6,500 to $6,999	238	2,071	1,984	–4.2
$7,000 or more	73	2,316	2,209	–4.6

SOURCES: MEDPAR data for the 100 percent beneficiary population, Medicare Impact Files, Medicare 100 percent Denominator Files, Area Resource File.

NOTES: Spending is measured as spending by Medicare per beneficiary by county of residence for beneficiaries in non-metropolitan counties. Adjusted payments are simulated payments excluding special payment amounts. Averages are weighted by the number of beneficiaries in each county.

EFFECTS ON HOSPITALS RECEIVING SPECIAL PAYMENTS

The Medicare special payment provisions are intended to provide additional revenue to the rural hospitals that qualify for special designations to help ensure continued access to their services for rural beneficiaries. The estimated payments in Table 8.8 show the estimated effects of the special payments on each of the four types of special payment hospitals. As shown in Section 4, the actual payments per stay for three of the four groups of special payment hospitals were higher than those for non-metropolitan hospitals with no special designation; only the Medicare dependent hospital had lower payments. When payments were adjusted to a standard PPS payment amount, the Medicare payments per stay declined by 10.6 percent for sole community hospitals, by 8.3 percent for rural referral centers, and by 11.7 percent for hospitals with both designations. As a result, the adjusted payments for sole community hospitals were lower than those for hospitals with no special designations, whereas those for rural referral centers and SCH/RRCs remained higher. Medicare-dependent hospitals had the lowest actual payments per stay of all types of non-metropolitan hospitals, and adjusted payments for these hospitals were only 4.8 percent lower than actual payments. This small difference probably reflects the fact that some hospitals were incorrectly identified as Medicare-dependent in the PSF and actually received the standard PPS payments for some portion of the three years. Thus, their adjusted payments were the same as or very close to their actual payments.

Table 8.8
Average Total and Medicare Payments per Inpatient Stay, by Type of Hospital,
Three-Year Average 1996–1998

Type of Hospital	Total Payment per Stay			Medicare Payment per Stay		
	Actual	Adjusted	Change	Actual	Adjusted	Change
Non-metropolitan hospitals						
No special designation	$4,660	$4,660	0.0%	$4,088	$4,088	0.0%
Sole community hospital	4,949	4,498	–9.3	4,332	3,874	–10.6
RRC	5,871	5,439	–7.4	5,177	4,747	–8.3
SCH/RRC	6,028	5,401	–10.4	5,347	4,723	–11.7
Medicare-dependent hospital	4,112	3,941	–4.2	3,541	3,373	–4.8
Metropolitan hospitals	9,682	9,682	0.0	8,493	8,493	0.0

SOURCES: MEDPAR data for the 100 percent beneficiary population, Medicare Impact Files, Medicare 100 percent Denominator Files, Area Resource File.

NOTES: Spending is measured as spending by Medicare per inpatient stay by county of residence for beneficiaries in non-metropolitan counties. Adjusted payments are simulated payments excluding special payment amounts. Averages are weighted by the number of beneficiaries in each county.

We show in Table 8.9 the average Medicare payments per inpatient stay and per beneficiary by categories of counties grouped by the share of total stays for county beneficiaries who were at special payment hospitals. For example, counties with 20 percent or fewer of total beneficiary inpatient stays at special payment hospitals had an average Medicare payment of $2,090 per beneficiary, of which $101 was for stays at special payment hospitals. By definition, the share of payment per beneficiary for special payment stays was larger in counties that had higher percentages of special payment hospital stays, and adjusting payments to remove the special payment component yielded a larger reduction in payment per stay. We estimated a reduction in payment per stay of less than 1 percent for counties with 20 percent stays at special payment hospitals and 7.3 percent for counties with greater than 80 percent special payment stays.

Table 8.9

Effects of Special Payments on Medicare Payments per Stay and per Capita for Non-Metropolitan Beneficiaries, by Level of Special Payment Stays, Three-Year Average 1996–1998

Special Payment Stays as a % of All Stays	Payment per Inpatient Stay			Payment per Beneficiary	
	Actual Payment	Adjusted Payment	% Change	All Inpatient Stays	Special Payment Stays
20 percent or fewer	$5,713	$5,689	–0.4%	$2,090	$101
21 to 40 percent	5,603	5,493	–2.0	2,035	496
41 to 60 percent	5,763	5,510	–4.4	2,073	849
61 to 80 percent	5,807	5,499	–5.3	1,984	1,112
Greater than 80 percent	5,795	5,373	–7.3	1,927	1,467

SOURCES: MEDPAR data for the 100 percent beneficiary population, Medicare Impact Files, Medicare 100 percent Denominator Files, Area Resource File.

NOTES: Spending is measured as spending by Medicare per beneficiary by county of residence for beneficiaries in non-metropolitan counties. Adjusted payments are simulated payments excluding special payment amounts. Averages are weighted by the number of beneficiaries in each county.

The geographic distribution of special payment hospitals will be reflected in the average actual and adjusted payments per stay by non-metropolitan county categories. Average actual Medicare payments per inpatient stay are shown in Table 8.10 for all stays for beneficiaries in a county as well as for stays at special payment hospitals. Estimates of the percentage reduction in payment with removal of the special payment portion also are reported. Estimated reductions in payments per stay for all inpatient stays replicate those reported in Table 8.5. They are reported again here to provide a comparison for the reductions for special payment hospital stays.

The percentage reduction for stays at special payment hospitals was similar for the five county categories, with estimated reductions ranging from 9.2 to 9.9 percent. Thus, beneficiaries who received care at special payment hospitals tended to use a similar mix of these hospitals, regardless of category of county of residence. For frontier counties, an estimated 11.5 percent of the payment per stay for special payment hospitals was attributable to the special payment provision. Beneficiaries in these counties appeared to make greater use of rural referral centers than other special payment hospitals, including hospitals designated as both sole community hospitals and rural referral centers, which according to Table 8.8, had the largest percentage of payment attributable to special payments (i.e., removed in the payment adjustment).

In Table 8.11, we report patterns of Medicare payments per beneficiary and the share of those payments made to special payment hospitals, by categories of non-metropolitan hospitals and frontier counties. The largest share was in remote counties with a city of 10,000 population, where payments to special payment hospitals represented an estimated 42.7 percent of the Medicare payments per beneficiary. The other two categories of remote counties and frontier counties also had higher percentages than counties adjacent to MSAs. These higher shares are the combined result of the extent to which beneficiaries in the more remote counties use special payment hospitals and the size of the Medicare payment per inpatient stay for each of those stays. We note that only 9 to 10 percent of the payment per beneficiary for special payment stays would be removed if payments were adjusted to eliminate the special payment provisions (see Table 8.10).

Table 8.10

Effects of Special Payment Amounts on Medicare Payments per Inpatient Stay, for All and Special Payment Stays, by Non-Metropolitan County Category, Three-Year Average 1996–1998

County Category	Actual Medicare Payment per Stay		Change When Special Payments Removed	
	All Stays	Stays in Special Payment Hospitals	All Stays	Stays in Special Payment Hospitals
All non-metropolitan counties	$5,721	$4,735	−2.6%	−9.5%
Rural county category				
Adjacent, city 10,000+	5,947	4,790	−2.2	−9.4
Adjacent, no city 10,000+	5,826	4,543	−1.5	−9.2
Remote, city 10,000+	5,700	4,960	−4.2	−9.9
Remote, town 2,500–10,000	5,454	4,691	−2.8	−9.2
Remote, no town	5,379	4,513	−3.4	−9.5
Frontier county status				
Frontier counties	5,798	4,473	−4.4	−11.5
Other non-metro counties	5,718	4,752	−2.5	−9.3

SOURCES: MEDPAR data for the 100 percent beneficiary population, Medicare Impact Files, Medicare 100 percent Denominator Files, Area Resource File.

NOTES: Spending is measured as Medicare spending per inpatient stay by county of residence for beneficiaries in non-metropolitan counties. Adjusted payments are simulated payments excluding special payment amounts. Averages are weighted by the number of beneficiaries in each county.

Table 8.11

Average Medicare Payments per Beneficiary to Special Payment Hospitals, by Non-Metropolitan County Category, Three-Year Average 1996–1998

County Category	Medicare Payment per Beneficiary		% Paid to Special Payment Hospitals
	All Stays	Stays in Special Payment Hospitals	
All non-metropolitan counties	$2,048	$554	27.1%
Rural county category			
Adjacent, city 10,000+	2,058	480	23.3
Adjacent, no city 10,000+	2,077	345	16.6
Remote, city 10,000+	1,989	849	42.7
Remote, town 2,500–10,000	2,039	629	30.9
Remote, no town	2,067	735	35.6
Frontier county status			
Frontier counties	1,906	734	38.5
Other non-metro counties	2,055	546	26.6

SOURCES: MEDPAR data for the 100 percent beneficiary population, Medicare Impact Files, Medicare 100 percent Denominator Files, Area Resource File.

NOTES: Spending is measured as Medicare spending per inpatient stay by county of residence for beneficiaries in non-metropolitan counties. Adjusted payments are simulated payments excluding special payment amounts. Averages are weighted by the number of beneficiaries in each county.

SPECIAL PAYMENT EFFECTS ON COUNTY PER CAPITA COSTS

As discussed above, the Medicare special payments for rural hospitals directly affect spending for hospital inpatient services for Medicare beneficiaries because these are the services to which the payments apply. Payments for inpatient services also affect Part A spending, of which they are one component. Other payments included in Part A spending are those for skilled nursing care, home health care, and hospice care. We estimated the effects of the special payment provisions on average total Part A spending per beneficiary for all Medicare beneficiaries and also for elderly beneficiaries (those aged 65 or older). The estimated effects for elderly beneficiaries can be compared to the 1997 Part A AAPCCs for elderly beneficiaries.

As shown in Table 8.12, the non-metropolitan counties vary substantially in the percentage of total Medicare Part A spending that is for hospital inpatient services. For all Medicare beneficiaries, all except 8.2 percent of the counties had inpatient service payments from 61 to 90 percent of total Part A spending; for 7.1 percent of the counties, inpatient payments are 60 percent or less of Part A spending. The distribution is shifted downward for elderly beneficiaries, with hospital inpatient payments being 60 percent or less for 9.4 percent of counties (compared to 7.1 percent for all beneficiaries), and reduction of the percentages of counties in the two highest categories (81 to 90 percent and greater than 90 percent).

Table 8.12

Distribution of Non-Metropolitan Counties, by Actual Hospital Inpatient Payments as a Percentage of Medicare Part A Payments per Beneficiary, Three-Year Average 1996–1998

Hospital Payment as a % of Part A Payments	All Beneficiaries	Elderly Beneficiaries
60 percent or less	7.1%	9.4%
61 to 70 percent	19.1	22.0
71 to 80 percent	44.3	44.0
81 to 90 percent	28.4	23.9
Greater than 90 percent	1.1	0.8

SOURCES: MEDPAR data for the 100 percent beneficiary population, Medicare Impact Files, Medicare 100 percent Denominator Files, Area Resource File.

NOTES: Spending is measured as Medicare spending per beneficiary by county of residence for Medicare beneficiaries residing in non-metropolitan counties, for all beneficiaries and elderly beneficiaries.

The distributions of non-metropolitan counties by average annual payments per beneficiary for Part A services and for hospital inpatient services are presented in Table 8.13, including both actual payments and the estimated adjusted payments with the special payment component removed. Only 7.9 percent of counties had *actual* annual Part A payments of less than $1,500 per beneficiary, whereas 9.7 percent of counties had *adjusted* Part A payments this low. The rest of the counties were fairly evenly distributed across the higher categories of payment levels. For hospital inpatient payments, average annual payments were less than $1,500 per beneficiary for 47.3 percent of counties for actual payments and 53.2 percent of counties for adjusted payments.

Table 8.13

Distribution of Non-Metropolitan Counties, by Average Medicare Part A and Hospital Inpatient Payments per Beneficiary, Actual and Adjusted Amounts, Three-Year Average 1996–1998

Average Payment per Beneficiary	Part A Payments		Hospital Inpatient Payments	
	Actual	Adjusted	Actual	Adjusted
Less than $1,500	7.9%	9.7%	47.3%	53.2%
$1,500 to $1,999	30.5	32.4	39.6	36.1
$2,000 to $2,499	28.1	27.7	10.9	9.2
$2,500 to $3,499	17.5	15.9	2.0	1.3
$3,500 or greater	16.0	14.3	0.3	0.3

SOURCES: MEDPAR data for the 100 percent beneficiary population, Medicare Impact Files, Medicare 100 percent Denominator Files, Area Resource File.

NOTES: Spending is measured as Medicare spending per beneficiary for all beneficiaries, by county of residence for beneficiaries in non-metropolitan counties. Adjusted payments are simulated payments excluding special payment amounts.

The distributions described above result in the average Part A payments per beneficiary shown in Table 8.14 for all beneficiaries and elderly beneficiaries. The overall average annual Medicare Part A payment for all beneficiaries was $2,772 per beneficiary, and the average adjusted payment without the special payment component was $2,720. The amounts were slightly higher for elderly beneficiaries. For both groups, the adjusted payments were 1.9 percent smaller than the actual payments, which compares to the 2.6 percent difference between actual and adjusted Medicare payments for hospital inpatient services (see Table 8.6).

Table 8.14

Average Medicare Part A Payments per Beneficiary, Actual and Without Special Payments, by Non-Metropolitan County Category, All and Elderly Beneficiaries, Three-Year Average 1996–1998

County Category	All Beneficiaries			Elderly Beneficiaries		
	Actual	Adjusted	Change	Actual	Adjusted	Change
All non-metropolitan counties	$2,772	$2,720	−1.9%	$2,810	$2,756	−1.9%
Rural county category						
Adjacent, city 10,000+	2,776	2,731	−1.6	2,803	2,757	−1.6
Adjacent, no city 10,000+	2,836	2,804	−1.1	2,870	2,838	−1.1
Remote, city 10,000+	2,673	2,588	−3.2	2,703	2,617	−3.2
Remote, town 2,500–10,000	2,763	2,705	−2.1	2,818	2,759	−2.1
Remote, no town	2,763	2,694	−2.5	2,824	2,752	−2.5
Frontier county status						
Frontier counties	2,537	2,453	−3.3	2,558	2,473	−3.3
Other non-metro counties	2,783	2,732	−1.8	2,822	2,770	−1.8

SOURCES: MEDPAR data for the 100 percent beneficiary population, NCH data for other Part A Services, Medicare Impact Files, Medicare 100 percent Denominator Files, Area Resource File.

NOTES: Spending is measured as Medicare spending per beneficiary by county of residence for beneficiaries in non-metropolitan counties. Adjusted payments are simulated payments excluding special payment amounts. Averages are weighted by the number of beneficiaries in each county.

The patterns of differences for the five categories of non-metropolitan counties and for the frontier counties mirror those for hospital inpatient payments, with smaller percentage reductions for the total Part A spending. The largest difference between actual and adjusted Medicare Part A payments was the 3.3 percent reduction for frontier counties, which compares to a 4.3 percent reduction in Medicare payments for hospital services.

ISSUES AND IMPLICATIONS

In considering the effects of the Medicare special payments for rural hospitals on Medicare Part A spending, we first examined the effects of these payments on hospital payments per inpatient stay, then looked at effects on payments per beneficiary for hospital inpatient services, and finally extended the analysis to effects on total Medicare Part A spending. This stepped approach allowed us to develop an understanding of the factors contributing to the ultimate effects of these payment provisions on Part A spending for non-metropolitan beneficiaries, including the costs per stay, rates of hospital inpatient utilizations, and the share of Part A spending that was for hospital inpatient services. Variations across counties in these factors also were examined in the analysis.

Overall, the special payments for rural hospitals represented 2.6 percent of the actual Medicare payments for Medicare beneficiaries, judging by the three-year average data for 1996 through 1998. The percentages of special payments as a component of total payment per stay varied across counties, however, as a result of variations in both the percentage of inpatient stays at special payment hospitals and the average payment per stay for different types of hospitals. Almost half the non-metropolitan counties had less than a 1 percent reduction in average Medicare payment per stay as a result of removing the special payment component, whereas 17 percent had a 5 percent reduction or greater.

The percentage of payments for inpatient stays attributable to special payment provisions varied somewhat across the five categories of non-metropolitan counties. These provisions had the greatest effects on payments for services to beneficiaries in the more remote counties and in frontier counties. Sole community hospitals, rural referral centers, and Medicare-dependent hospitals were not evenly distributed across categories of counties. Their shares of total inpatient payments were larger in the non-metropolitan counties that were not adjacent to MSAs and in the frontier counties, thus explaining the larger reduction in payments for those counties.

Although the special payment provisions have had a relatively small overall effect on Medicare spending for inpatient services, this analysis documented the importance of these provisions to the rural hospitals qualified for the additional payments. Without the special payment components, these hospitals would be paid 9.5 percent less per inpatient stay, on average, which could have a substantial effect on their financial viability. The hospitals designated as both a sole community hospital and rural referral center would experience the largest revenue reduction (an estimated average reduction of 11.7 percent). It was not possible to estimate effects for Medicare-dependent hospitals because this designation was in place for only part of the 1996–1998 period, so we could not estimate its true contribution to payment increases.

The 2.6 percent reduction in Medicare payment per beneficiary for inpatient services would translate to an average 1.9 percent reduction in Medicare payments for all Part A services. Again, variation across categories of counties was found, which mirrored the variation for hospital inpatient payments and reflected variation in the percentage of Part A services attributable to hospital inpatient services. The greatest reductions would occur in the most remote counties and frontier counties, where access to care poses the greatest challenges.

9. POLICY IMPLICATIONS AND RECOMMENDATIONS

In this section, we consider the implications of our research findings regarding the Medicare special payment provisions for rural providers and the goals they were intended to address. First, we explore findings regarding possible effects of the special payment policies on access to and costs of care for rural Medicare beneficiaries and implications for Medicare payment policy to further support these goals. Then we present recommendations for additional research to examine some of the specific issues involved with the numerous payment policies and their effects on access and costs of care.

IMPLICATIONS OF THE MEDICARE SPECIAL PAYMENT PROVISIONS

Special Payments for Rural Hospital Inpatient Services

Despite continuing concerns regarding the viability of the hospital infrastructure in rural areas, the findings of these descriptive analyses offer some evidence of stability in the supply of Medicare-certified hospitals during the 1990s. For example, the number of rural hospitals declined slowly, and hospitals increased staffing levels (which suggests growth in outpatient activity) and diversified into new services. These service changes likely were made to strengthen financial viability and competitive positions. In particular, rural hospitals with Medicare special payment designations appeared to play important roles in the delivery of services to beneficiaries in non-metropolitan counties, as shown by their shares of both inpatient stays and Medicare payments. The question remains about the extent to which these hospitals rely on the special payments for their financial viability.

Another general issue highlighted by the utilization analysis is that of the relationships between geographic access to hospital inpatient care, beneficiary health status, and observed utilization of inpatient services. Clearly, beneficiaries residing in the most remote rural counties, including the frontier counties, have to travel longer distances to hospitals, and access to hospitals with specialty capability may be even more difficult. Despite apparent access challenges, we found that beneficiaries in remote locations and in shortage areas (MUAs and HPSAs) had higher rates of inpatient utilization than other rural beneficiaries. Could this utilization include some hospital stays or rehospitalizations that could have been avoided if they had better access to outpatient services? We also found lower average payments per beneficiary for these beneficiaries, suggesting that their hospital stays were for less intensive procedures or that they were less likely to travel to urban hospitals for care. This issue argues for the special payment provisions for sole community hospitals and rural referral centers to help ensure that such facilities remain available in rural areas.

Effects of Rural Hospital Special Payments on Part A Costs

In considering the effects of the Medicare special payments for rural hospitals on Medicare Part A spending, we first examined the effects of these payments on hospital payments per inpatient stay, then looked at effects on payments per beneficiary for hospital inpatient services, and finally extended the analysis to effects on total Medicare Part A spending. This stepped approach allowed us to develop an understanding of the factors contributing to the ultimate effects of these payment provisions on Part A spending for non-metropolitan beneficiaries, including the costs per stay, rates of hospital inpatient utilizations, and the share of Part A spending that was for hospital inpatient services. Variations across counties in these factors also were examined in the analysis.

Overall, the special payments for rural hospitals represented an estimated 2.6 percent of the payments for inpatient services for Medicare beneficiaries residing in non-metropolitan areas. We found wide variation across counties in the effects of the special payment provisions, such that the special payment component represented less than 1 percent of the average payment per inpatient stay for almost half the non-metropolitan counties, whereas it was 5 percent of the average payment per stay for 17 percent of the counties. Special payments were the largest share of Medicare payments in the most remote counties and frontier counties, where access to care poses the greatest challenges. The 2.6 percent of Medicare payments for inpatient services translates to an estimated average 1.9 percent of Medicare payments for all Part A services.

Although the special payment provisions have had a relatively small overall effect on Medicare spending for inpatient services, these provisions have been important for the rural hospitals that qualified for the special payment designation. Without the special payment components, these hospitals would be paid 9.5 percent less per Medicare inpatient stay, on average, which could have a substantial effect on their financial viability. Given that Medicare patients tend to make up a large share of inpatient stays for non-metropolitan hospitals, and that many hospitals operate with small margins, these payments could be very important to them. This issue merits further analysis using Medicare hospital cost report data to estimate effects of special payments on hospital margins.

Rural Health Clinics and Federally Qualified Health Centers

Although RHCs and FQHCs differ in the scope of services they provide and, in many cases, the populations they serve, they both have become important health care resources for rural populations across the country. The supply of RHCs and non-metropolitan FQHCs increased substantially between 1992 and 1998, and the mix of facility types changed. With greater numbers of FQHCs and RHCs delivering primary care services to Medicare beneficiaries across rural areas, Medicare utilization and spending for these services increased accordingly. Medicare spending for all FQHC and RHC services (for rural and urban beneficiaries) was an estimated $54.5 million in 1991. Spending more than tripled to $175.8 million in 1994 and doubled again to $390.3 million in 1998. As of 1991, the highest utilization rates of FQHCs and RHCs were for beneficiaries in the most remote counties (with no town of at least 2,500), which are of special policy interest regarding access to care. The percentage of beneficiaries who used each type of facility also increased over time.

The distribution of Medicare spending shifted toward payments for provider-based RHC services during the 1990s. As of 1998, 28.8 percent of spending was for provider-based RHCs (up from 6.2 percent in 1991), 37.3 percent for independent RHCs (down from 47.1 percent in 1991), and 33.9 percent for FQHCs (down from 46.7 percent in 1991). Even with this shift in shares, the amounts of spending increased for all three types of facilities during this time. The average Medicare spending per beneficiary increased more than sixfold (from $1.54 per beneficiary in 1991 to $10.16 in 1998), indicating that only a small portion of the increased spending was due to growth in the size of the beneficiary population. Despite this rapid growth, the Medicare per capita costs remain small, with the 1998 amount of $10.16 representing less than one dollar per capita on a monthly basis (which is the basis for the AAPCC rates).

Physician Bonus Payments

The trends in physician bonus payments during the 1990s raise issues regarding the ongoing effectiveness of the bonus payment program. Some evidence was found that this program has been successful in supporting primary care providers and services and, possibly, enhanced services for beneficiaries residing in the more remote parts of our country, especially those in HPSAs. On the other hand, low levels of bonus payments in general, coupled with declines in those amounts since 1994, bode ill for its future potential to support physicians practicing in rural areas and, thus, to protect access for rural Medicare beneficiaries. For these goals to be achieved, physicians must use the bonus payments, yet they clearly are not taking advantage of the extra payment amounts available to them. If bonus payments continue to decline faster than basic Medicare payments for physician services, their effects will be further diluted.

Factors that could be contributing to these trends in bonus payments include the extent to which physicians are knowledgeable about bonus payments, the perceived value of the payments to physicians, and effects of administrative procedures on the ease of receiving the payments. Because the bonus payments are administered by the Medicare carriers, policies and procedures for informing physicians, administering payment requests, and auditing appropriateness of payments may vary widely across carriers, which could explain some of the observed regional variation. With the data used for our analyses, we are limited in our ability to explore the relative contributions of such factors to the declining trends in bonus payments.

When considering the policy option of extending bonus payments to NPP services, the small share of Medicare payments for NPP services makes it clear that such a policy would have limited short-term financial impact for Medicare, even if NPPs submitted claims for all eligible services. One might speculate, however, that NPP bonus payments would grow over time because these payments might be a stronger financial incentive for NPPs than for physicians to locate in rural areas.

FUTURE RESEARCH NEEDS AND UNANSWERED QUESTIONS

The Balanced Budget Act of 1997 and the Balanced Budget Refinement Act of 1999 made some significant changes to the ways that Medicare providers are reimbursed for the care they provide. In rural areas, the BBA and the BBRA will have the greatest impact on sole community hospitals, Medicare-dependent hospitals, rural health clinics and federally qualified health clinics. The provisions of the BBA and the BBRA include the following:

- Allowed sole community hospitals to rebase special payments on the basis of the hospitals' costs per discharge for the fiscal year 1996 reporting period, if the hospitals were paid during 1999 on the basis of either their 1982 or 1987 costs per discharges.

- Reinstated and extended the Medicare-dependent hospital designation from October 1, 1997, through October 2001; the BBRA further extended it another five years through October 2006.

- Created the Rural Hospital Flexibility Program through which participating states can regionalize rural health services and designate critical access hospitals (CAHs).

- Refined the definition of what constitutes a qualifying rural shortage area for RHC eligibility.

- Established criteria for determining which clinics may continue as approved Medicare RHCs in areas that lose designation as shortage areas.

- Placed limitations on waivers of some non-physician staffing requirements in clinics.

- Extended the all-inclusive rate and related payment limits to provider-based RHCs except in hospitals with fewer than 50 beds.

- Established rules to prevent "commingling" of RHC and non-RHC resources; and established a quality assurance program (HCFA, 2000).

We can anticipate that these new rules will contribute to changes in the supply and utilization of health care services in rural areas, which will affect access to and costs of services provided in these settings. An analytic capability should be in place to track these changes and extend the trend analysis begun in this research endeavor.

Continuing Trend Analyses

The analyses presented in this report document the historical trends for 1991 through 1998 in utilization of health care services by Medicare beneficiaries in non-metropolitan counties and the associated costs. Recent legislative action in the BBA and BBRA have shifted payment levels and potentially affected access to care in many rural areas.

Recommendation 1:   Continue the trend analyses to understand how these legislative changes influence future costs and access to care.

Recommendation 2:   Perform a focused analysis of the utilization and Medicare costs of care for CAHs and of the financial viability of these newly designated facilities.

In response to requirements in the Health Centers Consolidation Act of 1996 and to extensive comments received on proposed rules, HRSA is revising the criteria and procedures for designating HPSAs. The methodology is being changed substantially, and HRSA plans to publish a revised proposed rule in the near future. In an early analysis of the impact of changes to HPSA designations by HRSA, an estimated 50 percent of rural counties with a full-HPSA designation would lose that designation (Goldsmith and Ricketts, 1999). Changes to the HPSA definition have the potential to substantially influence access to health care services and affect many of the special payment programs including the bonus payment program and rural health clinics.

Recommendation 3:   Model the different criteria for designating HPSAs, and forecast trends in payments under Medicare special provisions for rural providers using these different models.

Observing the Impact of Special Payments on Hospital Financial Viability

Our analyses show that special payment policies are an estimated 1.9 percent of all Medicare Part A payments for services to beneficiaries in non-metropolitan counties. The hospitals receiving the special payments would be paid 9.5 percent less per Medicare inpatient stay, on average, if they were discontinued, which could have a substantial effect on their financial viability. How do the special payment policies influence the fiscal health of individual hospitals? What are the specific characteristics of those hospitals that remain viable over time? What happens to hospitals that lose their special hospital designations?

Recommendation 4:   Use hospital cost reports to estimate the contribution of the special payments to hospitals' net margin.

Patient Perspective on Care

The analyses we performed relied entirely on secondary data analyses that used Medicare claims and provider files for non-metropolitan counties. We cannot comment on the perceptions of Medicare beneficiaries in rural areas regarding issues such as quality of care, availability of services, or ease of physical access. We observed in our analyses that approximately 45 percent of Medicare payments for inpatient care received by non-metropolitan Medicare beneficiaries was in hospitals in metropolitan areas. Was their use of metropolitan hospitals consistent with their health care needs? Do rural Medicare beneficiaries have confidence in their local health care providers? Do they feel confident that they will be transferred to another hospital better equipped for their condition should they need it? Does trust in the system indicate the willingness to travel longer distances to get care? Who are the non-metropolitan beneficiaries who travel to metropolitan areas for their care; what conditions do they have and what services do they receive? Do they consistently receive their care in metropolitan areas? Do patients observe a difference when they go to their doctors depending on whether the doctors work in their own offices or whether they are employed by an RHC?

Recommendation 5:   Conduct beneficiary surveys to gather data on how rural beneficiaries perceive their care, including access to physicians and inpatient care and their perceptions of quality of care.

Recommendation 6:   Using claims data for Medicare beneficiaries residing in non-metropolitan areas, characterize the types of services received by those who received at least some services in metropolitan areas, with comparisons to those who did not.

Recommendation 7:   Conduct beneficiary surveys to understand how rural beneficiaries perceive care provided in a physician's office compared to the care provided in an RHC or FQHC.

Bonus Payments

Of all the Medicare special payment programs for rural providers, the bonus payment program appears to have been the least successful. Overall expenditures constituted less than 1 percent of total physician reimbursements in any year and they declined by 1998. Why do eligible physicians choose to claim or not claim a bonus payment? In part, physicians may not be aware that they are eligible to claim the bonus payment for services provided in a HPSA. They may also be reluctant to claim the bonus payment for fear of an audit from the Medicare carrier. Carriers may also play a role in encouraging or discouraging physicians from claiming a bonus payment. The regulatory burden of the bonus payment program is quite substantial compared to the size of the program. Do carriers fulfill their regulatory requirements for the program? Understanding the answers to these questions can be helpful in determining the future of the bonus payment program.

Recommendation 8: Survey physicians to gather data on their views about the bonus payments and how this option compares to converting their practice to an RHC, sampling from physicians who claim bonus payments and those who are eligible but do not make claims.

Recommendation 9: Interview Medicare carriers to gather data on how they administer the bonus program, issues they believe are important, and their perception regarding the burden it creates for physicians and carriers.

Currently, non-physician providers are not eligible to claim bonus payments for services provided in a HPSA to Medicare beneficiaries. Our analysis of the potential effect of NPPs on the bonus payment program was substantially limited because of data limitations. NPPs may function in their own independent practices or as employees or contractors to physician offices or clinics. Independent NPPs can bill Medicare separately, whereas the physicians or clinics bill Medicare for the services of NPPs that work with them. Until 1998, independently practicing NPPs could bill at 75 percent of the physician fee schedule rate. The BBA increased the rate to 85 percent of the physician's fee, and it also authorized PAs to bill Medicare directly without restriction in all health care settings. PAs are paid an amount equal to 80 percent of the lesser of the actual charge or 85 percent of the physician fee schedule. This fee structure creates a financial incentive for physicians and NPPs to forge relationships so the physicians can bill for NPP services under the higher payment rates for physician services. If NPPs were made eligible for bonus payment, would they be encouraged to bill independently rather than through the physician? Would making NPPs eligible for the bonus payment program increase access to care, particularly primary care?

Recommendation 10: Using claims data for a HPSA, including the actual provider of record (rather than the billing provider), analyze the role NPPs play in providing care in those populations and estimate the potential effects of allowing NPPs to claim a bonus payment.

Data Issues

We were faced with several limitations to our analyses because of the quality of the data available for analysis. The ARF was used to capture county-level characteristics including HPSA and MUA designations. We did not have enough detail in this data to understand the full effects of the special payment policies in partial HPSAs and MUAs. As a result, some of our conclusions were based on the average effect of these policies over a larger geographic region.

Additionally, the HRSA file with MUA designations reflected cumulative designations as of 1998. Using these designations for identifying MUAs in earlier years overestimates their presence. We had more data points to identify HPSA designations over time (1991, 1993, 1995, 1996, and 1997).

Recommendation 11: Develop more detailed data on HPSA and MUA designations in each year, including more accurate profiling of partial HPSAs and MUAs.

We had difficulty confirming the counts of RHCs and FQHCs, for which the annual Medicare POS files were the data sources. Our counts tended to be larger than those obtained by others. Our counts probably were higher because we included all facilities that were certified at any time during a year rather than at a point in time during the year (which we did because we were analyzing claims that occurred throughout the year). Also, some facilities may have discontinued Medicare in previous years but were not removed from the POS files. In addition, the POS counts of FQHCs should be larger than the number of corporate entities with Medicare certification because many of the FQHCs have clinics at multiple locations, with each clinic location having its own Medicare provider number. Each of these clinics is listed separately in the POS file which would yield larger counts than those for the corporate entities that own them. This fact also points out the lack of accessible data on "chain ownership" of Medicare providers.

Recommendation 12: Perform an internal review of data on RHCs and FQHCs in the POS files to assess the extent to which counts of these facilities in the files are inaccurate, including checks for facilities that are no longer Medicare-certified and for multiple clinic locations owned by larger organizations.

REFERENCES

American Medical Association (AMA), *Physicians' Current Procedure Terminology,* Chicago, IL, 1997.

Baer, LD, and LM Smith, Nonphysician Professionals and Rural America, in TC Ricketts III (ed.), *Rural Health in the United States,* New York: Oxford University Press, 1999.

Baldwin, LM, RA Rosenblatt, R Schneeweiss, DM Lishner, and LG Hart, *Rural and Urban Physicians: Does the Content of Their Practices Differ?* WWAMI Rural Health Research Center, Seattle, WA, 1998.

Bureau of Primary Health Care, *Community and Migrant Health Center Grantees,* Health Resources and Services Administration, Rockville, MD, 2001.

Buto, KA, Statement on "Rural Health Clinics" before the House Committee on Government Reform and Oversight Subcommittee on Human Resources and Intergovernmental Relations, Washington, DC, February 13, 1997.

Center for Medicaid and State Operations, Health Care Financing Administration, Letter to State Medicaid Directors, December 1, 1998.

Cheh, V, and R Thompson, *Rural Health Clinics: Improved Access at a Cost. Final Report Submitted to Office of Research and Demonstrations*, Health Care Financing Administration No. 500-92-0047 by Mathematica Policy Research, Princeton, NJ, November 25, 1997.

Cullen, TJ, LG Hart, et al., "The National Health Service Corps: Rural Physician Service and Retention," *Journal of the American Board of Family Practice*, 10(4), 1997.

Department of Health and Human Services (HHS), Office of Inspector General, *Rural Health Clinics: Growth, Access, and Payment,* OEI-05-94-00040, Washington, DC, July 1996.

Earle-Richardson, GB, and AF Earle-Richardson, "Commentary from the Front Lines: Improving the National Health Services Corps' Use of Non-Physician Medical Providers," *Journal of Rural Health*, 14(2), 1998.

Ghelfi, LM, and TS Parker, "A County-Level Measure of Urban Influence," *Rural Development Perspectives* 12(2), 1995.

Goldsmith, LJ, and TC Ricketts, "Proposed Changes to Designations of Medically Underserved Populations and Health Professional Shortage Areas: Effects on Rural Areas," *Journal of Rural Health* 15(1):44-54, Winter 1999.

H.F. 3426, The Medicare, Medicaid, and SCHIP Balanced Budget Refinement Act of 1999, as Incorporated into P.L. 106-113, Consolidated Appropriations for FY 2000, Enacted November 29, 1999, http://www.hcfa.gov/regs/bbra/.

Health Care Financing Administration (HCFA), *Carriers Manual Part 3, Chapter III,* Washington, DC, http://www.hcfa.gov/pubforms/14_car/b00.htm, 2000.

Health Care Financing Administration (HCFA), *Medicare Part B Supplier Files Layout,* Washington, DC, 2000.

Health Care Financing Administration (HCFA), Medicare Program; Rural Health Clinics; Amendments to Participation Requirements and Payment Provisions; and Establishment of a Quality Assessment and Performance Improvement Program, *Federal Register* 42 CFR Parts 405 and 491, 65(39), February 28, 2000.

Health Care Financing Review, *Unpublished Quarterly Report,* Washington, DC, 1993.

Health Care Financing Review, *Unpublished Quarterly Report,* Washington, DC, 1999.

Health Resources and Services Administration (HRSA), Designation of Medically Underserved Populations and Health Professional Shortage Areas: Proposed Rules, *Federal Register* 63(169): 46537-46555, September 1, 1998.

Health Resources and Services Administration (HRSA), Office of Rural Health Policy, *Comparison of the Rural Health Clinic and Federally Qualified Health Center Programs,* Rockville, MD, July 1995.

Health Standards and Quality Bureau, Health Care Financing Administration (HCFA), Letter to Administrators, Baltimore, MD, March 1991.

Krein, SL, "The Adoption of Provider-Based Rural Health Clinics by Rural Hospitals: A Study of Market and Institutional Forces," *Health Services Research,* 34(1):33-60, April (Part 1), 1999.

McBride, TD, JD Penrod, and K Mueller, Volatility in Medicare AAPCC Rates: 1990-1997, *Health Affairs,* 16(5):172-180, 1997.

McNamara, PE, "Income Differences and Rural Resident Outmigration for Inpatient Hospital Services," *Abstract Book Association of Health Services Research,* 15:40-41, 1998.

Medicare Hospital Manual, Chapter 4, Billing Procedures, updated June 14, 2000.

Mohr, PE, SJ Franco, BB Blanchfield, M Cheng, and WN Evans, "Vulnerability of Rural Hospitals to Medicare Outpatient Payment Reform," *Health Care Financing Review* 21(1):1-18, Fall 1999.

Moscovice, I, A Wellever, and J Stensland, *Rural Hospitals: Accomplishments and Present Challenges,* Rural Health Research Center, University of Minnesota, Minneapolis, MN, July 1999.

Mueller, K, *Rural Implications of the Balanced Budget Act of 1997: A Rural Analysis of the Health Policy Provisions*, No. P97-10, Rural Policy Research Institute Rural Health Panel, October 1997.

Mueller, KJ, and T McBride, *Taking Medicare into the 21st Century: Realities of a Post BBA World and Implications for Rural Health Care*, No. P99-2, Rural Policy Research Institute Rural Health Panel, February 10, 1999.

National Rural Health Association, *The Rural Health Clinic Services Act: Public Law 95-210,* Report of the Office of Rural Health Policy, Health Resources and Service Administration (HRSA), January 1991.

North Carolina Rural Health Research and Policy Analysis Center (NC-RHRPAC), *Mapping Rural Health,* Health Resources and Services Administration (HRSA), Cooperative Agreement (CSURC0004-01-0), Chapel Hill, NC, 1998.

Office of the HHS Inspector General, Health and Human Services, *Hospital Closure: 1990*, OEI-04-91-00560, 1992.

Office of the HHS Inspector General, Health and Human Services, *Hospital Closure: 1992*, OEI-04-93-00500, February 1994.

Office of the HHS Inspector General, Health and Human Services, *Hospital Closure: 1994*, OEI-04-95-00100, February 1996.

Office of the HHS Inspector General, Health and Human Services, *Hospital Closure: 1998*, OEI-04-99-00330, July 2000.

Office of the HHS Inspector General, Health and Human Services, *Trends in Rural Hospital Closure: 1987-1991*, OEI-04-92-00441, July 1993a.

Office of the HHS Inspector General, Health and Human Services, *Vulnerabilities in the Medicare Incentive Payment Program: Draft Report*, Department of Health and Human Services: Washington, DC, 1993b.

Physician Payment Review Commission (PPRC), "Bonus Payments in Health Professional Shortage Areas," Chapter 22, *1994 Annual Report to Congress*, Washington, DC, 1994a.

Physician Payment Review Commission (PPRC), "Improving Access to Health Services in Rural Areas," Chapter 17, *1991 Annual Report to Congress*, Washington, DC, 1991.

Physician Payment Review Commission (PPRC), "Increasing the Availability of Health Professionals in Shortage Areas," Chapter 5, *1992 Annual Report to Congress*, Washington, DC, 1992.

Physician Payment Review Commission (PPRC), "Medicare Capitation Payments," Chapter 5, *1996 Annual Report to Congress*, Washington, DC, 1996.

Physician Payment Review Commission (PPRC), "Medicare Risk Program Payment Policy," Chapter 5, *1995 Annual Report to Congress*, Washington, DC, 1995.

Physician Payment Review Commission (PPRC), "Non-Physician Practitioners," Chapter 24, *1994 Annual Report to Congress*, Washington, DC, 1994b.

Politzer, RM, LQ Trible, et al., "The National Health Service Corps for the 21st Century," *Journal of Ambulatory Care Management*, 23(3), 2000.

Prospective Payment Assessment Commission (ProPAC), *Rural Hospitals Under Medicare's Prospective Payment System*, Congressional Report C-91-03, Washington, DC, October 1991.

Rabinowitz, HK, and NP Paynter, "The Role of the Medical School in Rural Graduate Medical Education: Pipeline or Control Valve?" *Journal of Rural Health*, 16(3), 2000.

Rabinowitz, HK, JJ Diamond, et al., "Demographic, Educational and Economic Factors Related to Recruitment and Retention of Physicians in Rural Pennsylvania," *Journal of Rural Health*, 15(2), 1999.

Ricketts, TC, "Federal Programs and Rural Health," in TC Ricketts III (ed.), *Rural Health in the United States*, New York: Oxford University Press, 1999.

Ricketts, TC, LG Hart, et al., "How Many Rural Doctors Do We Have?" *Journal of Rural Health*, 16(3), 2000.

Ricketts, TC, KD Johnson-Webb, and P Taylor, *Definitions of Rural: A Handbook for Policy Makers and Researchers.* Technical Issue paper prepared for the Federal Office of Rural Health Policy (Contract No. HRSA93-857(p)), 1998.

Rogers, CC, AA Goldstein, and SG Cooley, "Population," Chapter 2, in JF Van Nostrand (ed.), *Common Beliefs about the Rural Elderly: What Do National Data Tell Us?* National Center for Health Statistics, *Vital Health* 3(28), 1993.

Rosenbach, ML, and DA Dayhoff, "Access to Care in Rural America: Impact of Hospital Closures," *Health Care Financing Review,* 17(1):15-37, Fall 1995.

Rosenblatt, RA, and LG Hart, "Physicians and Rural America," in TC Ricketts III (ed.), *Rural Health in the United States,* New York: Oxford University Press, 1999.

Rural Health Clinic and Federally Qualified Health Center Manual, "Payment," Chapter 5, updated January 11, 1999.

Schlenker, RE, and PW Shaughnessy, "The Role of the Rural Hospital in Long-Term Care," in GD Rowles, JE Beaulieu, and WW Myers (eds.), *Long-Term Care for the Rural Elderly,* New York: Springer Publishing Company, 1996.

Stearns, SC, RT Slifkin, et al., "Access to Care for Rural Medicare Beneficiaries," *Journal of Rural Health*, 16(1), 2000.

Taylor, P, D Puskin, SG Cooley, and J Braden, "Assess," Chapter 3 in JF Van Nostrand (ed.), *Common Beliefs about the Rural Elderly: What Do National Data Tell Us?* National Center for Health Statistics, *Vital Health* 3(28), 1993.

U.S. General Accounting Office (GAO), *Health Care Shortage Areas: Designations Not a Useful Tool for Directing Resources to the Underserved,* GAO/HEHS-95-200, Washington, DC, September 1995.

U.S. General Accounting Office (GAO), *Physician Shortage Areas: Medicare Incentive Payments Not an Effective Approach to Improve Access*, GAO/HEHS-99-36, Washington, DC, February 1999.

U.S. General Accounting Office (GAO), *Rural Health Clinics: Rising Program Expenditures Not Focused on Improving Care in Isolated Areas*, GAO/HEHS-97-24, Washington, DC, November 1996.

U.S. General Accounting Office (GAO), *Rural Primary Care Hospitals: Experience Offers Suggestions for Medicare's Expanded Program*, GAO/HEHS-98-60, Washington, DC, February 1998.

United States Code, Title 42, Section 13951.

Van Nostrand, JF, SE Furner, JA Brunelle, and RA Cohen, "Health," Chapter 8 in JF Van Nostrand (ed.), *Common Beliefs about the Rural Elderly: What Do National Data Tell Us?* National Center for Health Statistics, *Vital Health,* 3(28), 1993.

Walsh Center for Rural Health, *Importance of Provider-Based Rural Health Clinics for Parent Hospitals and Local Access to Care*, Project Hope Center for Health Affairs, 2001.

Williamson, HA, Jr., LG Hart, MJ Pirani, and RA Rosenblatt, *Market Shares for Rural Inpatient Surgical Services: Where Does the Buck Stop?* Seattle, WA: WAMI RHRC (Rural Health Working Paper Series, No. 21), 1993, p. 26.

Wisconsin Physicians Service, *Providers' Guide to Medicare Part B,* Madison, WI, 2000.

WWAMI Rural Health Research Center, *An Initial Report on the Impact of the Balanced Budget Act on Small Rural Hospitals*, University of Washington, September 1999.

APPENDIX

A. SPECIAL MEDICARE PAYMENTS FOR RURAL HOSPITALS

The scope and history of the Medicare special payment policies for inpatient services by rural hospitals reflect the diversity of issues faced by rural hospitals serving Medicare beneficiaries. By 1990, the full set of these special payment policies had been established for the following designated hospitals, although modifications continued throughout the 1990s:

- Sole Community Hospitals (SCH)
- Rural Referral Centers (RRC)
- SCH/Rural Referral Centers
- Medicare-Dependent Hospitals (MDH)
- Essential Access Community Hospital (EACH)
- EACH/Rural Referral Center

Because each special payment designation responded to a unique set of issues for rural hospitals, both the eligibility criteria and payment methodologies differ substantially. We summarize these provisions below. In addition, we describe two other provisions that increase payments for rural hospitals: reclassifying hospitals so an urban standardized amount or wage index is used to establish PPS payments, and higher DSH payments for certain rural hospitals. The provisions described here were applicable during the 1990–1998 time period covered by this research. The BBA and follow-up legislation subsequently modified many of these provisions.

SPECIAL PAYMENT DESIGNATIONS

Sole Community Hospitals

This designation provides payment protection for hospitals in isolated locations that are the sole source of inpatient services reasonably available to Medicare beneficiaries. Effective April 1, 1990, hospitals that qualified as sole community hospitals were paid the highest of three rates: (1) the updated hospital-specific rate based on the hospital's 1982 costs per discharge, (2) the updated hospital-specific rate based on its 1987 costs per discharge, or (3) the federal PPS rate, including any applicable outlier amount. A provision of the BBRA allows a sole community hospital to elect to rebase its special payments on the basis of the hospital's costs per discharge for its fiscal year 1996 reporting period, if the hospital was paid during 1999 on the basis of either its 1982 or 1987 costs per discharge. Sole community hospitals also receive special treatment under criteria for geographic reclassification and DSH payment adjustment (discussed below).

Designation as a sole community hospital remains in effect without need for reapproval unless there is a change in the circumstances under which the designation was approved. Hospitals that were granted exemptions from the hospital cost limits before October 1, 1983, were automatically classified as sole community hospitals. Any other rural hospital seeking designation must meet one of the following criteria:[24]

---

[24] A hospital not in a rural area may be designated as a sole community provider if it is more than 35 miles from other similar hospitals.

- More than 35 miles from other similar hospitals; or

- Between 25 and 35 miles from other similar hospitals, and

  - No more than (1) 25 percent of total inpatients or (2) 25 percent of Medicare inpatients admitted to hospitals from the hospital's service area are admitted to similar hospitals located within a 35-mile radius of the hospital or to larger hospitals within the hospital's service area, or

  - Has fewer than 50 beds and would admit at least 75 percent of the inpatients from its service area except that some patients seek specialized care it does not provide, or

  - Other similar hospitals are inaccessible for at least 30 days in each two out of three years because of local topography or prolonged or severe weather conditions;

- Between 15 and 35 miles from other similar hospitals, but because of local topography or prolonged severe weather conditions, the other similar hospitals are inaccessible for at least 30 days in each two out of three years; or

- Travel time between the hospital and the nearest similar hospital is at least 45 minutes because of distance, posted speed limits, or predictable weather conditions.

Rural Referral Centers

For discharges occurring before October 1, 1994, hospitals that qualified as rural referral centers were paid on the basis of the "other urban" prospective payment standardized amount, rather than the rural amount, adjusted by the DRG weight and the hospital's area wage index. Following that date, the same amounts were paid for "other urban" and rural standardized amounts. However, as discussed below, rural referral centers continue to receive special treatment under the payment adjustment and criteria for geographic reclassification, which qualifies them for the urban disproportionate share payments. To qualify as an RRC, a hospital must be located in a rural area and meet all of the following criteria:

- Have a case-mix index of at least 1.276 for fiscal year 1991, or one that equals the median case-mix index for urban hospitals (excluding hospitals with approved teaching programs) calculated by CMS for the census region in which the hospital is located;

- For the cost reporting period that began during fiscal year 1991, have at least 5,000 discharges, or discharges equal to the median number of discharges for urban hospitals in its census region, or have at least 3,000 discharges if an osteopathic hospital; and

- Have at least 275 beds or meet one of the following criteria:

  - More than 50 percent of the hospital's active medical staff are specialists,

  - At least 60 percent of its discharges are for inpatients who reside more than 25 miles from the hospital, or

  - At least 40 percent of all inpatients treated are referred from other hospitals or from physicians not on the hospital's medical staff.

CMS reviews referral center status every three years. Beginning on October 1, 1992, to retain referral center status, a hospital must meet the applicable criteria in the current year or for at least two of the last three years.

SCH/Rural Referral Centers

Some rural hospitals qualify for designation as both sole community hospitals and rural referral centers. Payments for these hospitals are the greatest allowed under either designation. In addition, special DSH payment adjustments are defined for hospitals with both designations.

Medicare-Dependent Hospitals

The designation of Medicare-dependent hospitals was first available to rural hospitals for cost reporting periods beginning on or after April 1, 1990, and ending on or before October 1, 1994. The BBA reinstated and extended this designation from October 1, 1997, through October 2001, and the BBRA further extended it another five years through October 2006.

Hospitals that qualify as Medicare-dependent hospitals are paid according to the sum of the federal payment rate applicable to the hospital and the amount by which the federal rate is exceeded by a specified percentage of the higher of (1) the hospital-specific rate based on the hospital's 1982 costs, or (2) the hospital-specific rate based on its 1987 costs. The applicable percentages for the hospital-specific rates are 100 percent for discharges occurring on or before April 1, 1993, and 50 percent for discharges occurring between April 1993 and October 1994 and occurring from October 1, 1997, through October 2006.

To qualify for this designation, a rural hospital must meet all of the following criteria:

- Have 100 or fewer inpatient beds;

- Not be classified as a sole community hospital; and

- Be dependent on Medicare for at least 60 percent of its inpatient days or discharges for its cost reporting period that began during fiscal year 1987.

Essential Access Community Hospital

Designated by participating states and approved by CMS, hospitals that qualify as EACHs are the referral hospitals for EACH/RPCHs. These hospitals are paid as sole community hospitals. A participating state could designate a hospital as an EACH if the hospital:

- Was in a rural area more than 35 miles from a hospital designated as either an EACH or a rural referral center, or met other geographic criteria set by the state;

- Had at least 75 inpatient beds or was more than 35 miles from any other hospital; and

- Had executed agreements with RPCHs participating in the rural health network to provide emergency and medical backup services, accept patients transferred from RPCHs, exchange data with RPCHs, and grant staff privileges to physicians who provide care at the RPCHs.

With the introduction of the Medicare Rural Hospital Flexibility Program, effective October 1, 1997, no new EACH designations may be made. Existing EACHs continue to be paid as sole community hospitals as long as they comply with the applicable requirements.

EACH/Rural Referral Center

Some EACHs also qualify for designation as rural referral centers. Payments for these hospitals are the greatest allowed under either designation.

HOSPITALS RECLASSIFIED FOR STANDARDIZED AMOUNT OR WAGE INDEX

The Medicare Geographic Classification Review Board has the responsibility for making determinations of hospital reclassification for purposes of payments under the Prospective Payment System. Rural hospitals may be reclassified to permit use of a higher standardized payment amount or wage index from another area in the PPS payment calculation. A hospital in a rural county may be reclassified as follows:

- The hospital must meet proximity criteria by being a sole community hospital or rural referral center, or must demonstrate close proximity to the area to which it seeks reclassification, such that the distance from the hospital to the area is no more than 35 miles, and at least 50 percent of the hospital's employees reside in the area.

- The hospital must meet financial criteria for reclassification for an area's standardized amount or wage index:

  ➤ To receive an area's standardized amount, the hospital must demonstrate that its incurred costs are more comparable to the amount it would be paid if it were reclassified than to its payment under its current classification.

  ➤ To receive an area's wage index, the hospital must demonstrate that (1) its incurred wage costs are comparable to hospital wage costs in the area, (2) the hospital average hourly wage is at least 108 percent of the average for hospitals where the hospital is located, and (3) the aggregate average hourly wage for all hospitals in the rural county is at least 84 percent of the average wage in the area, or the average wage weighted for occupational categories is at least 90 percent of the urban area's average wage.

- The hospital must be a participant in a *group of all hospitals* in a rural county applying for reclassification, the rural county must be adjacent to the metropolitan area to which reclassification is sought, and the group must demonstrate that:

  ➤ The rural county meets Census Bureau standards for redesignation to a metropolitan area as an outlying county, and

  ➤ The aggregate average hourly wage for all hospitals in the rural county is at least 85 percent of the average wage in the adjacent urban area, or the average wage weighted for occupational categories is at least 90 percent of the urban area's average wage.

SPECIAL PROVISIONS FOR DISPROPORTIONATE SHARE PAYMENTS

Adjustments are made to the federal portion of the operating cost DRG payment to allow additional payments for hospitals serving a disproportionate share of low-income patients. A DSH percentage is calculated for each hospital as the sum of (1) the percentage of Medicare Part A patient days attributable to patients who also are Supplemental Security Income (SSI) recipients, and (2) the percentage of total patient days attributable to patients entitled to Medicaid but not Medicare. A rural hospital qualifies for an operating cost DSH adjustment if it has a DSH percentage of:

- At least 15 percent for a rural hospital with 500 or more beds;

- At least 30 percent for a rural hospital that has more than 100 beds but fewer than 500 beds, or is classified as a sole community hospital; or

- At least 45 percent for a rural hospital with 100 beds or fewer that is not classified as a sole community hospital.

For each rural hospital group that qualifies for DSH payments, the adjustments are shown in Table A.1.

Table A.1
Adjustments to Payments for Hospitals
Serving a Disproportionate Share of Low-Income Patients

Type of Rural Hospital	DSH Payment Adjustment Factor
With 500 or more beds, and at least 15% DSH percentage	The same as for urban hospitals with 100 or more beds with a DSH percentage of at least 15%.
With 100–499 beds or a sole community hospital, and 30% DSH percentage	a. If rural referral center—4% plus 60% of difference between DSH percentage and 30%. b. If sole community hospital—10%. c. If SCH/rural referral center—the greater of (1) 10% and (2) 4% plus 60% of difference between DSH percentage and 30%.
With 100 beds or fewer, not a SCH, and at least 45% DSH percentage	4%.

B. DEFINITIONS OF RURALITY

Historically, two principal definitions of rural have been used by the federal government. The first definition is the "urban-rural" classification of populations developed by the Census Bureau. The bureau specifies "urbanized areas" and defines as urban all territory, population, and housing units located in those areas and in places or towns of 2,500 or more persons outside urbanized areas. All other areas not classified as urban are considered to be rural. An urbanized area is a continuously built-up area with a population of 50,000 or more, comprising one or more central places and the adjacent densely settled fringes with a population density of more than 1,000 persons per square mile.[25]

The second definition is the "metropolitan/non-metropolitan" classification of counties developed by the Office of Management and Budget (OMB). Metropolitan areas contain core counties with one or more central cities of at least 50,000 population or with a Census Bureau-defined urbanized area and a total area population of 100,000 or more, as well as fringe counties that are economically tied to the core counties. All other counties are considered to be non-metropolitan.

Policy analysis and research studies generally have worked with these definitions or adaptations from them, but the populations that are defined as rural differ substantially depending on which definition is used as the basis for classification. Therefore, the choice of definition is an important aspect of study design and should support the basic research or policy issues being addressed.

For the analyses of Medicare rural payment policies, the county-based definition of metropolitan/non-metropolitan groupings is a useful organization because many Medicare payment policies and related data sources are based on county boundaries. This definition loses much of the granularity of the urbanized area definition, however, which differentiates between areas with concentrated populations and those with more sparsely distributed populations, for which local health care services are likely to be quite different.

Two methods have been available to classify the metropolitan and non-metropolitan counties according to degrees of rurality. The Department of Agriculture developed the Urban Influence Codes (UICs) and the Rural-Urban Continuum Codes (RUCCs). The categories used by these two methods are listed in Table B.1. The methods differ in how they measure a county's urban population for categorizing the county. The UICs work with the size of the largest town or city in a county, whereas the RUCCs sum the total population for all towns and cities of more than 2,500 in a county. Thus, the RUCCs would classify a county with many small towns with populations totaling 20,000, but without a city of at least 10,000 population, as more economically centralized than the UICs would classify that county.

---

[25] The primary source for this discussion is Ricketts et al. (1998).

Table B.1
Two Classification Methods for Metropolitan and Non-Metropolitan Counties

Code	Definition
Urban Influence Codes	
1	Large central and fringe counties of metropolitan areas of 1 million population or more
2	Small counties in metropolitan areas of fewer than 1 million population
3	Adjacent to a large metropolitan area with a city of 10,000 or more
4	Adjacent to a large metropolitan area without a city of 10,000 or more
5	Adjacent to a small metropolitan area with a city of 10,000 or more
6	Adjacent to a small metropolitan area without a city of 10,000 or more
7	Not adjacent to a metropolitan area and with a city of 10,000 or more
8	Not adjacent to a metropolitan area and with a town of 2,500 to 9,999
9	Not adjacent to a metropolitan area and without a town of at least 2,500
Rural-Urban Continuum Codes	
0	Central counties of metropolitan areas of 1 million population or more
1	Fringe counties of metropolitan areas of 1 million population or more
2	Counties in metropolitan areas of 250,000 to 1 million population
3	Counties in metropolitan areas of fewer than 250,000 population
4	Adjacent to a metropolitan area, urban population of 20,000 or more
5	Not adjacent to a metropolitan area, urban population of 2,000 or more
6	Adjacent to a metropolitan area, urban population of 2,500 to 19,999
7	Not adjacent to a metropolitan area, urban population of 2,500 to 19,999
8	Adjacent to a metropolitan area, less than 2,500 urban population
9	Not adjacent to a metropolitan area, less than 2,500 urban population

SOURCE: Ricketts et al. (1998).

Rural health researchers tend to prefer the UICs to classify degrees of rurality for non-metropolitan counties because the availability of health service resources is strongly affected by the presence or absence of a city of substantial population. We chose to use UICs for this analysis for this reason. However, we recognize that the use of county-level boundaries sacrifices the ability to measure variations in the populations living in towns of at least 2,500 within each non-metropolitan county, which weakens our ability to capture the effects of related variations in health services and utilization.

The U.S. Department of Agriculture (USDA) recently released a new definition of "urban" and "rural" areas called the Rural-Urban Commuting Area (RUCA) codes, which were developed jointly by USDA's Economic Research Service and the HHS Office of Rural Health Policy. Like the UIC and RUCC systems, the RUCA codes are based on measures of urbanization, population density, and daily commuting. However, this set of 10 codes—three codes for metropolitan areas and seven for non-metropolitan areas—uses the much smaller census tract as its base unit instead of the county and metropolitan area. These codes are listed in Table B.2. The primary codes refer to the primary or single largest commuting share of a census tract. These codes are subdivided "to identify areas where primary flow is local but over 30 percent commute in a secondary flow to a larger area core" (Economic Research Service [ERS] web site on RUCA codes). The seven non-metropolitan codes form a unidimensional scale of rurality. Analysts are just beginning to experiment with the RUCA codes, and we hope to explore their applicability in subsequent analyses for this project.

Additional information about the various coding methods for classifying areas based on degree of rurality may be found at http://www.ers.usda.gov. Some addresses are listed here for reference.

What Is Rural?	http://www.ers.usda.gov/briefing/rurality/WhatisRural
Urban Influence Codes	http://www.ers.usda.gov/briefing/rurality/UrbanInf
Rural-Urban Continuum Codes	http://www.ers.usda.gov/briefing/rurality/RuralUrbCon
Rural-Urban Commuting Area Codes	http://www.ers.usda.gov/briefing/rural/data/desc.htm
Urbanized Area	http://www.ers.usda.gov/briefing/rural/data/urbanar.htm

Table B.2
Rural-Urban Commuting Area (RUCA) Codes

Primary Code	Sub-Code	Definition
1		Metropolitan-area core: primary flow within an urbanized area (UA)
	1.0	No additional code
	1.1	Secondary flow 30% to 50% to a larger UA
2		Metropolitan-area high commuting: primary flow 30% or more to a UA
	2.0	Primary flow to a 1.0 UA
	2.1	Primary flow to a 1.1 UA
	2.2	Combined flows to two or more UAs adding to 30% or more
3		Metropolitan-area low commuting: primary flow 5% to 30% to a UA
	3.0	No additional code
4		Large town core: primary flow within a place of 10,000 to 49,999
	4.0	No additional code
	4.1	Secondary flow 30% to 50% to a UA
5		Large town high commuting: primary flow 30% or more to a place of 10,000 to 49,999
	5.0	Primary flow to a 4.0 large town
	5.1	Primary flow to a 4.1 large town
6		Large town low commuting: primary flow 5% to 30% to a place of 10,000 to 49,999
	6.0	No additional code
7		Small town core: primary flow within a place of 2,500 to 9,999
	7.0	No additional code
	7.1	Secondary flow 30% to 50% to a UA
	7.2	Secondary flow 30% to 50% to a large town
	7.3	Secondary flow 5% to 30% to a UA
	7.4	Secondary flow 5% to 30% to a large town
8		Small town high commuting: primary flow 30% or more to a place of 2,500 to 9,999
	8.0	Primary flow to a 7.0 small town
	8.1	Primary flow to a 7.1 small town
	8.2	Primary flow to a 7.2 small town
	8.3	Primary flow to a 7.3 small town
	8.4	Primary flow to a 7.4 small town
9		Small town low commuting: primary flow 5% to 30% to a place of 2,500 to 9,999
	9.0	No additional code
	9.1	Secondary flow 5% to 30% to a UA
	9.2	Secondary flow 5% to 30% to a large town
10		Rural areas: primary flow to a tract without a place of 2,500 or more
	10.0	No additional code
	10.1	Secondary flow 30% to 50% to a UA
	10.2	Secondary flow 30% to 50% to a large town
	10.3	Secondary flow 30% to 50% to a small town
	10.4	Secondary flow 5% to 30% to a UA
	10.5	Secondary flow 5% to 30% to a large town
99		Not coded: Tracts with little or no population and no commuting flows